To the children of urban America
and to the many frontline educators deeply devoted
to their academic and social well-being

Building Civic Capacity

STUDIES IN GOVERNMENT AND PUBLIC POLICY

Building Civic Capacity
The Politics of Reforming Urban Schools

Clarence N. Stone, Jeffrey R. Henig,
Bryan D. Jones, and Carol Pierannunzi

University Press of Kansas

Published by the University Press of Kansas (Lawrence, Kansas 66049), which was
organized by the Kansas Board of Regents and is operated and funded by Emporia
State University, Fort Hays State University, Kansas State University, Pittsburg State
University, the University of Kansas, and Wichita State University.

Library of Congress Cataloging-in-Publication Data

Building civic capacity : the politics of reforming urban schools /
    Clarence N. Stone . . . [et al.].
        p. cm. — (Studies in government and public policy)
    Includes index.
    ISBN 0-7006-1117-7 (cloth : alk. paper) — ISBN 0-7006-1118-5
(pbk. : alk. paper)
        1. Education, Urban—Political aspects—United States—Case studies.
2. School improvement programs—United States—Case studies.   3. Community
and school—United States—Case studies.   I. Stone, Clarence N. (Clarence
Nathan), 1935–   .   II. Title.   III. Series.
    LC5131.B83 2001 371.19'0973—dc21   2001000887

British Library Cataloguing in Publication Data is available.

Printed in the United States of America
10 9 8 7 6 5 4 3 2 1

Contents

Acknowledgments

A book with four authors is a collective enterprise in several ways. Four is a group in itself and involves a complex dynamic, best understood by remembering that each author enjoys a system of support. A book that was more than a decade in the making, from initial conversations about an idea to publication, itself rests on an extensive body of supporters. Those named below are thus only a partial list of people to whom the four authors are indebted, but they are individuals who have our deepest gratitude.

First, this book is an outgrowth of the Civic Capacity and Urban Education Project funded by the National Science Foundation. That study involved research on eleven cities and a considerable body of researchers. The city teams were as follows:

- Atlanta—Carol Pierannunzi, Desiree Pedescleaux, and John Hutcheson;
- Balitmore—Marion Orr;
- Boston—John Portz;
- Denver—Susan Clarke, Rodney Hero, and Mara Sidney;
- Detroit—Richard Hula, Richard Jelier, and Mark Schauer;
- Houston—Thomas Longoria;
- Los Angeles—Fernando Guerra and Mara Cohen;
- Pittsburgh—Robin Jones;
- St. Louis—Lana Stein;
- San Francisco—Luis Fraga and Bari Anhalt Erlichson;
- Washington, D.C.—Jeffrey Henig

The field research for the project yielded 516 codable interviews. Bryan Jones directed the coding, with extensive work by Whitney Grace and Heather Strickland. In addition to this considerable body of scholars, several others participated in shaping the research design and the protocol for field research: the late Byran Jackson, Alan DiGaetano, Barbara Ferman, Valerie Johnson, Katherine McFate, Timothy Ross, Jorge Ruiz de la Vasco, and Marta Tellado.

Jeffrey Henig headed the task of collecting and analyzing a large body of demographic, program, and financial data. In this work he was ably assisted by Mark Kugler, Cheryl Jones, Connie Hill, and Kathryn Doherty.

A book such as this benefits enormously from the community of scholars, and our debt to members of that community are countless. We want to mention a few. Jennifer Hochschild tops the list. From the inception of the project to a hugely helpful set of comments on the completed manuscript, Jennifer has been a major participant in the dialogue from which this book emanated. She has also been a much-valued source of encouragement and a believer in the importance of what this work is about. In addition, we owe a very special debt of gratitude to Michael Kirst, a member of the community of education scholars, willing and able to contribute to a dialogue with members of the political science community. He too provided greatly helpful comments on the completed manuscripts and has also been a vital source of support and encouragement from the early days of the research project on. Others scholars who have been especially important sources of counsel and support include Marilyn Gittell, Betty Malen, Frederick Wirt, and Kenneth Wong. Their comments, advice, and encouragement have been of special value for many reasons, not the least of which is their own pioneering work in the politics of education.

This book grew out of a grant from the Education and Human Resources Directorate of the National Science Foundation (grant number RED 9350139), and we have had the special pleasure to work with and receive encouragement from then program officers David Jenness and Iris Rothberg and deputy director Larry Suter of the Division of Research, Evaluation, and Communication.

In the National Science Foundation project, Clarence Stone was the principal investigator and Jeffrey Henig and Bryan Jones were coprincipal investigators. Clarence Stone wishes to express special appreciation for the succession of truly extraordinary research assistants who have enabled him to keep on task, contributed to the ongoing intellectual discourse, and made life better: Kathryn Doherty, Connie Hill, Cheryl Jones, Anja Kurki, Timothy Ross, and Circe Stumbo. Clarence is happy to report that, despite (and perhaps because of) the stresses and strains of coordinating a complex and long-running project, they are among his most valued friends.

The four authors wish to express special appreciation to Fred Woodward and the staff at the University Press of Kansas. Fred has been a believer in the project from the beginning, a source of sage advice about matters of presentation, and a friend to us all.

Last to be mentioned but first in our hearts are the spouses of the authors: Mary Stone, Robin Marantz Henig, Diane Jones, and John Hutcheson. Mainstays in our respective personal and professional lives, they have also contributed immeasurably to the dialogue from which this book has emerged. The four authors are blessed that these partnerships run deep.

Introduction

America spent most of the twentieth century trying to take politics out of education. That was a mistake.

American school reformers survey the landscape of decrepit and poorly performing schools and conclude that what is needed is a high-intensity campaign to raise citizens' concern and catapult more dramatic reform initiatives onto the public agenda. That, too, is a mistake.

Education analysts collect specimens of seemingly successful school systems, study the form of the policies they pursue and the style of the leaders that put those policies into place, and abstract the "best practices" that can be transplanted directly into other cities with the expectation that they will take root and flourish. This is an error as well.

These, at least, are some of the arguments that we will make in the pages that follow. Successful educational reform ultimately requires a broad and sustainable coalition of support, and the route to this goes directly through, and not around, politics. Chicago, once cited as an illustration of all that was wrong with American education, more recently has been broadly characterized as a leading exemplar of urban school reform. But although others see this as the consequence of a particular set of policy initiatives—combining state intervention, replacement of the traditional school board with a structure more directly accountable to the mayor, centralization of certain management and financial operations, and decentralization to individual schools' authority to make certain decisions about operations and leadership—we consider it just as important that the focal point for reform is a master politician with an exquisite understanding of how to draw together disparate groups by providing clear and direct benefits to cooperation, defining an inclusive vision, and pragmatically zeroing in on doable tasks and realizable goals.

Successful education reform implies the implementation and institutionalization of policies, not just a public endorsement of the desirability of change.

Mediocre school systems are not attributable to citizen complacency or failure to appreciate the importance of education. Consider Atlanta, Detroit, or Washington, D.C., three of the eleven school systems that provide the empirical grist for the research we report here. During the 1980s and 1990s, each of these cities experienced dramatic initiatives, including the election of reform-oriented slates to the school board, hiring new superintendents with ambitious agendas, and much public discussion about the centrality of education as a vehicle for pursuing economic revitalization, crime reduction, and social equity. That these bursts of attention proved ephemeral and ineffective was not because various sectors of the city were indifferent, but because diffuse concerns and scattered activities never generated a community synergy that could be sustained in the face of slow progress and competing demands on the public's attention and purse. Overcoming such obstacles also requires the skills of the politician—the elected politician—the specialist in the democratic policy at resolving conflicting values in a manner that overcomes the "complexity of joint action."[1] But it also requires an attention to converting short-term alliances into institutionalized relationships, a step that not every politician remembers to take. Politicians often thrive by creating momentum and ad hoc coalitions perfectly timed to coincide with a critical election or legislative action. But the energy, enthusiasm, and willingness to join hands despite differences that characterize these peak periods are almost impossible to sustain. To break the cycle of school reform surges and retreats, attention must be paid to the task of creating institutional legacies that live beyond the moment.

Nor are good ideas and proven leaders the answer. Witness the spotty record of transplanted superintendents who were brought into town to put into place the programs and practices upon which they built their reputations. Joseph Fernandez, hailed as a dynamic and successful innovator in Dade County, Florida, lasted only four years in New York City, when he failed to build a local base of support. Franklin Smith, championed by Washington, D.C., reformers because of his accomplishments in Dayton, Ohio, was chased out of office just five years after his arrival, in spite of the fact that his District of Columbia agenda included the same themes and components that had worked for him before. His successor, General Julius Becton, had a track record of success as a military leader and was advised by national experts about model practices, yet even with an extraordinary grant of legal authority, owing to support from Congress and its appointed local financial control board, Becton, too, left office branded as a failure. Leaders are important, but not if they are cut off from the networks of relationships within a community.

Based on these observations, we have concluded that many of the conventional ideas about what education reform entails are wrongheaded, albeit well meant. We do not pretend to offer a full-fledged alternative that is comprehensive, precise, and sure. Indeed, part of our argument is that the desire for such panaceas contributes to the cycle of sporadic effort, frustration, and resignation that we encountered in our research. Moreover, we have great respect for many of the specific ideas and arguments that the community of education thinkers has developed and that play a role in the conventional wisdom we ultimately reject. Our goal is to add something to the mix of ideas and evidence currently drawn upon in the national debate. In doing so, we rely on some general insights that have established roots in the political and social sciences as well as original research that we will describe.

Our national aversion to politics in education has two intellectual roots. The first is a stunted vision of politics. Politics, in American thought, has come to be too closely associated with the wheeling and dealing, backroom maneuvering, and sometimes cynical corruption of the machine-style politics that dominated many large cities around the turn of the last century. Machine-style politics elevates material incentives over higher ideals as a motivating force and substitutes party and group interests for the pursuit of a broader public good. But politics comes in other flavors as well, and in some of its other manifestations it can be a critical tool for discovering and mobilizing collective action. Education reforms of the last century and this one, by building institutional walls to buffer education decision making from political "interference," ironically have deprived themselves of this critical tool.

Exaltation of technique and organizational form constitutes the second intellectual wellspring that feeds the misguided mission to create an educational system outside of politics. Americans have spent much of their reform energies trying to solve problems in schools by inserting the right curriculum, pedagogical style, or institutional structures. "If only we would commit ourselves to _____," children would learn more and better, with the blank filled by this or that notion-of-the-moment, be it whole language instruction, open education, back-to-the-basics, accountability through testing, longer school years, longer school days, charter schools, vouchers, or whatever you will. From this perspective, politics is either a direct threat or a necessary evil. Politics is a direct threat when it takes power out of the hands of the experts who, presumably, are in the best position to recognize a superior technology. Or it is a necessary evil—the distasteful course that must be taken to get the proper policies and programs into place—to be banished as quickly and completely as possible once that goal has been accomplished.

Political scientists by training and inclination, we came to this book with a different orientation. We share with many educators and school reformers a belief that education is immensely important if we are to achieve the levels of social equity and well-being to which we aspire, combined with a sense of deep disappointment that the realities of education fall so far short of what we believe is possible—especially for low-income and minority children and especially in some of our large, central-city public school systems. Unlike many scholars with whom we share these sentiments, however, we see the solutions as well as the problems as lying within the political realm. And we draw from our background and our previous research a different set of conceptual lenses and lessons to apply.

This book is based on a project titled "Civic Capacity and Urban Education." The "urban education" part requires no extended explanation; the project consists of a study of education politics in eleven large cities across the nation's major regions. The cities are typical in that all are racially and ethnically diverse and all contain sizable lower-income populations. There is a general concern about the state of American education, but the most acute worry surrounds schools in large cities. Although serving the neediest population, urban schools have the most disappointing performance. Moreover, closer state oversight, numerous programs, and much talk about the need for reform have had only limited impact. The sparse evidence of genuine reform leads some observers to talk about a weak political will.

Of course, many of the poor conditions evident in urban schools reflect broader forces that bring city schools face-to-face with tougher challenges than those confronting schools in places more sheltered. Any effort to pin the tail of responsibility solely on the back-end of local leaders is sure to be an oversimplification. But if city school systems are going to give city children the tools they need to break free from the disadvantages they inherit by virtue of the disinvestment, disorder, and decline that characterize their communities, they cannot wait for a magic wand to banish the inequalities that plague them. Local initiatives, sustained by local coalitions, must generate the capacity to get things started and draw in resources from the outside. Our project was animated by a desire to understand the conditions that do or could enable some communities to undertake more serious and sustained efforts to make collective investments in the human capital their children represent. It is to this that we are referring when we make use of the term "civic capacity."

What, then, is civic capacity, and does it shed light on the issue of political will? Is civic capacity a useful concept in the study of urban school reform, and, if so, why? These questions call for a more extended discussion, which we provide in Chapters 1 and 2. But our concept of civic capacity has roots in some broader theoretical discussions about urban politics, social capital, problem definition, and nonincremental policy change that it is appropriate to highlight here.

Civic capacity is about various sectors of the community coming together in an effort to solve a major problem. On occasions when city hall, business elites, and labor unions combine efforts to redevelop downtown or build a new convention center, a community's civic capacity has been activated. When a wide alliance develops enough of a common understanding to work in concert to reform urban education, civic capacity has been activated—but the target is human rather than physical development.

Urban scholars have been more attentive to the politics of redevelopment than to the politics of urban education, and more is known about how various sectors of the community come together around issues of physical development than is known about coming together around education and related issues of human development. Urban education involves a different mix of players from urban redevelopment, and the motivations appealed to are also somewhat different. Collective well-being and long-term benefit occupy a more prominent place in education reform than in redevelopment projects. With selective material incentives less central, civic-mindedness potentially has a bigger part to play. But for most students of urban policies and politics, this is an unexplored phenomenon. We perhaps know more about community conflict than we do about successful campaigns for communitywide cooperation.

Yet there is much relevant work to draw on, ranging from studies of social movements to ongoing research into civic engagement. And there is accumulating work on social capital. Indeed, if a central issue in school reform is degree of cooperation around a collective purpose, then why talk about civic capacity rather than social capital? After all, in the wake of significant work by sociologist James Coleman and political scientist Robert Putnam, much ink has been spilt over the concept of social capital. Why bring another term into play?

To begin with, much of the work on social capital concerns behavior that is largely interpersonal and private: the extent to which households in a neighborhood provide shared oversight and care for children, whether people bowl alone or in organized leagues, or the level of volunteer activity tied to church membership. By contrast, civic capacity centers on activities that are squarely in the public arena and involve governance institutions and major group representatives. When education reformers suggest bringing key stakeholders together, they are talking about assembling the *principal sectors* of the locality around a matter of communitywide import. We could think of such a gathering as a civic assembly, and it is one in which the public sector is central. At issue are questions about such matters as making collective attempts to change *public policy* or to enhance the power of the *public sector* to act through partnerships. In short, the fact of being in a civic arena makes salient broad considerations of a public kind. Even if the process does not involve a literal assembly, acting at the communitywide level and making appeals to others in that context has a public dimension that even highly altruistic microbehaviors lack.

Concepts like "social capital" and "civil society" provide many valuable insights and have surely increased the richness of public debate, but they have misdirected attention in at least two important ways. First, in emphasizing the naturalness and ease of cooperation in social realms apart from government, they tend to portray government and politics as corrupting forces that counterproductively inject lines of cleavage and conflict into otherwise harmonious relationships. In doing so, they fail to appreciate the several ways in which raising the scale from small group to collectivity genuinely and necessarily complicates matters. Second, by locating effective action in trust and interpersonal relationships, they fail to appreciate the senses in which formal institutions of governance can extend their force and authority without which the actions of even well-intentioned and like-minded people may sputter and fail.

Social capital implies sociability and social ties among individuals that can enhance collective problem solving. James Coleman describes it broadly as social relations "that facilitate action."[2] Robert Putnam has a more delimited concern. In his work, social capital centrally consists of such inclinations and skills as social trust and reciprocity, and they are important in part because they are deemed transferable. Reciprocity and social trust developed in one set of relationships, Putnam suggests, can be and are applied to others; they are not restricted to particular and bounded relationships.[3] When talking about a large public arena, however, a special caution should surround any discussion of social capital. Perhaps transferability occurs at the level of interpersonal behavior, but habits of cooperation that develop in small and close settings do not necessarily come into play when acting on a large and public stage.[4]

Education reform can, of course, occur at various levels—from the state government on down to a given school. In this book, our central concern is change at the citywide level. Hence we give special attention to intergroup relations and the ways they can hinder or facilitate collective action around a reform agenda. Although interpersonal bonds can provide a basis for cooperation in a small demonstration project or in a given school, the kind of personal interaction that holds sway at that level does not translate onto the citywide stage, where actions are often seen and judged in group terms. Frictions of race and class can be overcome in strictly face-to-face interactions much more easily than they can at an intergroup level. Past conflicts and injustices have strong staying power at the intergroup level, particularly when actors take on the role of group advocate. Anytime there is an effort to achieve fundamental reform, the group advocate role looms as a strong possibility. Fundamental reform involves major policy issues and heightens group differences, often making these issues highly contentious and providing a spawning ground for the kinds of intergroup maneuvering and symbolic politics that can erode prospects for pragmatic compromise.

Even when key players work out the terms for joint action at the citywide level, continued cooperation may be fragile. Misunderstanding may escalate rapidly, and intergroup relationships lack the same resilience and capacity for quick adjustment that personal relationships have. In an intergroup setting, tacit agreements are more readily overturned because more individuals have to stay in line. Since any of several individuals may balk at the interpretation of an agreement, differences are smoothed over less easily than in smaller and more intimate settings.

There are, then, conditions under which small-scale, interpersonal interactions are simply not the right mode of operation. Consider the implications for reform of what Norton Long calls an "ecology of games."[5] For most of the time in most American cities, policy is made through semiautonomous subsystems—one for law enforcement, one for transportation, one for education, and many others. The most active players tend to be the ones most directly affected through the jobs they hold, the property they own, or other immediate concerns they have; and they are the ones likely to direct the day-to-day activities of these subsystems. As a consequence, the policies pursued by members of the subsystem can deviate from what is in the best interest of the community.

Civic capacity involves mobilization by a broader array of community interests to remove policy-making authority from subperforming policy subsystems. Simply disrupting subsystems is not the point, however, even if the preexisting regime is inefficient or even corrupt. Policy making can slide back to old ways of doing things when broader political actors return to their "day jobs." Even worse, less-than-ideal but nonetheless working arrangements may be undermined with nothing to replace them besides chaos and uncertainty. If change is to occur and reform is to "stick," then subsystem relations need to be altered in a lasting way; an "institutional legacy" has to be established.[6] This is what makes fundamental reform so difficult. It calls for more than bringing short-term pressure to bear on an existing arrangement; instead, it calls for altering relationships. In an important sense, the old subsystem has to be replaced by a new or remade one. The disturbance involved in such a change can be far-reaching.

Education is not unique in confronting such challenges. Recent research on policy change has established that there is a common pattern in which policy subsystems experience long periods of relatively settled thinking and power relationships, occasionally punctuated by spasms of disjointed change.[7] During much of the twentieth century, the American education policy subsystem was characterized by stability and consensus, and ideologically and institutionally defended by a combination of deferral to experts and the reservation of potentially divisive decisions to local norms. The lurching and uncertain political dynamics that we find in the education policy arena today reflects the fact that this is a subsystem in which the equilibrium has been punctured—long-standing assumptions are being questioned, new stakeholders have asserted a claim to have influence, and settled arrangements are in disarray. This period of disequilibrium is more extended than the literature on policy dynamics leads us to expect. That may partly reflect a tendency of that literature to overly compress its characterization of the transition between periods of equilibrium; in emphasizing stability over extended periods of history, it may have underestimated the extent to which competing problem definitions and alternative institutional arrangements may coexist while political battles between the new and the old regime remain unresolved. But we also believe that there are differences among types of policy arenas, some being more vulnerable to disruption and more difficult to tame. Education, we suggest in Chapter 2, may be such a "high-reverberation" policy subsystem, where institutionalizing change is no easy matter at all.

To look at urban school reform in this way is to go beyond such things as pedagogical innovations at the school level, new management practices, or the addition of intensified professional development for teachers. It is to ask whether

or not basically different relationships are put in place. For reform to be fundamental, mobilization has to be sustained and has to institutionalize new practices
and relationships. Because the inner core of a subsystem—in the case of education, what Wilbur Rich has called "the public school cartel"—rarely reforms itself, some form of civic mobilization seems essential.[8] This is what civic capacity
is about, wide mobilization around a shared concern. Activating this process is
almost certain to necessitate overcoming some set of intergroup tensions.

Civic mobilization is, of course, a political action. It is not a magical kind of
consensus that simply emerges on occasion; it has to be created politically. Because in popular use politics often implies opportunistic pursuit of personal gain
or partisan advantage, some education reformers may be uncomfortable with
phrases like "political action." But politics also has an older meaning: The activity by which a diverse citizenry reconcile, put aside, or in some manner accom-
modate their differences in order to pursue their common well-being. This can
entail various actors expanding their normally narrow understanding, each developing a capacity to appreciate the needs and wants of others. It could turn on the
community developing a large vision of what it as a collectivity can and should
do. Or perhaps the different players gradually work out an overarching scheme in
which their sundry wants can be satisfied mutually or at least facilitated by an
understanding of mutual noninterference. Of course, it could also rest on some
combination of the above.

Politics will occur. Differences will be dealt with to pursue broad and shared
aims, to serve narrow and particular aims, or some mix of these. Politics is the
name attached to the activity that determines what the mix will be. Because urban
communities are diverse and because urban school children are a highly vulnerable group, urban education is an important testing ground for politics and whether
it can be made to serve worthy aims.

Put another way, members of an urban community share a common existence. This common existence can be characterized by narrow aims and opportunistic behavior, or it can be characterized by attention to broad and socially worthy
aims. How the community arrives at one or the other is politics, and so is the process of changing from one mode of common existence to another.[9] Attention to
politics therefore includes attention to how a community defines and pursues its
aims. Civic mobilization is a political action, and so too is any effort to shape policy-
making relationships through the creation of an institutional legacy. Change advocates who talk about systemic school reform certainly understand that piecemeal
innovations may have little impact, and they look toward altered relationships in
the education arena (or subsystem) as necessary for real change to occur. It is this
(sub-) systemic scope that we are most concerned to address in the writing of this
book.

Readers interested in these issues will find related themes developed in some
of the other books that have their origin wholly or in part in the Civic Capacity
and Urban Education Project. Clarence N. Stone, *Changing Urban Education*

(Lawrence: University Press of Kansas, 1998), is an edited volume that uses the civic capacity concept to frame and interpret case studies of reform efforts in nine city and suburban school districts. John Portz, Lana Stein, and Robin R. Jones, in *City Schools and City Politics: Institutions and Leadership in Pittsburgh, Boston, and St. Louis* (Lawrence: University Press of Kansas, 1999), explore how city and education leaders draw upon or are thwarted by local culture and institutional context in their efforts to build and activate civic capacity. Jeffrey R. Henig, Richard C. Hula, Marion Orr, and Desiree S. Pedescleaux, in *The Color of School Reform: Race, Politics, and the Challenge of Urban Education* (Princeton, N.J.: Princeton University Press, 1999), explore how race complicates the process of school reform in four cities—Atlanta, Baltimore, Detroit, and Washington, D.C.— in which the levers of local governmental authority have passed firmly into the hands of African Americans. Marion Orr, in *Black Social Capital* (Lawrence: University Press of Kansas, 1999), looks deeper, and with a longer historical sweep, into the political and social underpinnings of reform in Baltimore. And Susan Clarke, Rodney Hero, Mara Sidney, Bari Erlichson, and Luis Fraga, in *The New Educational Populism: The Multi-Ethnic Politics of School Reform,* a forthcoming book, focus on the volatile relationship between African Americans and the rapidly expanding Latino and Asian minorities in Denver, Los Angeles, San Francisco, and Boston. In addition to developing distinct but complementary arguments, these works provide more in-depth discussion of some of the case cities than we feasibly could cover in this book.

1

The Scope of the Problem

Significant educational improvements may not materialize unless the political life of schools creates and sustains authority for it.
Anthony Bryk et al., *Charting Chicago School Reform*

Americans are generally concerned about the state of public education, but it is the plight of the urban school that especially cries out for attention.[1] Education is closely linked to equality of opportunity and the potential for upward mobility in Americans' thoughts and values, but where the need for these is greatest, our capacity to deliver on the promise has been most attenuated. Children in urban school districts are more than twice as likely to attend high-poverty schools; in places like East St. Louis, Camden, Detroit, New Orleans, Hartford, Miami, Atlanta, Cleveland, and Dayton, more than four out of every ten schoolchildren are poor. Yet children in such districts also are less likely to have teachers who majored in the subjects they are responsible for teaching, and their teachers are more likely to call in sick and to quit their jobs before the end of the school year. Based on the National Assessment of Educational Progress, students in nonurban school districts are more than 50 percent more likely than urban students to score at the "basic" level in reading, mathematics, and science. Moreover, this urban performance gap is not due to poverty alone. It is true that urban districts house more poor children than do nonurban districts; urban districts account for 24 percent of all public school children, but 35 percent of those who are poor. But when one controls for poverty differences by comparing high-poverty schools in nonurban areas to those in urban areas, the performance gap is proportionally higher—closer to 100 percent—than when all schools are compared. Forty-six percent of nonurban students in high-poverty schools reach the basic level in reading, for example, compared with only 23 percent in high-poverty urban schools; in math the comparable rates are 61 percent to 33 percent achieving basic level, and in science they are 56 percent to 31 percent.[2]

The failure of central-city school systems to prepare youth to survive and thrive is both tragic and surprising. It is tragic because the global economy shows no mercy to individuals who lack basic skills. The manufacturing economy of the early and mid-1900s was more forgiving. High school graduates and dropouts could find entry-level jobs and earn a decent pay. Today, with manufacturing in decline and a change in the qualifications for manufacturing jobs that remain, jobs for workers without at least some college are increasingly hard to come by. Boston, Chicago, Cleveland, Detroit, New York, and Philadelphia each had declines of approximately 50 percent in jobs for people without high school diplomas between 1970 and 1980, at the same time that the number of jobs for workers with at least some college increased by one-third or more.[3] Thus, modern corporations, as others have detailed, do not need quite as many low-skill workers—even jobs low on the corporate totem pole increasingly require workers who are technologically literate—and when they do need them, they can find them in other countries where the costs of labor are far lower. The result is a growing inequality in income and, more striking, wealth, and the prospect that large concentrations of urban Americans may fall further and further behind.

This failure is surprising because urban public schools were once the nation's pride, because the mission of school reform has been high on the public agenda, and because local leaders and citizens have demonstrated a capacity to work cooperatively and effectively to meet public goals in other arenas—most notably the physical and economic development of downtown areas. Deindustrialization, emerging technologies of communication, and the automobile and suburban growth in combination altered the economic function of the city and sent many cities into a spiral of seemingly irreversible decline. But although these pressures led some observers to resignation and despair, in many places they set in motion impressive efforts to respond. Not surprisingly, the recasting of the city's physical landscape has occupied center stage, with urban renewal and the building of expressways establishing a direction that still prevails. Enormous resources, material and mental, have gone into developing new facilities, redesigning urban transportation, and altering land use. The dismal headlines of the earlier era have been displaced, in many cases, by optimistic declarations that "the city is back."[4]

But what about the *social* reconstruction of the city? Demographic change has accompanied physical change and given us central cities with huge concentrations of the poor. Such class composition has profound consequences, particularly for schools. In jurisdictions that house a largely middle-class population, the diffuse actions of private households provide a robust human-capital base on which educators can build, and children, believing that society strongly values them, meet life with hope and expectations. For lower socioeconomic populations the private household is a limited source of human-capital investment, and children may, with good reason, feel that society holds them in low regard. Educators of the concentrated poor, particularly, face a much different challenge than their counterparts who teach the offspring of the affluent middle class. Thus, the uneven distribution of resources and opportunities creates a severe underinvestment in the children of the poor, and low-performing schools are one result.

None of this is by grand social design; it is simply the consequence of diffuse actions pursued in a market-based society. There is every reason to believe that the pattern is reversible. Just as public-private partnerships employed the combined resources of the governmental and business sectors to reconfigure land use and redevelop the city physically, so the combined actions of the governmental and nongovernmental sectors can provide a compensatory response to underinvestment in children in urban school systems. However, the politics of collaboration around urban education is underexplored terrain. We know little about the ability of urban communities to develop and carry out a collective answer to the educational needs of the poor in a postindustrial world.

As we sought to examine the urban experience with systemic school reform, we centered on a two-stage question. First, what political conditions favor greater movement toward a broad effort to improve public education? The potential answer we examined was "greater civic capacity." And, if our research supported that answer, as turned out to be the case, the follow-up question would be: What facilitates greater civic capacity *around the issue of urban education?* That proved to be no easy puzzle to solve, although, as we shall argue below, our research provides useful clues.

What, then, is civic capacity, and why specify "around the issue of urban education"? Civic capacity has to do with the ability of a community to come together to address its problems. Our research taught us quickly, however, that civic capacity is not a generic quality; an ability to address educational improvement is not simply an application of a general community capacity to solve problems.

THE NORM IN URBAN SCHOOL REFORM: EPISODIC AND INEFFECTUAL MOBILIZATION

Observing the failure of urban school systems to respond more dramatically and effectively to the challenges before them, some analysts have pointed their fingers at a seemingly complacent American public.[5] "Self-deception *cum* complacency is a major contributor to the U.S. education disaster," according to Chester Finn, a former assistant secretary in the U.S. Department of Education. Others have blamed an education bureaucracy that they see as self-interested, rigid, unimaginative, and indifferent or actively hostile toward the children that it is meant to serve. Both of these perspectives encourage an overly simplistic conclusion:

Urban schools are failing because no one is trying hard enough to make them succeed. Defining the problem this way encourages reformers to focus their energies on the politics of agenda setting: raising the level of public information about poor school performance and beating the drum about how this failure hurts the country in both economic and social terms.

Recent research, however, has suggested that this characterization is wrong. Urban school systems are not ostrichlike deniers of the seriousness of the problems that face them. Nor are they reactionary devotees of the status quo. It is true that many large, central-city school systems are thickly bureaucratized, and many have teachers' and principals' unions that have opposed reforms that others see as vital. Yet even the systems with the most deserved reputations for unresponsiveness are more like bubbling cauldrons than frozen ponds. "Not only are districts pursuing an immense number of reforms," one researcher reports, "they recycle initiatives, constantly modify previous initiatives, and adopt innovative reform."[6] Another analyst refers to this as the tendency toward a "reform du jour."[7]

Not all cauldrons that bubble, however, provide a harnessed source of thermal power. Sincere and energetic efforts to bring about systemic education reform cycle in and out of the cities we studied. Reforms and initiatives launched by this or that innovative principal or in response to this or that foundation or government grant falter when the original instigator moves on, when funding dries up, or when dissenting voices emerge. The normal innovation, accordingly, generates movement but not progress; variation does not accumulate into systemic change. At sporadic intervals those outside of the education community take note. Local newspapers, activists, and business elites "discover" the education problem and mount frantic efforts to join hands in a collective movement of reform. But high hopes typically founder when the challenge proves more formidable than initially presumed. When the financial and personal costs of wrestling with urban school problems prove daunting and when test scores fail to rocket, reform coalitions unravel in a puddle of enervation and resignation.

Take, for example, the case of Atlanta. Atlanta has demonstrated a tremendous capacity to pursue a policy of urban redevelopment centered on the city's main business district. Yet Atlanta has consistently failed to draw key sectors of the community together around an agenda of educational improvement.

In 1993, a decade after the publication of *A Nation at Risk,* Atlanta seemed ripe for a thoroughgoing reform effort. Schools were performing at an abysmal level, with test scores even lower than in some of Georgia's rural counties. Moreover, the longer Atlanta students were in the education system, the worse they performed; high school scores were even more dismal than scores in the elementary grades. The drop-out rate was high, at an estimated 30 percent. Even with per-pupil expenditures higher in Atlanta than in many of the surrounding suburbs, enrollment in city schools had gone down at an astonishing rate. From 1975 to 1993 enrollment halved, declining from 119,000 to 60,000.

Atlanta's elected school board was scandal-ridden and rife with conflict, leading one observer to characterize it as "the most criticized and ridiculed" body in the city government.[8] One school board member had been removed for channeling funds at questionable payment levels to favored contractors, and another board member was under fire for accepting funds from the board's highly paid ($300,000 per annum) attorney. The board was sharply split along racial lines, and personal disputes within and across racial lines heightened the conflict level. Civility was at a low level, and an argument between a member of the board of education and the school superintendent nearly turned violent. Though school board proceedings were televised and therefore public, questions of education policy took a backseat to issues of who was in charge of what, contracts, jobs, and school employee compensation packages.

With school board elections upcoming, the time seemed right for coalition-building around a fresh start. If Atlanta were to build civic capacity around educational improvement, 1993 would seem to have been the time to do so. Business, recognizing the urgency of the situation, put aside its practice of disengagement and created a campaign organization, EDUPAC, to support a new majority on the nine-member school board. In an environment of rising opposition, four members of the board chose not to seek reelection. A biracial coalition came together in another organization, Erase the Board, seeking a completely new school board. Erase the Board was headed by the president of Concerned Black Clergy, and it enjoyed biracial support spanning a diverse set of groups: the Atlanta Council of PTAs (a racially mixed but majority black organization), 100 Black Men, Atlanta Parents and Public Linked to Education (Apple Corps., a small but well-organized group then headed by white women professionals), the education division of Jimmy Carter's Atlanta Project (a group with strong business connections), the teachers' union, and the Council of In-Town Neighborhoods and Schools (another racially mixed group). Whereas Erase the Board sought a complete ousting of incumbents, EDUPAC supported three incumbents, and those three were reelected. But two other incumbents were defeated, and the postelection board of education had six new members. The school superintendent also resigned, and the stage was set for a new era in Atlanta's education politics. For a time, racial division had taken a backseat to a move for change.

With business having a renewed interest in education, the chamber of commerce formed a Committee on Public Education as an organization to bridge the gap between business and schools. Already in place at that time was the Atlanta Partnership of Business and Education, concerned with such matters as adopt-a-school programs and teacher-of-the-year awards. In addition, like most cities, at this time Atlanta had a number of advocacy groups for children as well as organizations concerned with various aspects of youth development. Overall there was no shortage of actors interested in education and related matters. Diffuse concerns provide useful raw material, but in and of themselves they do not generate synergy.

With schools desperately in need of attention, with the education issue prominent in public discussion, with a diverse set of players coming together to elect a new school board, and with an opening to bring in a new school superintendent, Atlanta could have come together to build a high level of civic engagement around improving its education system. It did not. Interest in school reform existed, but it was scattered among several organizations, each of which continued to pursue its particular agenda. No one came forward to summon the disparate players to join efforts and form an encompassing coalition with a comprehensive program of action. Once the election was over, broad concerns faded, and the business community once again narrowed its focus to the conventional issues of containing costs, unbusinesslike practices such as tenure (subsequently eliminated by state legislation), and excessive bureaucracy. The new school board and new superintendent embraced a kindred outlook and soon occupied themselves with various financial matters such as the underfunded pension plan and with economy measures such as school closings. Such issues as the use of closed schools, underutilized space for prekindergarten programs, and services for families and children went unpursued.

The one move toward a comprehensive approach was the Atlanta Project of Jimmy Carter. Launched during the city's preparation for the Summer Olympics, this was a business-backed and nongovernmental effort to address poverty and show the world that Atlanta possessed a social conscience. It was a five-year program intended to spur volunteerism in Atlanta to new heights, but it came under criticism for its lack of focus, its paternalistic approach, and the unrealistic expectations it fostered.[9] It was weak on community consultation, and after its planned five years, the Atlanta Project closed shop, leaving only a few of the initiatives it launched still operating. With opened-ended aims but a firm promise to business to remain separate from local government, the Atlanta Project lacked sustaining power and possessed no institutional capacity to design programs to combat poverty and improve city schools.

Perhaps as an unintended legacy of the once-touted Atlanta Compromise,[10] education has proved to be highly resistant to civic mobilization. During the 1990s, the school system had four different superintendents (the fourth continues in office at this writing), and many of them have shown little inclination to court business involvement. Moreover, since the 1993 chamber of commerce study mentioned above, business has mainly been critical of Atlanta schools and their management practices.

Today, the striking feature of the Atlanta scene is the scarcity of people either seeking to enlist elites to come together on the education issue or to overcome the distrust among the masses. Despite the city's long history of biracial governance around urban redevelopment, Atlanta's education arena provides a striking example of weak civic capacity. As an issue, education remains tellingly disconnected from economic development.

The story of education reform in Atlanta—a story we find repeated elsewhere in broad form if not the specific details—is a story of spent energies, not complacency or indifference. Rallying the public for another round of exertion is not likely to solve the problem; indeed, each subsequent cycle of high hopes and frustrating results makes it harder to generate political support for a reform initiative the next time around. Discovering why some cities fall victim to this cycle and why this cycle is more common in the education policy subsystems than others are two of the questions that animate this book. But our goal is not just to understand failure. Our intent is to discover insights into the conditions for success as well.

NOT ALL NEWS IS BAD NEWS: SCHOOL REFORM THAT SEEMS TO WORK

Finding genuine cases of sustained and systemic urban school reform is more difficult than one might expect. Complicating matters is the very pattern of episodic enthusiastic mobilization that we have just described. Each local district that launches itself into the reform cycle tends to generate optimistic accounts about progress being made and anticipated. Reform leaders within these cities have an incentive to highlight, even exaggerate, such accounts to build confidence that efforts will be rewarded. Reformers in other cities, political entrepreneurs, and the national media often pick up on these reports; the distinction between proven results and enthusiastic projections often gets lost in the process. Popular accounts of "successful" reforms in other places, therefore, need to be regarded skeptically.

Nonetheless, there are reasons to believe that some places have managed to make more lasting, comprehensive, and sustained efforts than others. Chicago is one possible contender. Clearly, it has garnered substantial national attention, and, although close examination and considered judgment suggest that there may be some hype and premature celebration in the national accounts, there is some hard evidence to back up the soft anecdotes suggesting that genuine change is under way.[11]

Contrast with Atlanta Chicago's experience with school reform. After *A Nation at Risk* and other reports put the spotlight on public education, the weak performance of many school districts came under close scrutiny. During a 1987 visit to Chicago, then–U.S. Secretary of Education William J. Bennett labeled the city's school system the "worst in America" and said to Chicagoans: "You've got close to educational meltdown."[12] Bennett lent drama to what the city's research and advocacy groups had already documented: A high dropout rate and low test scores were damning proof of the failure of Chicago schools.

In 1987, the same year that Bennett's comments caused a stir, a prolonged teachers' strike (the ninth in eighteen years) brought matters to a head, and Mayor Harold Washington initiated a summit process, bringing major sectors of the community together to address the need for school reform. The mayor had already taken a preliminary step to draw Chicago business into a more active and open role.[13] After the strike settlement, Mayor Washington arranged for an all-day, open meeting on the city schools. "Attended by thousands," this meeting led the mayor to appoint a Parent Community Council, and he asked it to sponsor "parent and community forums throughout the city."[14] Though Harold Washington's death a short time later weakened the effort to create a tight-knit coalition around school reform, the process had nevertheless been set in motion, and the reform coalition achieved far-reaching legislation to create decentralization and parent participation through a system of powerful local school councils. Subsequently, however, with a shift in party control of the Illinois legislature, a business-dominated coalition gained state authorization for an additional form of restructuring superimposed on the recent decentralization. It provided for business-style management, controlled by city hall, to guide and monitor the school system overall. Mayor Richard M. Daley embraced this version of school reform and put in place a management team to operate it.

Chicago thus illustrates not a highly developed form of civic capacity but a loosely joined form. Short on continuity, it nevertheless represents a markedly higher level than the diffuse and fragmented capacity Atlanta displays. From the outset, Chicago possessed significant research and advocacy groups able to focus attention on systemwide problems. Chicago business has a long record of involvement in education, and its concerns are broader than the low-taxation, economy-and-efficiency concerns that Atlanta business displays. In addition, first under Mayor Harold Washington and later under Mayor Richard M. Daley, city hall has played an active role, of a more facilitative kind under Washington and of a more top-command kind under Daley. Significantly, however, parent and community-based groups have also played an important, albeit uneven, part, first in shaping the reform agenda and later in implementing decentralization. Although the major players have not always formed a tight-knit coalition, they have cohered to a significant degree around sundry efforts to improve schools.[15] Chicago shows, however, that civic capacity is not constant and does not always build cumulatively. Civic capacity can and does sometime regress.

Another strong candidate for acknowledgment as a reform model is El Paso, Texas.[16] In the early 1990s, confronted, as were many other cities, by weakly performing schools and a wide achievement gap between minority and Anglo students, El Paso moved to foster communitywide collaboration around educational improvement. Following extensive discussion among a cross-section of city leaders, a small group came together to form the El Paso Collaborative for Academic Excellence. The key figures were the superintendents of the three school districts that serve El Paso; the president of the University of Texas, El Paso; the president of El Paso Community College; the executive director of the Texas Education Agency's regional service center; the lead organizer of the El Paso Interreligious Sponsoring Organization (an affiliate of the Industrial Areas Foundation); the president of the Greater El Paso Chamber of Commerce; the president of the El Paso Hispanic Chamber of Commerce; the mayor of the city; and the county judge.

Unlike the loosely joined reform movement in Chicago or the totally scattered activity in Atlanta, El Paso formed and still maintains (unlike Chicago's short-lived summit effort) a tight-knit organization around a set of agreed-upon concerns. The collaborative has a professional staff, pursues activities that involve parents and the broader community, and has embarked on a project to develop "a cadre of community leaders and parents who are willing to support educational renewal for the long term" and help "keep the public engaged in the endeavor."[17] By maintaining a focus on essentials, especially teacher quality and training, the collaborative appears to have managed to meet the twin goals of raising overall student performance and substantially narrowing the gaps among racially and ethnically defined groups. In the 1992–1993 school year, 63.1 percent of white students, but only 36.2 percent of Hispanics and 32.3 percent of African Americans passed the standardized mathematics test used by the district. Five years later the passing rate for white students had risen to 94.2 percent, that for Hispanics reached 86.4 percent, and that for African Americans was 85.2 percent.[18]

The business sector has played a major part. In February 1998, city leaders came together in an Economic Summit identifying education and workforce development as a top priority for the city. The Greater El Paso Chamber of Commerce followed this summit with a business/education white paper, including a series of recommendations for how businesses could address the concerns identified.[19] Another period of community consultation followed, and in February 2000 the city held an Education Summit to move on a wide array of specific recommendations.

Several things are notable about El Paso's experience. One is that all sectors of the community are represented, including the leadership of the city's three school districts. Moreover, not only is there a major community-based organization involved, the development of parent and community leadership and the promotion of grassroots engagement are part of the ongoing activity of the collaborative. Another notable feature is the strong representation of institutional bases of power and resources: the three school districts, the state, the city, the county, two chambers of commerce, the university, and the community college. Yet another notable feature is the durable character of the collaboration. Significantly, it is formally organized and staffed, and it maintains a high level of visible activity. Perhaps related to this feature of El Paso's experience is the fact that collaboration focuses on concrete and specific courses of action; it is no mere expression of general sentiment. Further, grassroots and elite-level consultation and deliberation are ongoing activities. Finally, it should be noted that the collaborative has received important material and intellectual support from extralocal sources: the National Science Foundation (the Urban Systemic Initiative); the Pew Charitable Trusts; the Education Trust, headed by Kati Haycock; and John Goodlad's National Network for Educational Renewal.[20]

If Atlanta, Chicago, and El Paso are aligned along a continuum of systemic school reform, the question remains as to what factors account for the differ-ences among them. What accounts for the fact that some jurisdictions may do a better job of breaking out of the cycle of episodic and ephemeral reform? Is this a matter of preexisting differences in education resources, smart school leaders, better designed governing institutions in the education arena, or simply better ideas about what good education entails? Or are there other factors—factors more closely tied to networks of cooperation and lines of political conflict outside of as well as within the education policy subsystem—that are important parts of the tale?

OUR APPROACH AND RESEARCH DESIGN

As a centerpiece in the social reconstruction of the city, educational improvement is unquestionably a collective good with potentially great benefits. Understand-ably, then, educators and advocates of school reform often talk about the need to bring together and involve stakeholders. But this may assume away the central problem. Well-meaning calls for education stakeholders—parents, business lead-ers, teachers, school administrators, public officeholders, community groups, social-agency staff, foundation officers, and miscellaneous others—to join hands rest on the dubious premise that, in the past, these actors have been complacent or stubbornly resistant to cooperation. Yet this is not the case. Most central cities—perhaps all—have been staging grounds for efforts to build coalitions to improve urban schools. But many such efforts have been sporadic and short-lived. Instead of assuming that school reform is simply a matter of issuing the call to action, it might be better to start by asking under what conditions cooperation is more likely to occur, and, when it does so, whether this cooperation has policy consequences. These are the questions that have guided an eleven-city study, "Civic Capacity and Urban Education."

A Political Perspective

V. O. Key and Frank Munger once said, "In research the answers one gets depend in part on the kinds of questions [one] asks."[21] The authors of this volume and the larger research team conducting the eleven-city study are all political scientists. Thus, the questions we ask are about politics, and these, we believe, are questions that education reformers often neglect. Specialists frequently assume that policy making is a matter of selecting good, professionally sound techniques, and they often believe that, if information about good practice is widely disseminated, change will follow. In the case of education, some analysts believe that a reform template can be spread first from school to school and then from system to system. In this view, what the world needs is a replicable model, whether of curriculum, pedagogical technique, professional training, school organization, the market model, or some other technique. Yet the world of education is populated with applications of technique, many of which are effective in some cases but not in others, and many of which are untried in more than name. From all indications, the presence of successful "demonstrations" in one school is not the path to system reform.

Good technique is not a form of contagion, spreading readily from one case to another with all or most schools susceptible to its appeal. Indeed, the specifics of technique may be less important than the relationships that link school and community. Put another way, educational reform does not take place in a political vacuum. Reform has to come to terms with a wider set of relationships that encompass a city's schools.[22]

Educational reform is also not simply a matter of spending more money. For many years, to be sure, litigation over equitable funding was a major reform initiative, and such efforts continue—efforts to see that sufficient resources are available to poorer school districts to enable them to provide an effective education for all children, regardless of background and family income.[23] At the same time, it is clear that, useful as education money is—especially in the face of the heavy demands of special education—funding by itself is no guarantee of academic performance.[24]

Moreover, in a predominantly suburban nation, political reality runs against the likelihood that broad support can be organized around a program of redistribution that favors city schools. Putting substantially more money into urban schools at the expense of suburban schools (or into schools of color at the expense of white ones or into lower-income schools over higher-income ones) is, as one pair of authors observed, "politically inconceivable."[25] Marginal adjustments are possible, but urban schools face a funding dilemma. If they perform well, this may serve as evidence to suburban legislators that city schools don't need more resources. If they perform poorly, this is often taken as evidence that city systems waste the money they do have. Large-scale redistribution in education finance thus appears to be an unlikely path of reform.

To us, the question of change is one of how sectors of the community relate to one another, including how these relationships might be affected by the intergovernmental context in which they take shape. In conducting research for an eleven-city study, we used the phrase "civic capacity" to refer to the involvement of various sectors of the community in a problem-solving effort. Numerous cities have demonstrated an impressive level of civic capacity in addressing the problems of physical redevelopment by means of public-private partnerships (both formal and informal), but examples of robust civic involvement in the area of social reconstruction are not widely available. At the same time, there is evidence that some cities display a stronger tendency in this direction than others.

Our Cases

We selected eleven cities to study with several criteria in mind. There was no special magic about the number eleven; we wanted enough cases to allow some leverage in making analytic comparison and uncovering patterns, but few enough cases that we would be able to undertake substantial field research to gather the qualitative and historical data that we expected to be important. The decision to focus on eleven cities, instead of nine or ten or twelve, was driven less by abstract criteria than by a combination of resource availability and ad hoc opportunities.

We made an a priori decision to restrict our analysis to large, central-city school systems with sizable proportions of low-income and minority students. One optimistic possibility is that the severity of the problem will itself play a central part in determining the extent of the local community response: The more acute the problem, the more likely will a broad segment of the community respond and act. Hence, a high level of poverty might be cause for civic concern and mobilization. This view is optimistic because it presumes that our political system is generally self-correcting. Yet related studies caution us that the objective characteristics of a problem (including its intensity) rarely explain political mobilization.[26] The eleven cities we selected—Atlanta, Baltimore, Boston, Denver, Detroit, the District of Columbia, Houston, Los Angeles, Pittsburgh, St. Louis, and San Francisco are tough cases, then. We expected to find more evidence about obstacles than successes—and we did. We knew that some wealthier, more homogeneous, suburban school districts have had more success in building and maintaining coalitions to support education reform.[27] Even in those conducive settings, the challenge of undertaking sustained and systemic reform is more complicated than many imagine, but we were especially interested in what might account for variation across jurisdictions that had a harder row to hoe.

Precisely because we were interested in variation, our selection process was designed to include some schools districts that *were* doing a better job, or at least had some reputation for doing so. This is not to say that we began by carefully and precisely scoring and ranking a large number of school districts in terms of their school reform efforts. There are no uniform and broadly accepted measures of school district success that we could turn to in order to build a sampling frame in that way. Rather, we scanned the literature and questioned other researchers to roughly and initially categorize districts and selected some cities specifically because there were indications that they were being relatively more successful than others, at least in some regards. Ultimately, as we explain in Chapter 4, three of the districts we selected—Pittsburgh, Boston, and Los Angeles—showed evidence of a more developed civic capacity for undertaking school reform during the time period we studied; four—Baltimore, Houston, Detroit, and Washington, D.C.— fell into an intermediate position, and four—Atlanta, Denver, St. Louis, and San Francisco—were more disorganized and undirected in the efforts they mounted.

Accounting for these differences is the research question that lies at the heart of this study.

A third important criterion in selecting the eleven cities was regional variation. At the outset, our thinking here was rather conventional. Social scientists have found good evidence that things like political institutions, political culture, and demographic patterns matter and that these in turn tend to cluster geographically. Accordingly, we made an effort to select some cities in the Northeast, some in the Midwest, some in the Southeast, some in the Southwest, and some in the Far West. As our field research began to progress, however, our thinking about the regional variation became more specific and mature. Region, it was once written, is "an undifferentiated *potpourri*";[28] to attribute a causal role to region is to leave unanswered critically important questions about *what aspect* associated with regions is responsible.

Consistent with our focus on politics, we came to realize that the key factor underlying the regional differences we encountered had to do with political constituencies. Pluralist theory suggests that political reactions are filtered through society's group structure. In education, racial groups are especially important. We found that we could meaningfully divide our eleven cities into three categories corresponding to different kinds of racial-political dynamics. One is what we call black-led cities (Atlanta, Baltimore, Detroit, and Washington, D.C.)—cities in which the school enrollment is overwhelmingly African American. Thus, in racial terms the most directly affected constituency is African American. At the same time, the school board and upper levels of school administration along with city hall are also preponderantly in the hands of African Americans, the same racial group as the constituency most directly affected. To be sure, economic power and control of state levers of power remain largely in white hands, but local positions of power and the student body are racially aligned.

A second category is what we call machine-descendant cities (Boston, Pittsburgh, and St. Louis)—cities in which machine politics resting on a white ethnic base had been dominant once, but business leaders worked out policy accommodations around urban redevelopment with city political leaders. In education, however, these are cities in which the school enrollment is predominantly children of color and the electorate is majority white; thus, the most directly affected constituency and the balance of electoral power are not racially aligned.

The third category is labeled Sunbelt cities (Denver, Houston, Los Angeles, and San Francisco)—cities in which the school enrollment and the electorate are multiracial and changing. In three of these cities, Hispanic students were the largest racial-ethnic group, and in the fourth (San Francisco) Asian Americans were the largest group. Moreover, these four cities were the most volatile in demography and politics. In none of the four cities were African Americans the largest minority, but in all four African Americans had gained early access to education policy and administration through the desegregation issue. That "inside" position was, however, challenged by newer minorities. Hence there were tensions between minority groups as well as between once-dominant whites and minorities. Continuing change and rising tensions rather than racial alignment characterized the relationship between the most affected constituencies and official positions of power.

As we shall see later, the level of civic involvement corresponds closely neither to level of poverty nor to a constituency base identified racially. The political character of a city does not spring full-grown from its socioeconomic foundation.

Putting Local Education in Its Place: Two Key Assumptions

The project on civic capacity and urban education rests on at least two assumptions that should be made explicit. One is that education, if it ever was, is no longer an isolated arena of activity. To be sure, a degree of professional autonomy and specialized knowledge provides educators with room to maneuver. But the high turnover rate among big-city school superintendents underscores their close interdependence with the politics of the urban community. It is now widely recognized that education is interwoven with other areas of life, and educators are part of a complex web of relationships. The term *stakeholder* is one acknowledgment of this current reality. Thus our research treats school superintendents, not as administrative entrepreneurs capable of shaping a world of their own, but as one category of actor in a much larger field of players.

A second assumption we make is that cities have a widely recognized need to pursue and improve performance by their educational systems, but that recognition of a need does not in itself guarantee the political will to act on that need. Though urbanists have long been attentive to the challenges that emanate from a global economy, few have given close attention to education as a response to these challenges.[29]

Obviously, globalization is a significant occurrence for cities, and it can be related to much of what is taking place in education as in other policy arenas. The publication of *A Nation at Risk* is testimony to this point.[30] In a related move, concern with global economic competitiveness has activated corporate business, not only at the national level, but on the state and local level as well.[31] And so the place of education reform on the policy agenda owes much to the heightened awareness of the global economy.

Still, globalization is not the whole story. Global economic competition gives broad signals about the importance of education in the changing economy, but that is only one step toward action. Global economic competition does not offer comprehensive and immediate feedback that dictates policy. Actors at various levels can and do respond in a variety of ways, and their actions may be guided by concerns they see as more pressing than the global economy. Where multiple

demands on time and resources exist, relationships among civic and political leaders may facilitate action on some matters but not others.

Thus, in this study, our assumption is that though improved educational performance is recognized as an appropriate response to a global economy, that recognition becomes a factor only to the extent that it is converted into a frame of
action that motivates individual players to take concrete steps. How, then, is a frame
of action constructed? To begin to answer this question, we needed a research
design that would allow us to study education decision making within a broader
context than encompassed by most studies of school politics. We needed to understand how key stakeholders in the community—not just the education community—generally set and define their priorities and how formal and informal patterns
for cooperation keep conflicts from generating stalemates or cyclical tugs-of-war
that focus on which subgroup wins the battle for short-term power rather than how
the community can sustain genuine reform.

Method

The research methodology developed by the Civic Capacity and Urban Education
Project was designed to combine some of the advantages of in-depth case studies
with the critical leverage by making comparisons. Most studies of education politics and policy tend to concentrate on a single school district or many districts, with
relatively few striking a middle ground. The high degree of localism in American
decision making about schools makes in-depth case studies reasonable and, to some
extent, necessary. The single-case study is appropriate because many key decisions
may, in fact, depend on parochial idiosyncrasies such as local leadership and per-
sonalities, the configuration of local interest groups, and localized experiences of
handling past challenges such as school desegregation. Information about school
decision making is often closely guarded and data-gathering and measurements are
often ad hoc and inconsistent across jurisdictions, so an in-depth, single-case study
is sometimes the only feasible option. Although often rich and revealing, such studies can overemphasize the particular and fail to recognize broad patterns that are
common—albeit differentially presented—from place to place.

When contemporary education research *does* rise above the particulars of
single-case studies, it often rises so far that it loses contact with important aspects
of the local context. In a few areas—primarily where federal policies have dictated or made possible common forms of data collection—quantitative analyses
including large numbers of school districts are feasible and fairly common. Such
studies—focusing on demographic patterns, school finance, educational resources,
standardized test scores, and the like—have helped tremendously in our efforts to
disentangle causal relationships between family background, school organization,
and educational outcomes. But they have had little to tell us about the political
forces that shape and constrain public policy, primarily because the key political
variables are not easily measured. The one dimension of local political context

that *is* relatively easy to measure—the formal institutional framework—has possibly received undue emphasis simply because of that fact.[32]

To combine the detail and context of a single-case study with the analytical leverage provided by a multicase design, the Civic Capacity and Urban Education Project relied on eleven individuals or teams, each assigned to a particular school district. Each city study was headed by at least one professional political scientist already familiar with the history and context of political life within the city; indeed, we considered access to a local team leader with the requisite background and skills to be so important that it might be listed as the fourth major criterion that determined our choice of cases.[33] During the formative stages of the project, members of the overall study team met several times to help design the study and to discuss its implementation; this helped ensure that team members had a common understanding of the objectives and a similar understanding of key concepts and data instruments.

Using a common field research guide, scholars in each of the eleven cities collected a wide range of documentary evidence regarding demographic change, enrollment patterns, governmental expenditures, and school policies. In each city, researchers interviewed three types of respondents. *General influentials* were individuals who by position or reputation were likely to be important actors in local decision making across a range of policy issues not limited to education.[34] *Community-based representatives* were individuals active in children's advocacy groups, minority organizations, neighborhood organizations, religious organizations, and PTAs.[35] *Education specialists* were persons especially knowledgeable about the implementation of school system policies and programs.[36]

Researchers employed an interview template comprised mostly of open-ended questions; the sets of questions differed somewhat for the three broad types of respondents, although most of the questions were common across the groups.[37] We designed questions to elicit information about the broad political context, the way that education issues are conceptualized by central actors, lines of conflict and cooperation, and the kinds of program initiatives and reform efforts already in place. Interviews were taped, transcribed, and coded.[38] In all, 516 interviews were completed and coded. Readers who are interested in further details of the research design are directed to the appendices and to our web site, <http://depts.washington.edu/ampol/urbaned.htm>.

BUILDING BLOCKS FOR URBAN SCHOOL REFORM

In a recent examination of school reform, Paul Hill, Christine Campbell, and James Harvey offered the telling observation that "the normal politics of school systems cannot support fundamental reform."[39] Such reform never comes from people who are engaged in running routine operations. Even a highly innovative superintendent is unlikely to have a lasting impact without a strong foundation of community support: "Leadership must come from a longer-lasting source and one that is both more deeply rooted in the community than a superintendent and less protective of the status quo than a school board or district central office."[40] In applying this insight to understand the continuum of response that distinguishes Atlanta's school reform efforts from both its downtown development efforts and from El Paso's seemingly more cohesive and sustained school reform activities, we find it useful to think in terms of four conceptual building blocks.

We use the term *civic mobilization* to denote the degree to which various sectors of the community come together in sustained support of school reform and related efforts to improve educational opportunities and performance. We prefer *mobilization* to a more passive term like *coagulation* because we believe that it is intentional effort rather than simply the chemistry of the situation that brings groups together. We make and test the assumption that the broader the array of elements involved—with the core players being the parents of schoolchildren, the business sector, and the educators themselves (both teachers and administrators)—the more conducive the political climate is for school reform.

Issue definition is the second building block in our conceptualization of the conditions for school reform. The ability to mobilize across segments of the community will be applied to the particular challenge of educational improvement only when the members of the community acknowledge that inadequate schools constitute something in need of the attention of the community as a civic body. It is now widely appreciated that issues are not self-defining. For a problem to be recognized as a public issue requires not only that it be seen as a source of difficulties, but also that it be seen as something amenable to solution through civic or political action.[41] The actions of groups around an issue thus depend, in part, on how that issue is understood and what various players see as needed solutions. Issue definition, however, is unlikely to occur in a political void. It is important, then, to see what interests are politically mobilized as well as what understandings they share.

Issue definition and civic mobilization have a potentially synergistic relationship. A common issue definition could facilitate mobilization of diverse elements of the community. At the same time, coming together to consider emergent issues might provide an arena in which a shared understanding could be hammered out and elaborated, making it more likely that diverse elements can maintain themselves as a viable coalition. Yet there is nothing automatic about this process. As we shall see in a later chapter, our research suggests that political and civic leaders across the eleven cities we studied lack a tightly structured conception of the education issue. The absence of systemic reform is thus not surprising. Diffuse efforts at reform correspond to a diffuse understanding of the issue area.

School boards and school administrators in the normal course of events tend to focus on the immediate responsibilities of running a system, and, because they are an integral part of that system, their reflexes are to defend it. They do not ask fundamental questions about how effectively the community is being served. For those questions to be raised and pursued, people need to embrace a special kind of civic-mindedness. They do that by being brought together on a community-serving basis to confront a common need. This is what theorist Hannah Arendt regards as politics. For her, politics is not the everyday pushing and shoving around particular interests, but an activity *out of the ordinary* in which people become conscious of their common welfare and act upon it.[42]

In this light, we can think of civic mobilization and an orienting issue definition as necessary but not necessarily sufficient preconditions for our third building block: *civic capacity* to devise and employ formal and informal mechanisms to collectively solve problems. In its fullest form in education, civic capacity is a broad (that is, cross-sector) base of involvement along with a shared and durable understanding of public education as a major area of community concern and a high priority for action.

Civic capacity, as we conceive it, shares some elements with the conception of social capital that has recently become so prominent through the work of Robert Putnam and others. In Putnam's treatment, social capital comes about as people learn to work with one another, practice reciprocity, and develop trust.[43] Civic capacity, like social capital, can depend upon informal relationships and shared understanding built over time. But civic capacity also involves a more public and collective mediation among disparate interests and an integral relationship to formal institutions of governance. These elements make civic capacity a potentially more powerful force, but they also make it more problematic to generate and sustain.

Social capital as described by Putnam does not deplete from use: quite the contrary, use strengthens it. The more people work with one another and practice reciprocity, the greater the trust among them. And greater trust encourages more working together and wider practice of reciprocity. This view of social capital contains valuable insights about human behavior, but it seems to apply most readily to microbehavior—informal kinds of helping among people engaged in everyday activities. Repeated interactions provide opportunities for people to become comfortable with one another, develop understanding, and cooperate with minimal negotiations.

In education especially, civic capacity is about mobilizing various segments of the community to become engaged in considering and acting upon a problem in a way that is out of the ordinary. In many ways, civic cooperation is inherently unstable, especially when it operates out of the ordinary. Unlike the conventional social capital described by Putnam, civic capacity may not be self-replenishing. The public and collective nature of civic capacity and its connection to issues that are potentially controversial mean that a spirit of cooperation can be speedily eroded.

Our fourth building block, *systemic reform effort,* effectively serves as the dependent variable in this study. There is no single, universally accepted definition of systemic reform, but there are several widely accepted elements.[44] The strongest unifying themes are insistence that genuine reform comprises more than increased spending or indiscriminant dabbling in pedagogical fashions and fads. More substantive elements include introduction of less centralized and bureaucratic means of assuring accountability; attention to the ongoing interplay between schools and other important societal institutions such as family, work, and community; and the importance of combining clearly defined goals, a long-term orientation, and ways of measuring progress along the way. Befitting this somewhat amorphous definition, we adopt a multipronged and qualitative operational definition, as discussed more fully in Chapter 6.

It bears merit to emphasize that our study was not designed to be a program evaluation. Our concern was *not* to attempt to measure the effectiveness of various reforms, but to assess the degree to which a program for school improvement was in place.[45] Had we sought to measure the impacts of various initiatives, we would have encountered major obstacles. Most school systems give little heed to the establishment of experimental controls or even to the systematic collection of program data.[46] Moreover, the long time period required for realistic evaluation means that assessment needs to be extended over a period of several years. Experienced school reformers like James Comer and his coauthors remind us that real change takes time. Even at the individual school level, Comer sees five years as the minimum time needed to work through the inevitable missteps and give a program a chance to have an impact.[47] The Annie E. Casey Foundation's New Futures initiative took nine years to have a measurable impact in Savannah, Georgia—one of the foundation's most highly regarded ventures.[48] The quest for measurable impacts in the short run, some practitioners argue, has the effect of undercutting more fundamental changes. A short-run focus reinforces reliance on professional capacities already in place and may encourage caution rather than bold measures.[49] New expectations are an important part of any reform effort, and altering expectations and the relationships on which they are based is never an overnight process. Our concern, then, could not center on the long-term question of measurable impacts but on the more modest question of which cities are more extensively involved in efforts to lessen the isolation of schools and alter existing practices.

OVERVIEW

In the eleven-city study, we find that sundry elements of urban communities come together to *varying degrees* in support of school reform and other efforts to expand and improve educational opportunities for disadvantaged students. In short, civic involvement varies from city to city. Moreover, we find that greater cross-sector support generally yields a wider array of efforts to improve the performance of urban schoolchildren. However, although cross-sector mobilization varies, in none of the cities did it reach the highest level of civic capacity, and in several cities the level of cross-sector involvement in education was quite low. Thus, it is no surprise that we also find that none of the eleven cities produced a fully comprehensive effort to bring about an improved educational performance. Instead of the systemic reform that many educators talk about, we found a variety of pilot projects, demonstration schools, and innovative practices, but in sum total a pattern of partial and fragmented efforts. Action fell far short of rhetoric, especially short of the rhetoric of *comprehensive* change. Even so, our four building blocks in combination give us a way of understanding how educational change is brought about, especially how intentions enter the picture.

Daniel Bell points to a distinction between crescive change and enacted change.[50] Crescive change stems from broad social and economic conditions or from the impact of technological innovations and the modifications in mass behavior they sometimes encourage. And we often talk about structures to emphasize the stability of these foundations of behavior. This is the analytical arena, Bell argues, where social scientists are often most comfortable. *Enacted* change, according to Bell, poses a different analytical challenge. The intentions of change-minded agents come into play. There are, Bell says, occasions when the practical or political judgment of individuals engages "the tactical and strategic nuances of 'unique moments,'" and these conscious agents remake the situation in a profound way. They may expand the sense of what is possible, put together unprecedented alliances, or forge new institutions.[51] On a grand scale, the moment may be revolutionary, but we can imagine many less dramatic but nonetheless important occasions when actors alter the structure of the situation within which they operate.

Because there is nothing inevitable about a reshaping moment, it is better explained by the particulars of history than statistical trends.[52] With regard to civic capacity, we can see that there might be occasions in which stakeholders recognize their common fate and decide to shape it together. Or they can let the opportunity slip by, focusing on the more narrow and immediate concerns that separate them. Seen in this way, political history is not a matter of social determinism, but of choices made or forgone.[53]

Choices are, of course, made in a context. In Chapters 2 and 3 we consider the issue of context in two quite distinct ways. Chapter 2 addresses the question of whether and how the contemporary arena in which collective decisions about education are made differs from other policy subsystems or from the educational subsystem as it existed in other historical eras. Civic capacity is problematic in all policy areas, but we identify some senses in which the challenge is especially great where education is concerned. In doing so, we account for the otherwise puzzling fact that numerous central cities have much more effectively addressed the twin problems of physical deterioration and economic development than the tasks of social reconstruction and human capital investment in which schools are the key public mechanism. We also situate the contemporary school reform movement in a historical context of policy stability and change. In doing so, we simultaneously draw on the existing political science literature to understand school reform as a general case of policy subsystem dissolution and suggest some refinements of the general theories needed to account for the special cases of "high-reverberation subsystems" like education.

If civic capacity does not arise spontaneously or uniformly, one possibility is that it springs from the socioeconomic and demographics context of cities, and this is an issue we consider in Chapter 3. Perhaps greater poverty spurs a greater response, or a more highly educated or more homogeneous population comes together more readily around issues of school reform. In Chapter 3 we highlight some of the ways in which large, central-city school systems may be structurally disadvantaged, relative to other school districts, and how the eleven cities differ along such dimensions in ways that hypothetically might dictate their ability to respond.

Chapter 4 adds empirical flesh to the concept of civic mobilization and tests some basic hypotheses about how its variation relates to underlying differences in demography, political institutions, and interest group dynamics. The metropolitan distribution of poverty and fiscal resources, the racial-group context, and the institutional and intergovernmental setting of education politics are important parameters within which largely localized deliberations and interactions take place, but we argue in the end that these parameters shape but do not determine the prospects for civic mobilization and capacity to undertake systemic school reform. Politics is a process involving conscious agents who—within the limits of bounded rationality—see, assess, and act on problems in interaction with one another. Socioeconomic conditions render some connections or some concerns more likely than others, but it is still up to these agents interacting with one another to make what they will of the challenges and possibilities they face. Past or established institutional connections make a difference, of course, but institution building nevertheless remains an unfolding process within which new directions and new possibilities can be pursued.

Chapter 5 returns to the issues of problem definition. We introduce a four-dimensional schema for characterizing problem definitions, and using coded interview responses from respondents in our eleven cities we empirically explore patterns in three of those dimensions—complexity, elaboration, and content. We find, in general, complex but weakly elaborated problem representations for general community issues and simpler but more elaborated spaces characterizing problems of children and youth. We find little divergence in perspective between different sets of elites regarding general community problems, but considerable differences in regard to problems of children and youth. Most significant, we find evidence that problem definition is correlated with community mobilization. Elites in highly mobilized cities are more likely to propose solutions and the solutions they propose are different from those in low- or medium-mobilization cities.

In Chapter 6 we turn from the issue of how civic mobilization and constructive problem definition around education issues arises to the questions of whether and how these can lead to better education for inner-city youth. We score our eleven cities on various components of systemic reform effort. Even in the cities that seemed most capable of generating cross-sector alliances, systemic reform initiatives lacked the breadth and sustained momentum that we had hoped to see. Yet there are variations among the cities we studied, and, significantly, the more extensive efforts are associated with a higher level of civic mobilization. In Chapter 7, the final chapter, we consider the implications of this finding for the design and orientation of more successful efforts at systemic urban school reform.

2

The Challenge of Change in Complex Policy Subsystems

Structures of which we are unaware hold us prisoner.
Peter M. Senge, *The Fifth Discipline*

INTRODUCTION

Education specialists continually make the claim that urban education is different. In many ways, that claim is true. Education policy does not resemble the other
types of policy that traditionally have dominated the attention of urban leaders—
negotiating downtown development, providing city services to neighborhoods,
and controlling drugs, crime, building decay, and fire risk through a complex
system of regulation. Education policy making today is different from education policy making in an earlier time. And delivering high-quality education in
America's central cities presents different challenges from doing so in suburbs
and rural areas. In each case, urban education differs in ways that present special problems—to political and community leaders hoping to forge stable coalitions and to public officials hoping to implement comprehensive reform agendas.

A long and still-hallowed tradition in American thought holds that education
is indeed different. During the Progressive Era, a consensus emerged, among elites
if not necessarily more broadly,[1] that education was a specialized arena in which
decision making was best left to those with deep knowledge and expertise. Institutional reforms were widely adopted with the aim of buffering education decision making from the ideas and interests driving local government priorities in
other arenas. These reforms—including independent funding authority, nonpar-

tisan school board elections timed so they did not coincide with the elections of mayors, council members, and other more "traditional" political offices, and civil service status for teachers—were meant to set schools apart, and in large measure they succeeded.

But urban education is not so different, so unique, that it can or should be dealt with sui generis and apart from other public concerns. Educating and nurturing young people clearly *does* call for special kinds of knowledge about such matters as childhood development, psychology, cognition, pedagogy, and the like. But devising, implementing, and sustaining educational policies calls for a much broader range of knowledge, skills, and allies, and these may differ in degree but not in kind from those encountered in other areas of public action. Placing educational thought in an intellectual quarantine risks depriving those responsible for shaping school policy from potentially valuable lessons. And encouraging education decision makers to "go it alone" risks cutting them off from sources of sustenance and support that could enable them to better protect and project their priorities in the face of competing demands on public resources and attention.

Briefly put, we argue that politics, far from being harmful to schools, is crucial in aiding them to improve. Politics, of course, has many meanings. In an organizational setting we sometimes say, "it was politics," when we see a seemingly unqualified individual advance. But politics, or at least politics in democratic settings, also implies the setting and implementing of collective goals in a public setting. It is in this sense that we use the term.

In this chapter we identify some of the important ways in which education is like and unlike other policy areas and some of the ways in which the contemporary education decision arena differs from the past. Our immediate objective is to make it possible to draw lessons from other arenas that can help us meet the challenge of school reform. Lessons from the study of urban school reform also can enrich the theories that social scientists have developed to explain politics, governance, and public policy, and the discussion in this chapter will serve the additional purpose of providing a foundation for generalizing our findings to other realms.

SOCIAL VERSUS PHYSICAL RECONSTRUCTION

The Civic Capacity and Urban Education Project began with an observation and a puzzle. Physical and economic decline, in the middle of the last century, was so common among central cities that it was seen by some individuals to result from an overpowering "logic of metropolitan growth" that could not be effectively ameliorated.[2] Concerted action by business leaders and politicians in some cities stemmed or even reversed the seemingly unstoppable spiral of deterioration. Yet, we observed, some of the same cities—indeed some of the very same coalitions of actors—appear to falter when faced with the challenges of addressing social inequality and investing in human capital. Why should this be so? Why should the coalitions that were so effective in addressing physical decline be so impotent when facing the challenges of human capital development?

Social reconstruction, typified in efforts to improve the performance of urban school districts, differs fundamentally from the politics of physical reconstruction. Although both physical and social reconstruction have private and collective dimensions, social reconstruction is tied to the pursuit of a collective good in a way that physical reconstruction is not. Physical reconstruction has collective benefits; if economic vitality is stimulated, businesses, unions, and government services (via an improved tax base) all reap the rewards. But particular business interests and construction unions directly benefit through the subsidies that they receive. Moreover, politicians, by being able to focus attention on the massive and obvious changes that occur downtown, can raise their profiles and improve election possibilities.[3]

Investment in human capital development has collective benefits, and some interests benefit more than others. A changing urban economy requires a more educated workforce, so businesses can benefit disproportionately. But educational improvement lacks the direct, particularistic benefits of physical redevelopment. Underinvestment in the education of the poor is thus a distinct possibility.[4]

In American cities, redevelopment has enjoyed backing from powerful business interests with a direct and immediate stake in the effort. Moreover, the activity of redevelopment itself opens up abundant opportunities for contractors, developers, and others (what Robert Caro calls "the retainer regiment") to benefit materially from the process.[5] By contrast, school reform runs the risk of being perceived as an activity that takes individual material benefits away from these influential stakeholders. Education costs plenty of money, much of it raised via the local property tax. Increases in taxes can drag economic development down, threatening jobs in the already job-scarce economies of the nation's cities. Even if it is true that a strong school system ultimately contributes to economic development and growth, such a payoff is neither immediate nor assured. Although education might objectively fit Peterson's definition of a developmental policy, key political actors often perceive it as more akin to a redistributive policy and gauge their actions accordingly.[6] As a consequence, the traditional focus of business interests has been on economy and efficiency in schools rather than on the development of human capital.

Thus, social reconstruction involves a different kind of politics. Unlike the prime beneficiaries of redevelopment, in social reconstruction people in position to benefit in the most immediate ways are largely poor and unorganized. Whereas material benefits and personal incentives are primary *drivers* of efforts to physically rebuild central cities, such benefits and incentives are more likely to divert or *co-opt* the collective pursuit of social goods. Although investment in human capital can provide particular benefits in the form of jobs and career possibilities, for example, these can readily become ends in themselves rather than steps toward a collective goal. All the results of human capital development are long-term and uncertain. Many of the benefits of physical redevelopment are immediate and visible. All things considered, there is little wonder that physical reconstruction has held a more central place on the urban action agenda.

Yet, despite past frustrations, especially those accompanying the antipoverty efforts of the Great Society, social reconstruction has gained new prominence.[7] Education especially is a matter of great concern at all levels of government and across several sectors of society. Among other considerations, many actors now see that the economic vitality of the city is irrevocably tied to social conditions, and social conditions, in turn, are closely linked to education and related matters of youth development. School reform has thus emerged as a major policy initiative among those concerned with the revitalization of the city.

The aim of educational improvement represents a collective good in another way. As a policy initiative, it requires that various elements of the city be drawn into the effort. Neither businesspeople, educators themselves, nor any other segment of the community is sufficient alone to ensure that substantial progress occurs; success depends on a collective effort. Democratic theorists see the process as one in which diverse players are brought to understand that *political* change is not a matter of what each separately wants, but of what, working together, they are able to accomplish collectively.[8] Yet in a nation in which an adversarial approach to politics is deeply ingrained,[9] participation in a shared effort is no easy matter.

As embodied in educational reform, the social reconstruction of the city is, then, a special kind of policy. If the physical reconstruction of the city represents a collective good that can be advanced by a heavy mixture of selective benefits, social reconstruction has no comparable base in distributive politics. Educational improvement thus poses the question of what are the conditions under which a diverse set of players, governmental and nongovernmental, can be brought together around the aim of a social good.[10]

If the politics of redevelopment does not suggest a satisfactory answer to that question for education, it nevertheless reminds us that, from initiation through implementation, policy making is a meld of governmental and nongovernmental actions, and that is no less true in education than it is in redevelopment. Indeed, as we elaborate upon in the next section, successful education reform involves five strands that, although ultimately interrelated, are tied to distinct organizational milieus and generate their own independent dynamics. These five strands are revenue considerations, the allocation of students to schools, the school-community interface, bureaucratic politics, and classroom management. This complex composition has three critically important consequences for the prospects of systemic reform. First, it widens the gap between incremental and systemic reform, making it more likely that "business as usual" will generate piecemeal initiatives.

Second, it increases the importance of cross-sector coalitions at the stages of agenda setting and policy formulation. And third, it sharpens the distinction between agenda setting and policy formulation, because those involved in agenda setting may not have the same goals as those who get involved in policy formulation.

THE ONE AND THE MANY: FIVE STRANDS OF EDUCATION POLITICS

In a very real sense, the education arena has "not one politics, but many."[11] The politics of urban education is thus not a single activity, but, as Kenneth Wong argues, a mixture of many activities and interacting processes.[12] Many of these activities are widely studied and easily recognized: the politics of the board of education, the politics of the superintendent's office, the intergovernmental links between the local school system and education programs and mandates at the state and federal levels, the locally minded moves of governors and other state officials, the local links between the school district and city hall, the politics of the PTA and other community groups as they interact with school officials, collective bargaining by the teachers' union and other employee organizations, and the watchguard activities of taxpayer groups, to name a few. There is also a school-level politics involving the principal's office, principal-teacher interaction, parent-school interaction, and, of course, the most basic of all education interactions—teachers and students in the classroom.[13] The student-teacher relationship is a case of the micropolitics of education, but no less political for being "micro."[14] The varying mix of control, cooperation, resistance, and bargaining in which teacher and student play roles inescapably has a political dimension. Even this long list of activities and processes is only part of the picture. Schools are what organization theorists call "open systems," profoundly affected by their external environment.[15] The "exit" process by which families make housing choices or opt for private schools to seek educational opportunities for their children shapes schools, sometimes more profoundly than the combined activities of the many interest groups at work.[16] Broadly understood, the politics of education encompasses as well those actions through which families and communities imbue children with expectations, provide opportunities, and bring to bear a range of social supports.[17] Because these processes do not occur in a vacuum, the politics of education also intertwines with the system of stratification of the larger society.[18] Hence the politics of urban education reaches far beyond those activities directly connected to formal school organizations.

Although education politics takes place on many levels and at various sites, there are connecting strands that tie these levels and sites together. Moreover, the various elements of an education system react to a shared context. As a city's demography, economic base, and political position change, so also do its schools. We need, then, to acknowledge the varied dimensions of a locality's education system while seeing how they might form a connected experience.

There are at least five major strands of education politics. Although they are conceptually distinct, in practice they have enormous effects on one another, and it is these effects that need close attention. These five strands are:

1. Raising and spending money—level of taxation, sources of funding, spending priorities, and scope of effort.
2. Who sits in the classroom with whom—school district lines, attendance zones— (especially their class and racial character), choice mechanisms, tracking and placement practices, and the exit option.
3. The school-community interface—the role of the school board and more broadly the nature of accountability, the formation of alliances and cleav-ages around education issues, the use of schools as focal points in commu-nity development, and various school-community interactions such as parent participation in site-level school councils, formal and informal procedures by which individuals petition on particular issues, the nature and extent of parent "partnerships" in the education process, and other forms of partnership.
4. Bureaucratic politics—inter- and intraorganizational relations (especially forms of hierarchical control and direction), the nature and place of various forms of specialization, the relation between schools and nonschool service agencies, organization norms and standard operating procedures, the protec-tion and promotion of employee benefits and perquisites, and career advance-ment strategies.
5. Classroom interaction—especially around the relations between order main-tenance and learning.

Exploring these five strands, we can see how urban education has evolved over time. As cities change, education politics changes, and the way these five strands interrelate also changes.

Revenue. Schools need money. We spent, in the United States, an average of just over $6,900 to educate each public elementary or secondary student in the nation in 1998. In the United States, money for schools comes from different levels of government. At one time, the bulk of the revenues came from local governments. In 1929, local revenues constituted about eighty-three cents of each dollar spent, with the states accounting for almost all of the rest. Today, states and local gov-ernments each account for about forty-seven cents, with the national government chipping in a little less than seven cents.[19] Each of these levels comprises a deci-sion-making arena with its own array of competing interests, institutional tenden-cies, and traditional priorities.

Money is power, at least potentially. For many years, the growing state role in funding was not accompanied by dramatic increases in state influence; tradi-tions of local autonomy, generally weak state legislatures, and dubious political gains to be made combined to induce most states to adopt a hands-off approach. Over the past two decades this has been changing fairly dramatically. Governors, legislatures, and state judges increasingly have insisted on a say in how local schools are run. This has been happening at the same time that central cities have become politically weaker within the state arena.[20] That has meant oftentimes that interests and values more prominent in suburban and rural areas have been imposed on local schools. At the extreme, states have taken over local school systems.[21]

Although this intergovernmentalization of school finance is important, it also is the case that much of the decision-making authority continues to be exercised at the local level. Much of the money coming from states and the national government comes with few or weak strings attached. Although the threat of greater intervention looms, on a day-to-day basis the key maneuvering to set educational priorities and practices tends to be at the local level.

Historically, the local politics of spending money on education pitted business interests, as primary sources of revenue, against parents, as the primary service users, and against educators themselves.[22] In an earlier era, business managed to keep down spending in most cities, producing modest salaries for teachers, construction programs that often lagged behind population growth, and, in some cases, large classes and even shortages in textbooks and other classroom supplies. Yet for many years, with enrollment on the rise and a sizable middle class as a core constituency, urban schools were a growth industry and could generate political support, a high degree of internal peace, and increasing budgets.[23]

Collective bargaining has advanced salaries, but sometimes at the expense of deferred building maintenance.[24] Textbook shortages and antiquated equipment also remain as significant problems, in some instances owing as much to bad management as lack of funds. Urban schools face special needs from the high level of poverty among students, the number of children for whom English is not the native tongue, and the costliness of meeting special education mandates.[25]

Costs have risen concurrently with declining city tax bases, as both business activity and middle- and higher-income wage earners have become increasingly suburban. Cities have thus become substantially dependent on state funds to meet education costs. However, city political clout in state politics has perhaps reached an all-time low. Suburban predominance in state legislatures has become an overriding fact of life, as is the large suburban vote in gubernatorial and other statewide contests.[26] Greater state funding for education is thus no guarantee that special financial needs of cities will get a receptive hearing. Even litigation over funding inequity has had limited results. Well-off suburbs are reluctant to take any less for themselves than what they pay into the state tax coffers. Hence, funding formulas to target students from disadvantaged backgrounds often encounter determined resistance.

The political disjuncture between taxpayers and service users has widened. Not only does business resistance to increased taxation continue, but many individual taxpayers have little identity with urban schoolchildren. Urban student populations are overwhelmingly poor and minority, but individual taxpayers are preponderantly white, middle-class, and suburban, and in increasing cases do not have children in the public schools of either the city or the suburb.

Though education expenditures have continued to rise, the prospects for future increases are somewhat dim. Financial resources have tightened and run a major risk of compressing even further. With city school systems no longer home to large numbers of middle-class students, political support for spending by these systems has become tenuous. Educators can no longer assume that taxpayers see urban schools as operations in which they have a substantial stake.[27]

Classroom composition. Separating students by ability once enjoyed professional backing, but now is questioned. Whatever professional educators might argue, parents have always had their own inclinations about with whom their children go to school. Thus, many schools have long been segregated de facto by race and class, reflecting the dominant housing pattern in the United States. The consequences of residential segregation are reinforced by the fragmented nature of local school districts.[28]

Urban areas were once the major arenas for struggles over racial desegregation, but with continuing suburban growth the issue has quieted in most large cities. Weariness over past battles might account for that in part. So might the fact that some of the mechanisms developed to handle the desegregation challenge, such as magnet schools and public school choice, have become institutionalized and broadly accepted. Probably most important, though, is the fact that demographic realities simply have changed. The most contentious conflicts around issues of desegregation have involved African Americans, and the size of the black student population in urban areas has dramatically stabilized. In 1972, 32.5 percent of central-city elementary and secondary public school students were black; this crept to a high of 36.0 percent in 1985 and has since fallen slowly to 31.8 percent in 1995.[29] Although the black population stabilized in central cities, it has grown substantially in suburban districts. In 1972, 6.3 percent of suburban elementary and secondary public school students were black; by 1995, this had increased to an all-time high of 10.7 percent.[30] As a result, suburban districts are today the more likely battlegrounds for racial balance issues that take on the traditional form of black versus white.

The hot and sharply defined conflicts involving integration of black students into previously white districts have abated, but today's schools confront a more complex and multidimensional form of heterogeneity. Public schools throughout the nation are now much more likely to have student bodies from multiple racial and ethnic backgrounds. Hispanics constituted 10.8 percent of the central-city public school population in 1972 and 24.3 percent in 1995. The comparable figures rose from 4.4 percent to 11.6 percent in suburban schools and from 3.6 percent to 6.5 percent in rural areas.

At the same time, sensitivities to the socioeconomic composition of student bodies have become more prominent. Large cities typically have predominantly lower socioeconomic status (SES) students, including many from very poor families, and the drive to achieve desegregation seems largely spent. In any case, social class integration was never a policy goal and it remains largely off the education agenda. The ability of middle-income parents to practice the exit option, either by moving to another jurisdiction or placing their children in private schools, stands as an imposing barrier to any effort toward bringing social classes together in the classroom.

Tracking practices, especially at the elementary level, have come under severe criticism[31] but remain widespread.[32] Magnet schools and classes for "gifted and talented" students often serve as a means to prevent or slow the exit of middle-class students from urban school systems. However, in most places, it seems that they contribute little to the aim of integrating diverse students into a common school experience. The reality for most urban city school districts is a huge concentration of poor children, with the integration option long since foreclosed.

The school-community interface. Early in the twentieth century, progressive reforms replaced ward politics with citywide, largely nonpartisan politics. In many communities, business and blue-ribbon groups gained the upper hand on school boards, and professional educators enjoyed wide discretion to shape the agenda and initiate action.[33] Voter turnout was typically low, and school boards more often legitimized policy decisions than formulated them.[34] Even though the authority of professional expertise has declined from its peak earlier, the policy role of most school boards continues to be quite modest, and members play mainly a constituent-service role.[35] Professional educators succeeded initially in presenting themselves as having special expertise and as being largely sufficient on their own to handle the process of education. That belief has begun to yield ground to the alternative view that education requires a broad partnership with parents and others,[36] but it is unclear how much actual practice is changing.

A strong case can be made for parent participation, and parents can reinforce the importance of academic effort as well as be of direct assistance by reading to children, volunteering in school, and monitoring homework. The key to such participation, however, is school staff who are welcoming and encouraging of parent involvement.[37] Parent participation in school governance is a more controversial step, and some parents feel that any form of involvement is resisted by principal and teachers. For their part, street-level educators often see parents as uncaring or indifferent or as a source of bothersome special demands.

Any move toward parent-school partnership faces potential opposition. As Bernard Crick has observed more generally, "the more one is involved in relationship with others, the more conflicts of interest, or of character and circumstance will arise."[38] Educators are keenly aware of Crick's point. With specific regard to schools, Seymour Sarason argues that parent and community involvement, for educators, makes life "more complicated, messy, and even unpredictable." He adds that, though educators have difficulty seeing it, this broad involvement can also make life "more interesting, exciting, less isolating, protective of the existence of public schools, and potentially an aid to their improvement."[39] Oft-criticized as they are, many educators find this possibility highly resistible.

Overall, the issue of school-community interface is in flux. Old beliefs about professionalism have been severely challenged, and the widespread introduction of local school councils, the increasing number of school-business partnerships, and a heightened emphasis on parent involvement, especially when linked to community organization, all serve to change the landscape in potentially significant ways.[40] Of course, middle-class parents have long been involved in school affairs through PTAs as well as on more personal and informal bases. But for urban school systems an unanswered question is the extent to which lower-class and more generally minority parents have come to engage teachers and various school officials, either through formal channels or informal ones. Many lower-SES parents find contact with school staff to be discomforting. Typically they themselves did not have a good experience with school, and they may feel at an educational as well as overall class disadvantage.[41]

Bureaucratic politics. The term "principal" is an abbreviation for "principal teacher." In an earlier period, most school employees were teachers, and most administrators were school-based and thus close to the classroom. Over time, particularly in large urban districts, the superintendent's office grew into a large headquarters staff with numerous areas of specialization.[42] At the school level, the principal's role also increased in administrative scope, and the office of assistant principal took hold and expanded. Federal and state mandates and special grant programs have added to both school- and district-level specialization, and an elaborate array of regulations has grown up around these programs, often focusing their administrators more on satisfying requirements set at the state and federal level than on coordination with classroom teachers and meeting their needs.[43] Collective bargaining has also contributed a body of regulations that are part of the work environment in contemporary schools.

Over the years, then, school administration and the accompanying body of regulations have become increasingly remote from the classroom, particularly from pedagogical matters, often leaving teachers with an increased feeling of isolation.[44] Reformer John Goodlad finds school administrators unduly preoccupied "with collective bargaining, desegregation, declining enrollments, vandalism, and the like, to the neglect of the centrally educational issues."[45] Rules have become so complex that central office staff spend considerable time granting waivers, as schemes of regulation prove to be exasperatingly cumbersome. Careers can be built around the mastery of rule-book detail.

Even the role of principal, although a school-level position, has often become a rung in an administrative career ladder. One observer notes:

> In most large school systems . . . the principalship is now seen as a step in a bureaucratic career—say from counselor to assistant principal to program di-

rector to division chief to assistant or deputy superintendent. The requirements increasingly become aptitude for success in the bureaucratic career. . . . Being an outstanding teacher or showing the potential for creating a good educational community are not a salient part of the dossier.[46]

In any big urban school system, administrative career opportunities abound. Taking Baltimore as an example, one finds an administrator for every eight teachers,[47] and that figure is not atypical, but quite in line with other large jurisdictions in Maryland and elsewhere. Because school systems also adhere generally to the "differentiation" principle (hierarchy requires that even lower-level administrators receive greater compensation than the teaching staff), administrators are paid more highly than teachers by a wide margin. There is, then, a significant material incentive for teachers to move into administration.[48]

Intergovernmental programs and mandates create multiple channels of reporting and thus work against school- or district-level coordination. One study refers to the "complex maze of programs, rules, and regulations, and conflicting mandates" in which urban schools operate.[49] On the larger scene, the institutional independence of education makes an integrated policy for children and youth unfeasible. Though there have been a few moves toward greater mayoral involvement in (and in a few cases toward control over) education, channeled thinking along narrowly functional lines remains dominant.[50] Few Social reformers would dispute that fragmentation of effort is the dominant pattern, and a quest for coherence is an understandable theme of school reform.[51]

Classroom interaction. By all accounts, classroom teaching is a demanding and unrelenting job. One observer characterized it as "the educational equivalent of whitewater rafting."[52] The teacher's classroom task centers on producing learning and exerting enough control to maintain order.[53] As the lower-SES composition of a classroom increases, order maintenance tends to become a greater concern for the teacher.[54]

At the same time, we should not overlook the fact that, within the same SES level, there is variation in classroom experience. Some teachers are more skillful than others in advancing learning and some pedagogical approaches are more effective in engaging students. The fact that lower-SES classrooms tend to present greater obstacles to learning increases, rather than decreases, the importance of teachers who *do* make a difference.[55]

Because classroom interaction is the core activity in education, it gives education policy a special character. It is not about the kind of material transactions that abound in urban redevelopment or transportation policy.[56] Although teachers as a group are certainly not unmindful of salary matters, salary has little to do with day-to-day teaching, and faculty norms reinforce that disconnection.[57]

In the student-teacher interaction, inner motivations are central. Much depends on what teachers and students find personally fulfilling. The skill of the teacher can expand what is mutually satisfying and lack of skill can contract it. That is only part of the story, however. For students, especially as they move up in grades and age, their expectations, previous experiences, and cumulative accomplishments have an impact that is largely beyond the control of the teacher. So even highly motivated teachers, especially in the upper grades, find that the nature of their relationship with students depends greatly on the context within which interaction takes place.[58]

For any given classroom, an important part of the context is what is taking place and has taken place in other classrooms. The general norm among teachers is one of mutual noninterference, encouraged by the "egg crate" structure of most classrooms,[59] but the formality of classroom autonomy and the practice of mutual noninterference are not the full reality of the situation. For any given class, student expectations are influenced greatly by previous and concurrent classroom experiences. Teachers, then, are constrained by what their fellow teachers have been and are doing.[60] Moreover, even highly dedicated and skillful teachers have found that their individual efforts "were overwhelmed by the indifference, incompetence, and in some cases the corruption of the larger system."[61]

In addition to what transpires in the school system itself, extraclassroom socialization and experiences also have a large impact on what students bring to their interaction with teachers. Several questions are salient: Do students expect that academic achievement will lead to worthwhile opportunities? Is academic achievement valued by students, or is it seen as a betrayal of one's peers or of one's class, race, or ethnic identity? At the high school level especially, several observers point to an autonomous youth culture and the extent to which it has weakened respect for an academic orientation.[62] Various segments of the youth population see an academic orientation as being a "nerd" or as acting "uppity," "white," or "Anglo."[63] As Goodlad reports, "it may be socially difficult in some schools to be smart unless one is regarded also as good-looking and athletic."[64] Yet a recent survey of American teenagers finds that they see "getting an education" as important to their future.[65] However, academic success is valued more for its instrumental uses than its intrinsic worth. As one high school student put it, "I can't wait to graduate and go to college, get a good job, get rich."[66]

Nevertheless, complex motivations are at work among students, and some teaching situations are more challenging than others are. It is not surprising, then, that teachers display increased stress in lower-SES schools, and given an opportunity to move away from such assignments, many do so, or move out of the teaching profession altogether. The attrition rate among new teachers is particularly high.

With the changing demography of the city, urban school systems have thus experienced a greater challenge, in part because the proportion of lower-SES students has increased. Not only has the population changed, but the expectation has grown that all students will complete high school.[67] With the decline of low-skill industrial jobs,[68] dropouts are now seen as an indicator of school failure, and the pressure is on schools to hold on to youths who, in previous eras, would have drifted into the workforce. This contributes to the proportion of students, especially at the high school level, who are reluctant participants in classroom learning.[69]

Education historians link declining standards to these changes and attribute to it the growing propensity for urban high schools to become "holding" operations for adolescents with limited alternatives.[70] Diversity and unevenness in motivation, in turn, encouraged a trend away from a core academic curriculum and toward "the shopping mall high school" with its assortment of "life experience" and "entertainment" courses.[71] Even so, these changes and the relaxing of standards did not prevent dropout rates from remaining at a high rate.[72]

Recent efforts to upgrade educational standards and increase the academic content of the curriculum consequently serve to put urban schools through added stress about performing, but without altering the basic conditions that surround these schools and their students.[73] Thus, urban educators find themselves under heightened pressure to show academic improvement, and perhaps the most acute stress is experienced by classroom teachers in the poorest neighborhoods. Teacher burnout has come to be recognized as a widespread problem and one that urban school systems experience at a heightened level.[74]

It should be pointed out that, important as race is in American education, the pattern described above is not attributable solely or even mainly to racial differences between educators and students.[75] Although many big-city school systems have undergone transition and now have preponderantly minority teaching and administrative staffs, stress and burnout continue as problems.[76] After all, the racial composition of school staff does little by itself to alter the larger structure of opportunity and its impact on the experiences and expectations of students. Educators might, then, understandably ask if it is appropriate to hold them accountable for the academic achievement of students who have limited confidence that academic effort will improve their life chances.

The strands interrelated: The failure syndrome. As we put together the various strands of urban education, we can see how they might be conducive to a syndrome of failure. The segmenting of American education into local districts, politically and financially independent of one another, puts city school systems into competition with the suburban districts around them and provides suburbs with a strong incentive to maintain independence. So big-city systems face major challenges without a strong political or financial base.[77]

Within the urban community, the tradition of an autonomous education profession puts teachers and administrators in the position of coping with the consequences of a welter of social problems beyond their control, but nevertheless manifest in the experiences, expectations, and habits of mind of their pupils. Students disadvantaged by the larger socioeconomic order pose a particularly sharp challenge to educators. Many of these students lack the same depth of social supports enjoyed by most middle-class students.[78]

That the larger population expects little of those from lower-SES backgrounds is itself a major barrier to academic improvement.[79] The situation is further complicated by the widespread belief that the personal ability of each child, not the effort made, is the key to academic performance.[80] If the long-term prospects for educational achievement and personal success really do depend on a cluster of factors that is pretty much determined by the time a child reaches school age, how could students of whom little is expected be motivated to learn? Or, for that matter, how can their teachers be motivated to try hard to bring about an atmosphere of academic achievement?

Although there is some recognition among experts that background factors strongly influence educational attainment, American ideology of upward mobility and effort has continued to stress excellence in schools. In comparison to an earlier era when education for the poor centered on the basics and on citizenship training, today's school systems that serve the poor are expected to do much more. These expectations, contrasting so vividly with the often cognitively and emotionally impoverished backgrounds of the urban poor, can buffet educators, leading them to feel overwhelmed by the challenges they face and powerless to turn matters around.[81] Schooling may then become a kind of holding operation. To the extent that happens, cynicism has fertile ground in which to grow, and educators can develop a defeatist attitude. They may see themselves not as professionals but simply as "survivors."[82] James Comer talks about schools in the grip of "the hand of hopelessness."[83] That frame of mind, in turn, becomes a further barrier to change as it undermines confidence that new practices can make a difference.[84] It can also weaken personal effort and commitment. In an occupation in which intrinsic reward is so important, an atmosphere of futility is sure to devitalize personal engagement and, even for those who survive the difficult initiation period, the urban school experience may encourage "time-serving."

Because learning is affected by the broad school environment,[85] the number of "time-servers" can have a cumulative effect. In a given school, as the proportion of "time-servers" grows, the teaching task of others becomes increasingly difficult—thereby heightening the likelihood that they too will succumb to feelings of defeat and futility.

As "time-servers" seek less stress-inducing positions, they may gain entry to administrative posts and foster cynicism there as well. Of course, the picture is not totally bleak; capable educators with positive motives also move into administration. No one knows the precise mix that makes up the supervisory staff of various urban school systems, but the level of cynicism is high and the potential consequences are considerable. Given a defeatist attitude, administrators would be little inclined to pursue bold initiatives or see experimentation as a way to foster improvements. Instead, "circling the wagons" to protect against criticism and devising ways to deflect blame are more likely patterns of action.[86] The failure syndrome may also produce a reluctance to involve outsiders in school operations or to seek partnership with parents or other community groups. Nor would those in the throes of futility be inclined to embrace research and evaluation. As one author observed: "Most urban school cultures are resistant to change, even when there is widespread recognition that children are poorly served under current conditions—partly because fear is more likely to breed defensiveness and rigidity than to foster risk-taking behaviors."[87]

Under these conditions, job protection is likely to be an overriding concern, with risk-taking avoided and little energy devoted to efforts at improvement. In failing systems, school administration is likely to resemble the management of a declining industry. Investment in new initiatives is less likely than simply trying to hold existing ground, retrenching to fend off the threat of deeper losses. Deferred building maintenance is especially probable. It is less conflict-laden than reallocations of personnel. With a shrinking pool of resources in relation to need, reallocation poses the risk of internal division and therefore increased political vulnerability for top-level administrators.[88]

Although many urban schools perform well, urban school *systems* overall do not. Nor have suburban systems distinguished themselves as they began to age and face a more diverse and less affluent student body.[89] That some individual schools perform well is evidence that it can be done.[90] That urban school *districts* generally are weak performers is, however, an indicator that systemic problems are a powerful factor, and that education is highly susceptible to the impacts of social inequality.

The following can be observed in many big-city systems of education:

1. Given the fragmented pattern of metropolitan governance, especially in education, city school systems have concentrations of the poor and nonaffluent, but weak access to compensatory funding and other forms of support.
2. Educators have the formal responsibility for schooling, but family and community background have a major effect on student performance. Shaped by signals of marginality from society at large, family and community influence, in turn, are channels through which social and economic inequalities tend to be perpetuated. Significant forces are therefore largely beyond the control of educators.
3. Education is labor intensive, and urban school districts represent a huge bundle of material resources—jobs, contracts, and opportunities for professional advancement. Educational performance, however, turns heavily on intangible factors, embodied in the inner motivations of students and teachers. And, because there is no ready formula by which money promotes academic achievement, the scramble for material benefits can take on a life of its own. In the worst cases, school boards and other community leaders despair of educational improvement and see the schools as, in the words of one former board member, "the community employment agency."[91]

4. Educators themselves have huge material and psychic stakes in professional autonomy. Yet urban school systems have shown almost no capacity to reform themselves; educators are often caught up in a "culture of resignation" or, as James Comer observed, "a culture of failure."[92]

5. Thus, despite their great resource needs, urban school officials have had little success in demonstrating that more money makes a difference in level of achievement. Indeed, even sympathetic observers suggest that larger budgets alone would not be enough.[93] In short, urban schools face a crisis of confidence both internally and externally. Many educators themselves are beset by doubts that urban schools as presently constituted can perform, and the public shares these doubts.[94]

Requirements of change in complex subsystems. Others, of course, have noted the complexity of the education policy subsystem. School politics has been characterized as "hyper-pluralistic," to highlight the extent to which they are subject to competing demands by a shifting array of stakeholders.[95] School organizations are sometimes described as "loosely coupled" systems, highlighting the senses in which the decentralization of discretion makes it difficult for those in the upper level of the formal hierarchy to effectively exercise oversight, authority, and control.[96]

Although such characterizations are complementary to our characterization of the five strands, we draw a somewhat different set of implications. Most others note the disorder and complexity that confound the process of getting things done and issue calls for administrative restructuring. We suggest, instead, that the interweaving of various strands characterizing the education subsystem sets a higher hurdle for school reform, especially within the urban context. To be successful, school reform must be systemic.

The term *systemic reform* is a popular one these days, but its meaning is often fuzzy. Some use it as little more than a shorthand term for emphasizing that reform needs to be "major." For others, the term also carries a connotation of organizational comprehensiveness; that is to say, systemic reform will require changing all parts of the educational subsystem, not simply a little tinkering here and there.

Our use of the term signals the need to consider the overall picture, far beyond the confines of the educational system alone. Lasting and meaningful change requires acting on a complex set of relationships, both within the school system and in the school-community connection. Yet talk about systemic reform in these senses runs against the grain of a long attachment to specialization. Only reluctantly have education reformers come to recognize that specific needs such as improved math and science training are embedded in a larger context of schooling, and schooling itself is embedded in and influenced by the wide context of the whole community. Even reformers who have come to understand this often shy away from the implication we draw: School reform is political at its heart.

For many observers, the temptation is nearly irresistible to mentally detach school performance from its environment and argue that schools be fixed from the inside out. This inside-out perspective of reform is contradicted by the now overwhelming evidence that schools are powerfully constrained and even shaped by the conditions that surround them.[97] In contrast, we take it as a given that what happens in a particular classroom is *not* independent of the school environment, and the formation of the school environment is *not* unconnected to the larger community from which students, parents, and other stakeholders come.

Rather than buffering schools from external pressures, we believe it is necessary to consider how schools can better align themselves with broader community forces. Rather than focusing on reform as an administrative or technical puzzle, we see it as necessarily a political challenge. It is a political challenge not just in the instrumental sense of politics as power, as a way to bring pressure to bear, but also in the broader sense of politics as a process of reorienting the way society operates collectively by changing public institutions and public ideas.

Thus, not only is the politics of urban education different from the politics of downtown redevelopment, but the politics of systemic educational change is different from the politics of promoting particular initiatives. Until relatively recently, a powerful line of thinking within political science held that disjointed and incremental policy change was the norm in the United States, and indeed nearly inevitable. Many lauded that approach as best for policy change, because the inevitable mistakes could be more easily corrected with small policy steps than with large ones. Newer strains hold that broad and sharp shifts in ideas and power do occur in America, with great policy consequences. We can gain some insights into the urban school reform challenge by considering how education decision making compares with other policy arenas that undergo episodic nonincremental change.

EDUCATION AS A HIGH-REVERBERATION SUBSYSTEM

For both institutional and process-related reasons, American politics has long been regarded as especially prone to incrementalism and political stalemate. Institutionally, both vertical fragmentation, associated with our federal system, and horizontal fragmentation, associated with the enthronement of various checks and balances in power across branches of government, are seen to provide multiple "veto points" that make it easier for those advantaged by the status quo to stymie challenges. A pluralistic political process, which establishes a relatively open arena in which multiple interest groups pull and tug, alone and in coalitions, also is seen to promote incrementalism, because the balance of power among these various groups tends toward an equilibrium state and because some interests ultimately gain institutional beachheads in the form of close alliances between interest groups, elected officials, and bureaucratic agencies.[98] Added to this mix is what some scholars have characterized as a "mobilization of bias" against change; a tendency of dominating norms and perceptions to marginalize and delegitimate potentially disrupting ideas before they can take root and flower.[99]

Against this backdrop, it would be tempting to see the difficulties of instituting school reform as little more than a confirming case of a general rule. Educational policy may be seen as a complex set of policy subsystems, occurring mostly at the local level, but with formal and informal linkages to policy makers, educational professionals, and interest groups at all levels of government. We refer to this complex network as *the* educational subsystem and acknowledge the costs of the necessary simplification. In any case, educational policy making is subject to forces similar to the more compact policy subsystems classically referred to as "iron triangles."

The absence of change may characterize policy subsystems for long stretches of time, but more recent theory and evidence suggest that such periods of relative stasis typically follow—and in turn are precursors to—relatively abrupt and complete transitions in which subsystem elites and the ideas that helped sustain them in power are displaced.[100] This more sophisticated understanding of what constitutes the norm in American politics can help to illuminate our conceptions of the nature of the battles that constitute the politics of school reform. At the same time, however, the sheer obstinacy of the educational subsystem presents something of an anomaly, suggesting that the newer ideas about policy stability and change may need to be elaborated.

One of the things we can learn from the recent literature on policy change concerns the importance of reigning ideas about problems and solutions. Subsystem elites and their privileges are protected less by the direct assertion of political power than by the broad acceptance of certain ways of understanding what items are legitimate issues for the exercise of public power. Problem definition is how major political actors think about political issues. Problem definition establishes priorities, links conditions to particular causes, and establishes strong claims about what kinds of policies are likely to be feasible or infeasible, effective or not.

For decades, the education subsystem was characterized by a relatively stable constellation of norms and ideas that helped to insulate reigning institutions and practices from serious criticism. At the core of the dominant issue definition were two powerful sets of beliefs, one related to individual well-being and one to the public good. Education was broadly seen as the most important tool available to families to obtain upward economic mobility for their children. It was also widely accepted that public schooling was the most important social institution for creating the conditions needed for collective economic competitiveness, cultural integration of diverse populations, and political stability. These norms and ideas fueled public investment in education and protected the subsystem from competing demands upon the public purse. Further ensuring a stable subsystem were ideas about professionalism and expertise, which invested in the educational bureaucracy the prerogative to choose the technically "best" ways to operate. Also important as an institutional safety valve were dominant norms of local control, which allowed potentially destabilizing normative conflicts over matters like race and religion to be "settled" within relatively homogenous communities.

The relatively placid decades of subsystem stability were jarred by two assaults in the latter half of the twentieth century. The first wave of assault, roughly commencing with the 1954 *Brown v. Board of Education* decision, involved issues of equity, primarily associated with integration and race. The second wave, roughly commencing with the 1983 publication of *A Nation at Risk,* involved issues of academic excellence and international economic competitiveness. As predicted by the political science literature on policy stability and instability, these assaults involved new political actors who were able to discomfit the existing elites only because they armed themselves with competing visions of the purposes and conditions of education, raised doubts about existing practices, and offered alternatives that would be feasible and effective.

Although these assaults have shaken the education subsystem, they have not led to its dissolution and displacement. Education—particularly public education—no longer has the unquestioned support of a public convinced that it is critical to personal and social progress. Educators and their institutions no longer can count on public willingness to defer to them. Seriously weakened, however, the basic parameters of the traditional arrangements remain intact.

This prolonged and seemingly open-ended period of subsystem contention leads us to suggest the need for an elaboration of the existing theories. We suggest that education should be seen as an example of a "high-reverberation" policy subsystem. High-reverberation subsystems are characterized by frequent reshuffling of mobilized stakeholders, multiple and strongly-felt competing value and belief systems, deeply held stakes by both educators (the professional providers of education) and parents (the consumers), and ambiguous boundaries, making the prospects for establishing a new equilibrium more problematic than is normally the case. Although educators, parents, and local public officials are relatively constant actors in the decision arena, other actors—the media, courts, business, religious organizations, federal and state government—ebb and flow in their involvement.

Of course, other policy subsystems experience shifting actors too. The difference is one of degrees. In contemporary education more than most arenas, these episodic actors get involved more frequently and carry disproportionate power when they do (immediately destabilizing the preexisting balance of power). Although value conflicts are hardly unique to education, recognition that schools can play a critical role in transmitting values and socializing the young raises the stakes underlying various "culture wars," making it more likely that conflagrations will be sparked and less likely that those who lose a battle will resign themselves to defeat.[101] And, with growing recognition of the ways in which education is interwoven with such vital and dynamic issues as concentrated poverty, globalism, family status, protection of cultural minorities, and crime, there are very few grounds on which to exclude "outside" actors who suddenly assert a claim to the right to have a say. Yet because of the continued strong appeal of the ideology of public schools and the continued power of stakeholders, no new policy settlement has emerged to replace the traditional public school model. Hence ideas and interests continue to reverberate throughout the system with neither the attackers nor the defenders able to establish a traditional equilibrium.

It is not just sensitivity to value and ideological debates that accounts for the high reverberation character of the education policy subsystem. "Producers" always have a big stake in a policy area and educators share that feature, but the stakes in education are amplified by the fact that the school system is often the top employer or one of the top employers in the city. Educators are thus a formidable political, social, and economic force in the local community. Education also reverberates because its budget is so large—typically half of a locality's budget if its school system is not an independent taxing authority, and, if the school system is independent, then its budget is often roughly equal to that of the general local government.

In addition, parents are not just stakeholders; they are stakeholders with deep emotional commitments because their children are involved. The intensity of these commitments gives an edge to decisions about schools that is sharper than that found even in other often controversial arenas, such as parks and transportation. Although local citizens can get incensed about traffic congestion that adds to their commute or shopping time, for example, the same households often make choices that involve huge transportation inconveniences to get their children to a desirable school. Parents of all classes, races, and social groups care enormously about what schools are like for their kids. Often this is true of other family members as well—grandparents, aunts, uncles. For parents, if they can afford a choice, place of residence may be largely dictated by views about schools, their effectiveness, their safety, their prestige and reputation, and the opportunities they offer to students. School sports teams and such may add a dimension of sentimentality that itself carries weight.

Add to the picture the fact that the reputation of the school system, because it affects choice of place of residence and image of the city, also influences the attractiveness of the community as a place to do business and invest. Overall, the reverberation is wide in number and range of people who care and get involved, but it is also deep in terms of how much they care.

THE POLITICS OF OVERCOMING THE FAILURE SYNDROME

Realistic efforts to improve urban education cannot simply rest on the simple issuance of mandates or declaration of new standards.[102] Improvement almost certainly turns on changing relationships, and such change is fundamentally a political process, whether those involved in the change effort recognize it as such or not. The politics of systemic reform, then, amounts to more than the struggle and resistance that surrounds particular plans. Change is likely to be systemic only if it comes about through the mobilization of a broad set of players in a concerted effort to alter what has been labeled "a culture of failure." Most efforts to change urban education fall far short of that standard.

Because there are many barriers to a broad mobilization and particular barriers are sometimes what is most visible, we need to keep the big picture in mind. The conventional approach to school reform has called for identifying a problem and bringing professional expertise to bear on it. That approach has produced disappointment and frustration. But if broader mobilization is what is needed, how does a community deal with what James Morone calls "a fragmented policy environment"?[103] That issue confronted the early warriors against poverty,[104] and it continues to pose a challenge today.[105] Thus social reform strategists find themselves in search of a comprehensive approach, and for that reason use the language of "bringing stakeholders together." This language and the related term we use, "civic capacity," are thus not about rallying support around particular programs or projects, but, as Bryk and others suggest, they are about reshaping the political life surrounding schools.

Unfortunately, mobilizing civic capacity almost always involves a major dislocation of the existing way of doing things. It means forging a viable consensus on some set of solutions to the complex educational problem. That invariably means some at least limited destruction of the existing policy subsystem, because policy subsystems are invested in the current set of implemented solutions to the educational problem. Harnessing civic capacity to the goal of educational reform means *both* bringing in educational and noneducational actors *and* instituting major changes in the way current educational professionals do business. These coexisting constructive and destructive elements make creating and sustaining coalitions difficult indeed.

Such reshaping does not occur in a vacuum. It pits efforts to change against a set of concrete problems and the political relationships in which those problems are embedded. Thus, we need to set the stage by starting with the diverse elements that, in combination, make up the political picture of urban education. That involves considering the behavior of political stakeholders both within and outside the traditional education community, a task we take on in Chapter 4. And it involves considering the particular role of competing issue definitions, which we address in Chapter 5. But it also involves a more extended consideration of the social and economic context of education, particularly as manifested in the distinct setting of central-city public schools.

Though education is in an important sense a policy subsystem, it does not function with complete autonomy. We need to be realistic about what changes in school practice can accomplish and not ask too much. Tyack and Cuban caution that school reform "has often diverted attention from more costly, politically controversial, and difficult social reforms."[106] Instead of using schools to try to reform society on the cheap, we might better consider how broad social reforms could make the job of schools easier.

Schools, we believe, are not closed systems, capable of being fixed without regard to their surrounding environment. Because the strands of education politics are intertwined, each not only affects the others, but the strands are also connected to the social environment in powerful ways. As a study of Chicago put it, "the root cause of each school failure is not inside each individual school, but rather in the external environments they share."[107] Thus, although up close it might seem that a problem, such as a high dropout rate, can be isolated and treated effectively, in a larger context that problem solving requires a broad set of interrelated approaches. Instead of operating in isolation, specialists need to be part of a comprehensive effort. Indeed, in a recent study of school reform in Newark, New Jersey, Jean Anyon contends that "educational change in the inner city, to be successful, has to be part and parcel of more fundamental social change."[108] She questions whether most reform proposals are "going to be powerful enough to overcome the decades of accumulated want and despair that impede students every day."[109]

Yet structural thinking has its own shortcomings. Unrelenting attention to the big structural picture can cause us to overlook social parallels to what environmentalists call instances of "local robustness."[110] Desirable as structural change to racial and class inequalities might be, awaiting that scope of change would leave urban schools in their plight for an indefinite future. The study of the politics of urban education reported here took as its field of inquiry the middle ground between a continuing flow of incremental reforms and a still-to-be-activated movement to transform U.S. society. Talk about systemic reform is about school-community relationships, but it is more modest in scope than transforming society. Similarly, talk about bringing stakeholders together is a large move, but one far more modest than seeking to launch social revolution. The focus is how school and community can be related in a constructive way. For reformers, the challenge is how to mobilize around a large enough sphere of activities to make a difference, but not so large as to constitute an impossible task.

Education politics is at a crucial stage. There is an important national policy debate under way. State educational activity is at a high level. Both levels are enormously important. Even so, the study focuses on the city level in the belief that crucial choices are being made, though perhaps with only a partial understanding of all that is involved. It is our aim to increase that understanding and focus on a feasible scope of reform activity. Education politics at the turn of the century affords an unusual opportunity to examine the process of system change if we look neither too minutely by concentrating on specific initiatives, nor too broadly by considering only national and global structures. "Local robustness" in school reform may prove to be a disappointment, but, if not, it would be a shame to overlook a potential for cities to turn around the performance of their school systems.

The politics of systemic change for urban schools is different from the politics of systemic change for middle-class suburban schools. Although the formal organization of schools may be the same in middle-class and poor communities, they are subject to fundamentally different pressures and they function in quite different ways.[111] This is not to deny that curriculum is important or to contend that pedagogy does not matter, but it is to suggest that how educational practices are put into effect can be greatly influenced by the class character of a school, specifically by the experiences, opportunities, and expectations that attach to life in the lower strata as contrasted with life among the affluent.

But recognizing the special constraints within which central-city systems operate need not, and indeed should not, induce fatalism. It is important to distinguish between economics as a powerful force and economics as an irrevocable determinant. It is with that in mind that we move to Chapter 3.

3

The Urban Context: A First Look
at the Case Cities

There are nearly 15,000 school district in the country, serving about 45 million elementary and secondary school students.[1] Compared with other nations, the U.S. system is highly decentralized, with these local districts playing important roles in determining funding, organization, teacher standards, and curriculum. These districts differ greatly, however, in size, wealth, and population characteristics. Although much of the public and media attention to the education "crisis" focuses on large districts including 25,000 or more students, most districts in the nation are much smaller than this. In the 1993–1994 school year, only 208 districts (1.4 percent) had 25,000 or more students. By comparison, there were 3,294 districts (22.1 percent) with total student enrollments of less than 300.[2] Although most school districts are small, however, most children attend districts that are relatively large. Districts with 25,000 or more students account for over 30 percent of all the country's public school enrollment, and more than half of the nation's public school children are in districts with 7,500 or more.

Big cities—and the special cases they present in terms of concentrated poverty and race and ethnic divisions—play a somewhat curious role in many of the popular debates about school reform. Dismal test scores and troubling anecdotes from large, central-city school districts are featured in the arguments of those who insist that we are in the midst of an educational crisis. But the specific programmatic and institutional reforms that are promoted, as well as the explanations offered for why reform is difficult, are framed in universalistic terms. The result can sometimes be a "blame the victim"[3] message: If big cities persist in failing to improve their schools, despite the fact that universalistic solutions are open to them, the fault must lie with local leaders. This can develop into a rationale for doing nothing ("they made their bed, now let them lie in it") or for extraordinary intervention by external actors, such as the courts, state legislatures, or Congress. But we are in a poor position to frame an intelligent response to the problems of education in large, central cities until we have given more serious thoughts to the ways in which they may present problems that are different in kind as well as in scale.

The eleven cases that constitute our primary focus are among the nation's largest. They range in size from about 40,000 (Pittsburgh) to over 600,000 students (Los Angeles). Nine of the eleven districts (all but Pittsburgh and St. Louis) are among the 100 largest in the county. The boundaries of cities and school districts in the United States do not always coincide, and among these eleven cities Los Angeles and Houston stand out as cases where the two are sharply distinct. For example, the Los Angeles Unified School District includes most of the city of Los Angeles plus parts of twenty-seven other cities.[4]

In this chapter, we address elements of the magnitude of the basic problems faced by urban school districts, focusing on the attributes of the populations they serve. Demographic forces, many of which are outside of local officials' capacity to control, are an important element of the broad context within which schools operate. All school districts in the country are engaged in a common enterprise, and they share many goals and many modes of operation. But large urban school districts operate in an environment that presents distinct and difficult challenges.

Population size, composition, and change combine to frame the context of urban education along at least three dimensions. First, they establish the *direct educational context*. Changes in the family background of the population (income, education, family status) affect the kinds of challenges teachers face in the schoolhouse and in the classroom on a day-to-day basis. The slogan that "every child can learn" has become popular in many school systems, where it serves the useful symbolic role of counteracting the kind of fatalistic determinism that leads some to conclude that family background consigns some children to a life of ignorance and failure before they reach the ripe old age of five. That slogan can become fatuous and misleading, however, when it is allowed to imply that differences in the socioeconomic circumstances of their students do not constitute major, even dominating, challenges to the schools and teachers who are attempting to educate the very poor. The evidence of the effects of poverty, and especially concentrated poverty, on educational outcomes is as clear and convincing as social science produces.

The evidence regarding the added consequences of being from a relatively disadvantaged racial, ethnic, or language minority is also compelling. We have reviewed some of the evidence as it affects classroom composition, classroom interaction, and parent involvement in Chapter 2. In this chapter we indicate where the eleven cities in our study stand in regard to these demographic conditions and trends. Although they share many of the characteristics that have come to signify the special "urban" challenge, they differ among themselves in the severity of the educational task, differences that are important in understanding the successes of educational reform.

Population size, composition, and change also affect the *fiscal context* in which educational funding and policy decisions are made. Our federal system, in law and in practice, delegates much of the responsibility for public schooling to local districts. In 1994, local governments were the source of 45 percent of all spending on public elementary and secondary education, almost exactly the same proportion as was contributed by the states and more than six times the contribution from federal sources.[5] Although local governments play much less of a funding role than they did during the first half of the twentieth century, in more recent years the local contribution has increased in both real and relative terms.[6]

The central role of local governments in funding public education is much noted, but its consequences are often underappreciated. The spatial distribution of populations with disparate characteristics would have direct educational consequences regardless of the overarching institutional context, but the overlay of governmental units and their assigned responsibilities for revenue raising and distribution gives these demographic forces added potency. Urban school districts frequently confront greater needs but have access to fewer resources with which to meet them. Redistributive aspects of fiscal federalism, in which national and state governments aid local districts, financially ameliorate some of the consequences of relying on limited geographic entities to fund education. This results in differences in per-pupil expenditures across districts that are much less pronounced than the baseline socioeconomic differences among them. In spite of this, large urban school districts face special fiscal challenges, and with intergovernmental redistribution have come a greater dependence and vulnerability to external intervention.

Finally, demographic forces affect the *political context* in which key stakeholders define their interests and shape their tactics for exercising (or *not* exercising) political voice. Shifts in the racial and ethnic composition of the cities have been accompanied by heated battles for political power, and the lines of cleavage and coalition formed in these battles continue to affect civic capacity to undertake school reform. Shifts in the composition of households (the proportion with school-age children, the proportion attending public schools) affect the size of the baseline constituency most inclined to support school spending. Shifts in the allocation of population and wealth between city and suburbs affect the magnitude of the relative burden experienced by central-city districts and the extent to which the exit option may undercut efforts to mobilize local residents to engage in collective movements for school reform.

As large, central-city-centered school districts, all of the eleven cases share some important characteristics, but there are differences among them as well. Some of these differences are idiosyncratic products of their particular histories. Yet, as we noted in Chapter 1, we have found that the eleven cities can be usefully categorized into three clusters, based on some common demographic, regional, and political characteristics. The four "black-led" cities (Atlanta, Baltimore, Detroit, and the District of Columbia) have predominantly African-American populations, overwhelmingly African-American student populations, and predominantly black leadership within the education policy community and the city government. The critical role of the racial transition in control over the local levers of governmental authority in these cities raises interesting issues about the relationship among race, power, governance, and education.[7] The three machine-descendant cities (Boston, Pittsburgh, and St. Louis) retain a more substantial white population within their boundaries, harbor strong working-class and ethnic traditions in many of their neighborhoods, and reflect stronger and more lasting histories of traditional machine-style politics. In these cities some of the most pressing issues involve the transition from an economy based heavily in manufacturing and with locally owned businesses to a more modern, service-based, and globally integrated economy, and the different ways that the three cities have handled the resulting tensions—between parochial politicians and a more cosmopolitan corporate sector and between a deep-rooted public bureaucracy and reform constituencies.[8] Compared to the other cases, the Sunbelt cities (Denver, Houston, Los Angeles, and San Francisco) tend to be "younger" cities—their institutions less entrenched, their populations and ethnic composition more fluid, their boundaries with surrounding suburbs less well defined. In these cities, it is the competition among Anglo, African-American, Hispanic, and, in some instances, Asian populations—each with somewhat distinct needs and interests, each with substantial political resources, and none with a secure position of dominance—that sets the defining context.[9]

We do not mean to imply that this typology represents more than a convenient tool for organizing our analysis. The boundaries between the groups are neither sharply defined nor permanently fixed.[10] Nor do we mean to suggest a form of regional determinism. We do conclude from our analyses that the different regional, racial, and political contexts affect the real and perceived costs and benefits of various alternatives for political alliance and educational reform, and that these, in turn, make some outcomes more or less likely. But we also believe that there is meaningful room for local actors to chart different—and collectively more fruitful—policy courses. Demography is not destiny.

POPULATION AND RACE

Each of the eleven cities has large minority populations; only in the three machine-descendant cities and Denver was a majority of the population white in 1990 (Figure 3.1). The particular configuration of racial and ethnic groups differs, however. Blacks constitute a majority of the population in Atlanta, Baltimore, D.C., and Detroit; the Hispanic and Asian populations in those cities are not large.[11] In the four Sunbelt cities, in contrast, Hispanics outnumber blacks; Asians are the largest minority group in San Francisco. In those districts, the classroom context may include language challenges that are not so pressing in cities where African Americans are the dominant minority group.

As the city populations have become more dominated by racial and ethnic minorities, the change in the population of students has been even more sharply

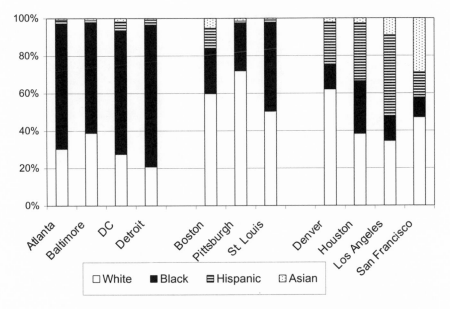

Figure 3.1. Race and ethnicity, 1990

defined. Although four of the eleven case cities had majority white populations in 1990, only one of the school districts (Pittsburgh) had a majority of whites among the public students enrolled. Figure 3.2 compares the proportion of whites in the population to the proportion of whites enrolled in public schools for all school districts with 100,000 or more students in 1990. The diagonal line represents what the racial distribution of students would be if it were the same as the racial distribution for the population at large. The proportion of students who are white is almost always lower than is the case for the overall population. For all large districts the difference averages 9 percentage points. The difference is greatest where the population is most racially diverse; in districts where whites make up between 30 and 70 percent of the population, the average district has a white enrollment that is 12.8 percentage points lower than the percent white for the overall district population. The eleven districts in our study average almost 15 percentage points fewer white students than white residents, indicating a somewhat larger disparity than other large districts, although, as indicated in Figure 3.2, they do not fall very far outside the normal pattern in this regard. For all of the districts in our study, then, the classroom context determines that educating *students* means educating *minorities*.

Most Americans' visions of large, inner-city schools are framed by images of racial turnover, "white flight," and declining enrollments. During the 1960s and 1970s, when battles over desegregation dominated the local school agenda, increases in the black population and decreases in the white population often combined to create an environment of racial instability and rapid change. The set of

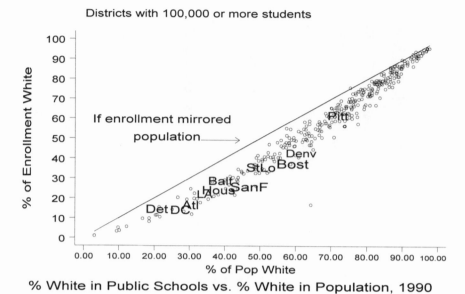

Figure 3.2. Percent white in public schools versus percent white in population, 1990

images that evolved during that period was perhaps unduly influenced by a few especially vivid cases, but that broad pattern of racial and population change and instability was common in many of the large, central-city school districts.

This set of images needs to be reconsidered. Total population is continuing to decline in all of the black-led and machine-descendant cities except Boston, which between 1980 and 1990 recovered a little of the population it had leaked during the previous two decades. But the recent history of these cities has seen moderation of the earlier demographic trends. As indicated in Figure 3.3, in the seven cities with large black populations the period of rapid racial turnover had begun to abate by 1980. This is clearest in D.C., which was the first of the cities to become majority black, sometime between 1950 and 1960. Since 1970, the white population in D.C. has been relatively stable.

Rather than continued out-movement of whites, a substantial process of black suburbanization is now under way. It is clear that the process of rapid racial and ethnic change presents complications within schools for educators who must adjust to a different clientele, as well as in local politics, where newcomers and old-timers joust for positions of power. However, most of the black-led and machine-descendant cities in our study have had considerable time to come to terms with the demographic shifts that they experienced. In the four Sunbelt cities, the demographic situation is a bit more volatile. Total population is growing or relatively stable, but the racial/ethnic mix is more dynamic and complex. Whites, who had long enjoyed numerical domination, have lost that advantage; along with blacks, Hispanics, and, in San Fran-

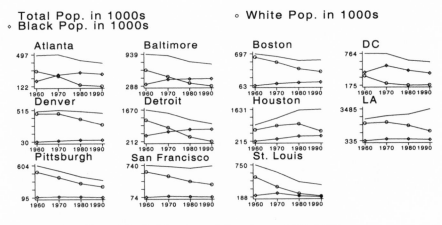

Figure 3.3. Racial and population change, 1960–1990

cisco, Asians, they find themselves in a pluralistic setting in which multiple racial/ ethnic groups are on relatively equal footing in terms of numbers of people.

INCOME AND EDUCATION

With racial and ethnic change has come greater concentrations of poverty. The 1989 poverty rate in the eleven case districts was 21.4 percent. This compared with a poverty rate of 12.3 percent in the other 330 districts with populations of 100,000 or more. This disparity is most intensely felt by youth. Just under one of every three children in the eleven districts was living in poverty in 1989, compared with 17.3 percent in other large districts. Poverty rates also varied substantially among our cities, as Figure 3.4 illustrates.

Economic disparities continue to follow race and ethnicity. Across the eleven cities, the median household income for blacks is about half of that for the whites remaining in these cities, with Hispanics doing marginally better than blacks in about half the cities and marginally worse in the other half (see Figure 3.5).[12] Minority income relative to white income is lowest in Atlanta, D.C., and Pittsburgh. In D.C. this is attributable entirely to the extraordinary high incomes of the whites who remain in the city (roughly one-third of the population). Indeed, D.C. blacks have a higher median income than those in any of the other cities. In Pittsburgh, by way of contrast, the high degree of racial disparity is wholly attributable to the particularly low incomes of its black citizens. Blacks in Pittsburgh have the lowest median incomes among the eleven cities; whites, although well-off compared with blacks in the same city, have relatively modest incomes compared with whites elsewhere. In Atlanta, which shows the greatest racial disparity,

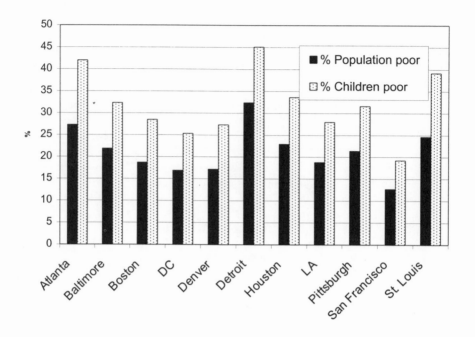

Figure 3.4. Poverty among population and children, 1990

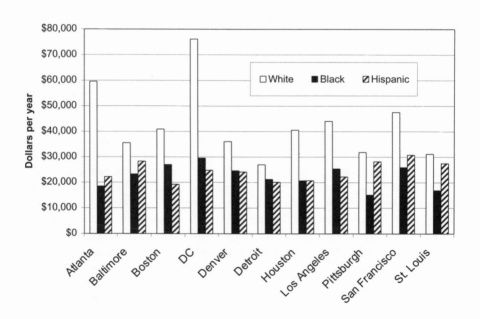

Figure 3.5. Median household income by race and ethnicity

blacks have lower incomes than blacks in all of the other cities save Pittsburgh and St. Louis, whereas the median white Atlantan household is better off than its counterpart in every city but D.C.

Parents' education levels are especially important in setting the stage for students' academic performance, and here the story for the eleven cities includes some positive signs. The percentage of adults who dropped out before completing high school has declined substantially in all of the eleven cities, and the proportion having completed college has dramatically increased (Table 3.1). This favorable trend includes the black population; increases in college education among blacks within the eleven cities have also been steep. Although the proportion of blacks

Table 3.1. Changing Education Levels, by City and Race

Percent Adults Not Graduating from High School, Total and Black, 1960–1990

City	All Adults		Black		Change	
	1960	1990	1960	1990	All	Black
Atlanta	59.5	30.1	79.0	40.2	−49%	−49%
Baltimore	71.8	39.3	71.9	42.7	−45%	−41%
Boston	55.4	24.3	63.8	33.3	−56%	−48%
D.C.	52.0	26.9	66.5	36.2	−48%	−46%
Denver	46.6	20.8	56.1	25.0	−55%	−55%
Detroit	65.6	37.9	73.5	37.4	−42%	−49%
Houston	54.8	29.5	73.8	33.7	−46%	−54%
Los Angeles	46.6	33.0	56.4	30.1	−29%	−47%
Pittsburgh	64.6	27.6	74.9	33.7	−57%	−55%
San Francisco	49.0	22.0	60.9	27.6	−55%	−55%
St. Louis	73.7	37.2	76.3	43.7	−50%	−43%

Percent with a College Education, Total and Black, 1960–1990

City	All Adults		Black		Change	
	1960	1990	1960	1990	All	Black
Atlanta	9.3	26.6	3.8	11.1	186%	192%
Baltimore	5.8	15.5	4.1	8.6	167%	110%
Boston	7.6	30.0	4.8	14.0	295%	192%
D.C.	14.3	33.3	7.2	15.3	133%	113%
Denver	12.2	29.0	6.7	14.5	138%	116%
Detroit	5.3	9.6	2.9	8.4	81%	190%
Houston	10.7	25.1	4.7	13.4	135%	185%
Los Angeles	10.6	23.0	6.5	13.3	117%	105%
Pittsburgh	6.4	20.1	2.5	8.8	214%	252%
San Francisco	11.1	35.0	6.6	14.9	215%	126%
St. Louis	4.5	15.3	3.4	8.0	240%	135%

with college degrees at least doubled in each city, this rate of increase was as steep as that for the overall population in only four of the cities.[13]

Scholars noting the close relationship between parental education and student achievement have almost uniformly inferred that raising adult education levels would, ipso facto, lead to better performance in subsequent generations. They have assumed, in other words, that the link between parent education and student achievement is direct and based on absolute levels of education. This might be the case, for example, if the process of education tends to make adults themselves more appreciative of the value of education, and to provide them with a better understanding of how to stimulate learning on the part of their children. The research on which they have based this perception, however, has almost always been cross-sectional in nature. The empirical evidence holds only that children of better educated parents perform better than children of less well-educated parents *at any given point in time.*

Our observation that adult education levels have increased dramatically in these eleven cities, when coupled with other evidence about the dismal performance of the schoolchildren in those districts, raises the possibility that the link may be indirect and relative. Rather than directly affecting child-raising practices, higher education levels may provide parents with competitive advantages in the economic sector, and it may be the concomitants of this economic success that lead their children to do well. Rather than absolute education, then, what matters may be parents' education levels relative to others with whom they are competing for economic advantage.

This vision of the link between parent education and student achievement as indirect and relative presents very different policy implications from the view that the link is direct and absolute. The latter view supports the presumption that each gain in educational achievement will generate positive ripples for the future. The former supports a less optimistic conclusion: Educational gains in central cities will not translate into student performance unless those gains actually narrow the gap between city and suburb, minority and nonminority, rich and poor.

CITY VERSUS SUBURB

Racially and ethnically patterned inequality in incomes within the cities coincides with growing inequality between cities and their suburbs. Figure 3.6 presents the ratio of each city's median household income to the median income in its entire metropolitan area. City-to-suburb disparities are growing in all eleven cities, although the problem is not as severe in the Sunbelt as it is in the black-led and machine-descendant cities.

Does the cities' economic standing relative to their surrounding suburbs really matter? Or is it absolute levels of income and economic vitality that are important? There are at least four senses in which it may be important to consider the cities' economic status in the context of their broader metropolitan context. First, to the extent that income is indicative of potential tax revenues, the loss of higher-income families may translate into a reduced capacity to meet education needs through local resources. That the slippage is relative to neighboring jurisdictions, which may compete with central-city school systems for the best teachers, exacerbates the problem. Second, to the extent that the socioeconomic status of residents is positively correlated with higher levels of political involvement, the relative decline of central cities may translate into reduced political leverage at the state level where some key decisions about educational funding and policy are made. Third, to the extent that this growing disparity reflects the out-migration of higher socioeconomic households, it may serve to make "exit" an increasingly attractive alternative to political action for families who are discontented with central-city schools.[14] A fourth possible consequence of the growing city/suburb disparity centers on the possibility that these economic differences may correlate with a relative increase in students who are especially difficult or costly to educate, an issue to which we turn our attention next.

As we noted above, a long line of research confirms the existence of a strong relationship between family background and a child's subsequent performance in school.[15] Much of that same research supports the existence of a strong peer effect; the presence of a large number of lower-SES children in a classroom can be expected to depress the academic achievement of their classmates as well.

For these reasons, schools and school districts that serve a disproportionate share of children from poor families face an especially difficult challenge. Figure 3.7 presents information on the extent to which central-city school districts are faced with a disproportionate share of the poor children who live within their metropolitan area. The indicator used is the ratio of the city's share of the metropolitan area's poor children to its share of the area's total population. A city that has 40 percent of the metro area poor children and 40 percent of the metro

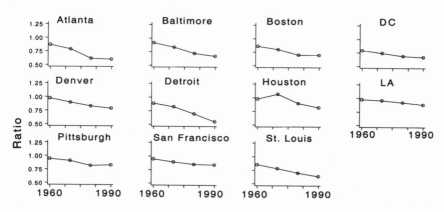

Figure 3.6. Ratio central city/metro income, 1960–1990

area population would receive a score of 1.00 on this indicator. Scores above 1.00 indicate that a city has a disproportionately high share of the region's poor children. All of the eleven cities have borne more than their proportionate share of poor children for at least the last twenty years. In all but three cases (Pittsburgh, Los Angeles, and San Francisco) the imbalance has been steadily increasing from decade to decade. In six of the cities, the 1990 share of the metro area poor children is more than twice what would be expected based on their population alone.

These metropolitan disparities are closely tied to the racial composition of their central cities. Figure 3.8 illustrates this relationship. Among the eleven cities in this study, those with the highest percentage of black residents are most likely to have a disproportionately high share of the region's poor children. The bivariate correlation between the share indicator and percent black is .87 (p < .0005). Compared with the cities with high black populations, Sunbelt cities do much better on this indicator because they are younger and have had more elastic boundaries.[16]

THE FISCAL CONTEXT

The linkages among local economic vitality, residents' income, and the capacity to financially support strong schools are strong but not determinative. In general, healthy local economies produce higher incomes for local residents and more tax revenue to support public education. In some metropolitan areas, however, many of the best paying jobs in the central cities are held by suburbanites, and the cities' ability to capture the fiscal benefits of that activity can be constrained by the nature of the taxing options left to them by their respective states.[17] On the other

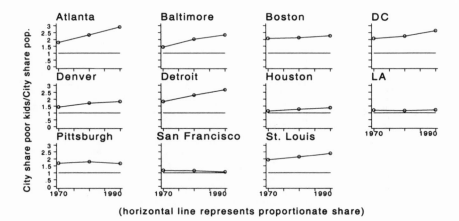

(horizontal line represents proportionate share)

Figure 3.7. Disproportionate city share of poor children, 1970–1990

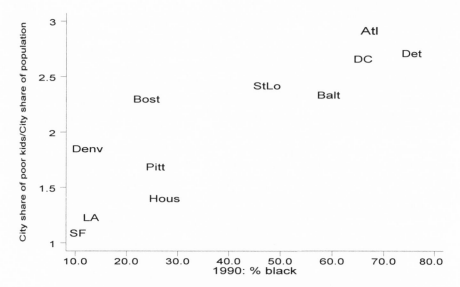

Figure 3.8. Disproportionate share of poor children, 1990, by percent black

hand, state and federal aid can potentially compensate for limits on local revenues, reducing or even reversing the disadvantages experienced by poorer jurisdictions.

Measured by total expenditures per student, the eleven cities are doing reasonably well. Based on 1989/1990 data from the Census Bureau's Survey of School District Finances, the eleven core districts spent, on average, nearly $6,200 per student during the 1989/1990 school year, almost exactly $1,000 more than the

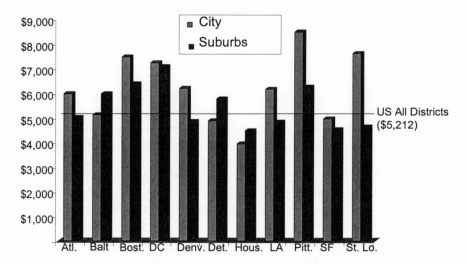

Figure 3.9. Expenditures per pupil, 1989 (city versus surrounding suburbs)

average for all districts nationwide (see Figure 3.9).[18] At that time four of the districts fell below the national average and three spent less on average than their surrounding jurisdictions.

That the central-city districts generally spend more than their suburban counterparts may initially seem surprising in light of their relative economic disadvantage documented earlier. The explanation lies largely in the role that intergovernmental financing has played in redistributing revenues in the cities' favor. Figure 3.10 illustrates the extent to which each of the eleven districts derives its educational resources from federal, state, and locally raised revenues. Education is primarily a state and local function; federal funds represent a relatively small part of the revenue stream for all eleven districts. More important, state involvement in local education varies substantially among the cities we studied. The districts' reliance on state as opposed to local funds varies dramatically. In Boston, Houston, and Atlanta local revenue accounts for about twice as much as state revenue; in Los Angeles and San Francisco, in contrast, the state accounts for three times the local revenue contribution.

Among the eleven cities, variation in federal support is only modestly correlated with indicators of poverty, and the degree of state support is not related to poverty at all. San Francisco, for example, with the lowest poverty level among our eleven cities, has the highest proportion of state fiscal support. Atlanta, with one of the highest poverty levels, gets a relatively small proportion of its school revenue from higher levels of government. Considerable fiscal need-based redistribution is nevertheless occurring. The redistributive character of state and federal support becomes very apparent in a comparison between central-city school districts and their surrounding suburban jurisdictions. The federal contribution to the eleven cities averaged about 8.7 percent in 1989–1990, but averaged only about 3.4 percent for the suburbs surrounding those cities. The state contribution averaged about 44.5 percent in the central cities[19] versus 34.8 percent in their suburbs.

The implications of the lack of severe disadvantage in the amount of money America's central cities can spend per pupil is not clear. Although central school districts are not particularly disadvantaged on a per-pupil basis, they harbor much larger special populations in need of aggressive intervention. Moreover, they can ill afford to ignore the needs of the "best and the brightest." Although a substantial body of literature—going back to the Coleman report of 1966—holds that school spending per se has little impact on school outcomes,[20] the aggressive stance that wealthier communities have taken in defending their spending advantages reinforces the belief of most parents and politicians that money still matters. Recent research supports this position as well.[21]

In spite of the ongoing conflict surrounding the "does money matter?" debate, two general conclusions are well established. First, spending *in and of itself* neither brings about improved educational attainment nor does it narrow existing achievement gaps. Championing the cause of greater financial support for central-

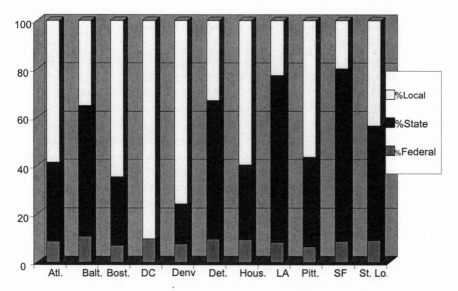

Figure 3.10. Education revenue by source

city school systems makes no sense if additional resources will simply be diverted into patronage, frills, or unnecessary administrative support. Second, in light of the special challenges they face, central-city school districts may need more money per student if they are to have any real chance to provide equal opportunity or equal results. Compared with more advantaged communities, large, central-city school districts serve a student population that enters kindergarten with a more complex array of personal and family problems. In large, central-city systems, aging buildings and deteriorating physical infrastructure generate severe and ongoing claims on the educational dollars that are available. Central-city students, moreover, are more likely to go home to neighborhoods of concentrated poverty after school is over—neighborhoods in which stunted information networks, limited positive role models, temptations to engage in illegal activity, and few positive outlets for youthful energy combine to erode some of the progress made between nine in the morning and three in the afternoon. Finally, because the physical and educational settings are less hospitable, central-city school systems may need to pay higher salaries if they are to have any chance at all of attracting and holding on to skilled classroom teachers and principals.

Fiscal capacity is a necessary but insufficient condition for educational reform. Knowledge, institutional capability, political will, and sustainable constituencies are other factors that determine whether the money that is available will be spent wisely and well. Civic capacity, not simple fiscal capacity, is critical for educational improvement.

DIMINISHING VOICE? DEMOGRAPHIC CONTRIBUTORS TO A WEAKENED PUBLIC SCHOOL CONSTITUENCY (THE EXIT OPTION)

In a classic analysis, Albert O. Hirschman outlined the ways in which the option to exit from an undesirable situation can serve as an alternative to political mobilization. When exit becomes easier, mobilization becomes relatively less attractive to rational individuals. Because voice requires responsive institutions and a continuous application of energy and innovation, Hirschman suggests that there may be "an important bias in favor of exit when both options are present."[22] Over time, the availability of an easy exit option can erode the basic foundations for collective political action. Citizens with children in schools have two major forms of exit, suburbanization and transfer to private schools.

The loss of families with children to the suburbs can undermine political pressure for reform of schools in several ways. The first has to do with the absolute numbers of families who opt for suburbia. Population decline can mean that the city accounts for a smaller and smaller proportion of the state electorate, at the very same time that states are becoming increasingly important as the source of both education funding and reform initiatives. Absolute numbers also can affect the political dynamics at the local level. If parents of school-age children become a smaller share of the central-city electorate, local public officials may find it easier to push school issues off the agenda in favor of competing priorities, including those of keeping taxes low, crime control, and downtown development. Other possible impacts have less to do with absolute numbers and more to do with the specific characteristics of those who leave. If families who leave tend to be those who care the most about their children's education and have the resources to act as effective educational advocates, then suburbanization may selectively deplete the supply of those who are most likely to constitute an effective leadership core around which a political movement for reform might be built.

As we already have illustrated, in the black-led and machine-descendant cities there has been a general trend of population loss. Although dissatisfaction with the city schools certainly is not the only factor going into such decisions, it also is clear that families with school-age children are especially likely to make that choice. Figure 3.11 compares the changes in total population to the change for the age group of eighteen years or younger. In the cities losing total population, the rate of loss among children and teens is dramatically higher; in the two cities with growing populations, the rate of growth among children is dramatically lower.[23]

Among families that do remain in the city, private school is another kind of exit option. On average, almost one out of five children living in the eleven cities attends private school.[24] The private school option, when combined with the choice of suburban versus central-city residence, generates a powerful racial bias to the

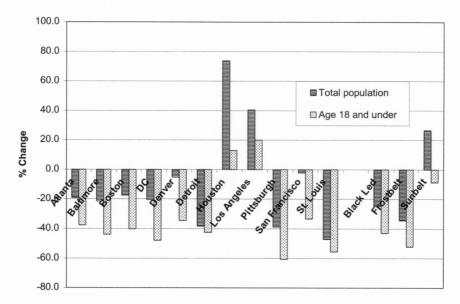

Figure 3.11. Change in population, children and total, 1960–1990

exit option. As indicated in Figure 3.12, based on 1990 census figures, the proportion of public school children that is white is sharply lower than the proportion of whites in the population at large. Roughly half of this appears to be attributable to selective residential patterns, which generate a white central-city population that is disproportionately composed of households without school-children. Roughly half is attributable to the greater likelihood that white children will attend private rather than public schools.

At the same time that population trends are tending to weaken the constituency for public schools within the city body politic, the relative loss of total population tends to weaken the clout of the city in state politics. Among the eleven cities in our study, all but Los Angeles lost population relative to their metropolitan area from 1960 to 1990, and this loss was especially pronounced in the cities with large African-American populations. Margaret Weir has made the case that this population shift has left central cities in a generally weaker position to defend their interests at the state level.[25] Moreover, this is happening during a period in which states generally have been taking on a more prominent role in monitoring and intervening in the performance of local school districts. As we have already noted, states are the source of more than $4 out of every $10 available to these eleven districts for educational spending, and central-city districts are substantially more dependent on this external support than their surrounding suburbs. In a range of areas—such as performance accountability, teacher

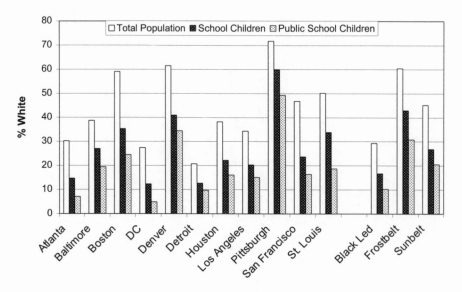

Figure 3.12. Race and exit from central-city public schools

standards, and charter schools—states have become much more willing to directly intervene in educational decision making once considered the province of local officials. Thus, the weakened role identified by Weir may have special meaning when it comes to the politics of school reform.

In many respects, schools and schooling in large cities look very much like their counterparts in the suburban and rural areas of the nation. To the teacher standing in front of the class, hoping to provide those in the room with new ideas, skills, and basic knowledge, the task is similar no matter what the type of neighborhood the children go back to at the end of the day. Many of the tasks faced by school administrators are similar too; no matter their location, school buildings must be constructed and maintained, revenues raised, salaries paid, hiring carried out, and so on. The urban context does not alter the central elements of the schooling equation. The demographic and fiscal context does, however, pose special challenges to those who wish to develop more effective education systems that truly meet the needs of inner-city youth.

Inner-city education poses special challenges within an environment that imposes critical constraints. Failing to recognize both special challenges and unique constraints leads to facile recommendations for reform. Many reform proposals are based on the premise that observed troubles in urban school systems are attributable to ineffective governments and educational policies, but that can only be part of the story.

On the other hand, the constraining elements of the urban context do not create a destiny of failure. Communities facing similar challenges mobilize in different ways, and some do so more effectively than others. None of the eleven communities we studied has mounted so broad and sustained a reform effort as might be possible, but some communities better manage to draw together disparate groups into broad reform coalitions with significant results. In the next chapter, we focus on this issue of variation in civic mobilization around the challenge of urban school reform.

4

Civic Mobilization
in Eleven Cities

The local political stratum has not been strongly reformist, certainly not on social and economic matters . . . local reform movements have concentrated on defects in the political system, not the socioeconomic structure of society.

Robert Dahl, *Who Governs?*

Improving urban education is not simply a matter of calling attention to a problem and summoning concerned stakeholders to embrace the idea of change. If simple endorsements were all that were needed, the task of undertaking systemic school reform would be an easy one.

Among both elites and the mass public, awareness has grown that the well-being of cities is closely tied to the strength of their educational systems. Poorly performing schools make cities unattractive as sites for investment as well as less appealing places to live. For that reason, contemporary reformers talk about the need to bring stakeholders together to promote educational improvement. In principle, stronger school systems serve the interest of all segments of the community—parents, business, voluntary organizations seeking to remedy social ills, racial minorities, and community residents in general as well as educators themselves. Good schools would make everyone better off.

At first blush, then, it might appear easy to convene various segments of the community for the purpose of advancing educational improvement. Who could be opposed? But, as with so many worthy social purposes, agreement in principle is far from sufficient to advance the cause. Agreement about an abstract idea often comes apart in the face of concrete realities, unforeseen tradeoffs, and the sheer intractability of established arrangements.

Sought-after improvements in urban education are far from immune to these forces. The harsh reality is that, for many reasons rooted in fundamental social and economic inequalities, heightened academic performance for students from lower-SES backgrounds is a difficult task to achieve.

In the United States, the task of education has traditionally been left to education professionals. Progressive Era thinking emphasized removing politics from education; Americans generally seemed to want to eliminate politics from schools. The considerable dissatisfaction expressed about the educational practices suggests that this model has not adequately addressed major educational issues.

As in most policy-making subsystems, major change cannot emerge from within. Instead, change entails active commitments of energy and resources and a willingness to build new relationships with traditional educational policy makers, and at the same time bring new ways of thinking about urban education to the educational policy subsystem. Communities differ in their abilities to interject new ways of thinking about education and in their abilities to bring together diverse interests from a broad segment of the community to solve problems collectively. We refer to this ability as *civic capacity*.

The dynamic element of the accumulation and exercise of civic capacity is *civic mobilization*. This is a term that stands for an effort extending across various sectors of the urban community. It has kinship with the term "stakeholders," but it goes further with its emphasis on active engagement in problem solving.

The end result of mobilization is civic capacity, and it rests on two factors. One is the commitment of resources—physical, personal, and communal. Capacity is partly a matter of the resources that can be brought to bear in a problem-solving effort. Few resources equal weak capacity; more resources mean a stronger capacity. The other factor is a shared understanding. Without some generalized agreement on the direction and magnitude of the desired reform among collective problem solvers, reform is likely to founder on the shoals of misunderstanding and mistrust. The need for a broad-based reform coalition active in solving educational problems has been a consistent theme of reformers. John Goodlad, for instance, argues that "schools will get better and have continuing good health only to the degree that a significant portion of our people, not just parents, care about them."[1] Caring alone is not enough; for problems to be solved broad segments of the community must move beyond caring to active engagement.[2] In this chapter we examine the degree and form of civic mobilization in our eleven cities and begin to consider some of the factors that enable some cities to do a better job than others to convert words to deeds and good intentions to effective actions.

As will be clear, we do not believe that there is an easy-to-follow recipe for building civic capacity. Although personal leadership is important, there is plenty of evidence that bringing in a proven leader cannot suffice to stimulate broad mobilization. Entrepreneurial superintendents might, for example, combine their standing as professional experts with their managerial skills to bring about major changes in educational practice. But this approach has potential drawbacks, one of which is that the professional standing of school administrators appears considerably weaker in the current era than it was at an earlier time. Today, for example, big-city school superintendents on average enjoy a tenure of less than three years.[3]

Nor is it simply enough to identify key stakeholders and call them together for a session of hand-shaking and motivational speeches. Chicago, Dallas, and New Orleans are among the cities that have called "summit conferences" to improve schools in recent years. With the possible exception of Pittsburgh, however, none of the eleven cities studied in the Civic Capacity and Urban Education Project has convened such summits.[4] Such summits may be a significant step toward civic mobilization, but their real significance hinges on follow-through measures. By itself, a single conference to highlight a shared concern falls short of a genuine mobilization of community elements to contribute to problem solving. Some follow-through, whether it be a formal entity for programmatic action (like LEARN in Los Angeles[5]) or a more informal mode of cooperation, is a necessary ingredient in genuinely building civic capacity.

Nor can even well-financed and carefully orchestrated planning by powerful organizations outside the public eye substitute for the kind of open engagement and coalition building that we emphasize. Peter Marris and Martin Rein point to the Kansas City Association of Trusts and Foundations as an example of a strategy of unobtrusive manipulation, working here and there to put together a series of experimental programs in the schools and in complementary activities such as preschool programs, special scholarships, and work-study for likely dropouts. Through its executive director, the association used its grants to build a network of influence through which changes could be promoted. Such "political opportunism," as Marris and Rein label it, shares with civic mobilization the strategy of building a coalition of cooperating elements, but it differs in working gradually through an established agency, as opposed to openly bringing diverse elements together on behalf of an explicitly comprehensive approach.[6] In some sense, the "political opportunism" embraced by Marris and Rein is a limited version of civic mobilization.[7] The Kansas City Association did, after all, represent a means through which diverse elements of the community could be drawn, albeit piecemeal, into a broad effort.

We focus on open collaboration and collective engagement, because both are central to the democratic process and because our empirical analysis shows them to be more likely to generate the sustained commitment necessary to break the common cycle in which school reform burns brightly on the local agenda for short bursts, then burns out before real changes are made and institutionalized. As will be argued in this chapter, the explanation for civic capacity has to do with historical factors—relationships, habits, loyalties, and expectations that build gradually over time. More than just working together, it also involves a foundation of shared understanding. If various concerned parties are operating on behalf of different and competing considerations, then the mere fact of their participation may result in little capacity. It is only when various groups mobilize behind a common effort that capacity becomes substantial.[8] In this chapter, we focus on civic mobilization. The role of shared vision and problem definition is the focus of Chapter 5.

CIVIC MOBILIZATION IN ELEVEN CITIES

In examining the experiences of our eleven cities, the indicator of civic mobilization we used was the extent to which different elements of the community came together behind the cause of educational improvement. The level of mobilization was assessed along three dimensions: breadth, cohesion, and durability of the education reform coalition in place during the period (1993–1994) in which the field research was undertaken. The participants in a coalition for educational improvement could be readily identified. Judgment entered in trying to assess the cohesion and durability of alignments in what was a somewhat volatile process. For example, in 1993 and 1994 Boston was moving toward a greater coalescence of effort, whereas Baltimore's coalition became shakier over an experiment with the privatized management of a small subset of city schools. Detroit and Houston had significant mobilizing efforts, but the Detroit effort came largely unraveled when the reform school board was voted out of office, and the Houston effort was hampered by litigation surrounding conflict between African Americans and Latinos over naming a new superintendent. For reasons such as these, the assessment of civic mobilization was essentially a qualitative call. Accordingly, we avoided the temptation to assign precise—but potentially unreliable—mobilization scores and we limited ourselves to a broad ranking. In order to achieve a mix of expertise and distance, a member of the team who had not engaged directly in any of the field research but who had carefully read all field reports performed the initial ranking. These rankings, in turn, were discussed fully by the rest of the project staff, and adjustments were made accordingly. We are confident that our estimates capture the relative rankings of civic mobilization among the cities we studied. Two additional points bear emphasis. First, mobilization scores were based solely on the nature of the relationships among coalition partners and did not involve any consideration of the wisdom or effectiveness of the specific policy initiatives the coalition favored.[9] Second, our assessments necessarily are time specific. In judging durability, we looked at the situation at the time and in the preceding years but could not, of course, project into the future.

Though none of the eleven cities displays a complete form of civic mobilization in education and in none is civic mobilization totally absent, the eleven cities offer substantial variation. In Table 4.1 three cities—Pittsburgh, Boston, and Los Angeles—are at the upper end. Four—Baltimore, Houston, Detroit, and Washington, D.C.—fall into an intermediate position, and four—Atlanta, Denver, St. Louis, and San Francisco—are quite low.

Table 4.1. Civic Mobilization by City: Level of Involvement by Selected Actors in Educational Reform

City	Business	Parents	Teachers	Superintendent	Other
Pittsburgh	Broad and institutionalized	Some, but not among the top actors	Included in reform coalition	Active promoter	Foundations, state government, and community-based organizations
Boston	Broad and institutionalized	Varied, but not a cohesive force	Included in reform coalition	In transition to active promoter	Foundations, mayor, state government, and community-based organizations
Los Angeles	Broad and institutionalized	Very little	Included in reform coalition	Active promoter	Foundations, advocacy groups
Baltimore	Somewhat broad and institutionalized	Very little	Very little	Highly selective promoter	Foundations, mayor, state government, and community-based organizations
Houston	Rising and institutionalized	Very little	Very little to minor	New, but with reform support	Foundations, CBOs
Washington, D.C.	Institutionalized but guarded	Narrowly based	Resists reform	Lacks firm political base	U.S. Congress
Detroit	Institutionalized but contested	Mixed, but quite small	Resists reform	Reform superintendent ousted	Foundations, state government, federal courts
Atlanta	Small	Small	Very little	New appointee following a nonleader	State government, CBOs, Jimmy Carter's Atlanta Project
Denver	Small	Small	Quietly resists reform	Old no; new selective promoter	Foundations, nonprofits, state government, federal courts
St. Louis	Small	Very little	Very little	Very little	Foundations, federal court, mayor
San Francisco	Very little	Very little	Very little	Active promoter	Federal court and advocacy groups

Our research gave close attention to the office of school superintendent as potentially a major player in school reform. After all, this office is the apex of educational expertise as an institutional force in the urban community. Even so, in the eleven cities studied the superintendent was not an independent force powerful enough to shape the political terrain on her or his own terms. Turnover in the position of superintendent was significant among our eleven cities, as it has been among big-city school systems in general. Thus we concluded that the office of school superintendent was often *a* core player but never *the* core player in the education arena. At best the superintendent acted as a promoter of educational interests in the community, but the superintendent alone does not commonly act as a change agent in big-city school systems.

A second significant feature in Table 4.1 is the absence of the board of education as a major actor *in broad efforts to promote educational improvement.* This is not to suggest that school boards are never a force for educational improvement, and, as the bodies that make decisions about hiring and firing superintendents, they clearly exercise significant power. However, they do not appear to be significant institutions in themselves for shaping new directions in educational policy. It is the superintendent's office that is the source of policy expertise and the main source of operational proposals.

Below the level of superintendent, education professionals appear to have a narrow range of interactions. Our interviews included, along with subordinate school administrators and other education specialists, interviews with related specialists outside the education bureaucracy (for example, Head Start and Job Training administrators). We asked both sets of specialists which groups they currently have contacts with, which groups they would like to have more contact with, and which groups are important for policy innovation in the human-capital area. For some of the groups, the two sets of interviewees gave similar responses. For example, contacts with business were reported by 14 percent of school-based specialists and 16 percent of nonschool specialists. For groups they would like to have more contact with, 61 percent of both categories of respondents identified business. Significantly, however, only 13 percent of education specialists reported contacts with the school board and external education groups (suggesting that contacts outside the school bureaucracy are channeled through the superintendent's office), whereas 32 percent of nonschool specialists reported such contacts (hence their contacts appear to be less tightly channeled). And this pattern occurred in the face of school specialists placing greater weight on these elements as important for policy innovation, 23 percent compared with 10 percent. Another striking contrast is in contact with city hall and the city bureaucracy. Virtually all (99 percent) of the nonschool specialists report such contacts, but only 55 percent of school specialists have such contacts. In other words, in the human-capital arena, specialist-to-specialist contact within the city bureaucracy appears to be more common than contacts across the school–city hall divide. Contacts with universities are reported by only 7 percent of school specialists, but no nonschool specialists report such contacts. And both categories of respondents unanimously see universities as lacking importance for policy innovation. Among nonschool specialists, 71 percent see city hall (that is, general government officials) as important for innovation, but only 38 percent of school specialists attach that importance to city hall. Interestingly, 86 percent of nonschool specialists see the school system as important for policy innovation, but only 27 percent of school specialists view their system as an important force for policy innovation. This again suggests that the atmosphere within the school bureaucracy may be confining in ways sensed by insiders that external actors don't sense. Thus, whereas nonschool specialists see the two major governmental institutions, city hall and the school system, as central to policy innovation, school specialists have a more diffuse understanding. And, except for a slight amount of university contact, they have less interaction outside their own hierarchical organization. The nature of the work of superintendents brings them into a wide set of contacts, but below that office contact seems limited, even in comparison to nonschool specialists working in the area of human-capital programs.

These reported interactions are classic patterns in subsystem politics. Specialists are in contact with a limited set of actors who are responsible for administering similar policies, but have little contact with important players in the community. In such systems, networks tend to settle down into an "equilibrium of interests"[10] that balance one another and are reinforced by patterns of authority and communication. Because of the patterns of authority and interactions and because of the press of day-to-day problems that must be solved, there is little opportunity or incentive for major change.

For their part, board of education members seem much more engaged in constituency service than in general policy formation and oversight. For this reason, they sometimes back into a general policy stance. For example, school boards tend to resist moves to decentralize perhaps because such a move renders the central office, to which they have the greatest access, less useful as a source of assistance in constituency service. School boards can, of course, serve as channels for the expression of voter sentiments. But, as part-time officeholders with little or no legislative staff, members of school boards have limited knowledge about school operations and about the actual or potential consequences of policy alternatives.[11] School board members appear to have policy significance when they speak for an organized coalition, and, in these circumstances, it is the coalition they represent rather than institutional position that appears to be the guiding policy force.

This finding about the relatively peripheral role of school boards is surprising. First, it runs counter to at least some normative visions about democracy and education, which place the elected school board in a pivotal role as the linchpin between voters and school policies.[12] Second, it appears to run counter to the findings of some past empirical studies that attributed a major role to school boards. In his classic study, *The Politics of School Desegregation,* for example, Crain found that "the school board sets the tone of the integration decision and the superintendent plays a less important role."[13]

At first glance, too, our conclusion that school boards are not central to civic mobilization around reform appears at odds with some of our own empirical findings. Our interviews with general influentials, education specialists, and community advocates revealed that respondents consider school boards to be visible educational "players," and our case studies uncovered instances in which communities exhibited an intense burst of attention on school boards, sometimes culminating in the election of reform-oriented slates. We asked respondents in our eleven cities to tell us what groups and actors are especially important in education in their city. Table 4.2 reveals that almost half of all respondents mentioned the school board, just slightly fewer than those who mentioned business or city government in general.[14] This was more than twice as many as mentioned the superintendent.

One explanation for the apparent disjunction between this and our finding that the boards tend not to be central to reform mobilization involves the distinction between general activity and visibility, on the one hand, and incorporation

Table 4.2. What Groups and Actors Are Especially Important in Education Decision Making?

Actor	% of respondents mentioning	Average per city
Business or chamber of commerce	53.5	52.7
City government in general	49.2	50.7
School board	47.5	47.2
Mayor	29.4	29.5
Community groups	26.7	27.1
Teachers	21.7	21.7
Superintendent	21.4	21.5
Parents	19.7	20.8
State	14.7	14.9
Nonprofit organizations	13.7	12.8
City council	11.7	11.8
Federal government	7.0	7.0
Colleges and universities	7.0	7.7
Racial or ethnic groups	6.7	6.9
Religious organizations/leaders	6.4	6.3
Unions	6.0	5.3
Media	1.7	1.3
Citizens' groups	1.3	1.5

Note: Up to five groups or actors were coded for each respondent, although most mentioned fewer than five.

into a working reform partnership on the other. School board members play highly active roles in many of our cities, but their activity and visibility tend to be tied to much narrower issues than the broad system reform focus that concerned us in Table 4.1. Often, the board is the key access point for parents seeking input on relations that are school-specific (Can we get our playground equipment upgraded?) or even child-specific (Can you help us transfer Johnnie to a different school?). On broad policy initiatives, they lack the staff and information to challenge the superintendent's leadership, and as a result they tend to follow the superintendent's policy leadership except when issues become highly visible and controversial.

To the consternation of many superintendents, school board acquiescence on issues of broad policy guidance does *not* necessarily translate into a reluctance to micromanage narrow issues on which the board members, or their constituents, take special interest. As mentioned, communities occasionally do mount broad reform movements that center on board elections, and around the time of our interviewing such reform boards were visible in Atlanta and Detroit. In Atlanta, an organization called "Erase the Board" was founded in 1993 with a stated goal of replacing all members of the faction-ridden school board. Although it enjoyed initial success, the board's postelection effort was mainly managerial. In Detroit, a reform slate labeled the "HOPE Team" had been elected in 1988, and by the time of our interviewing had become the focus of a popular backlash culminating in their loss of majority control at a subsequent election. These short-term bursts in school board centrality do not contradict our general conclusion that school boards tend to be marginal actors in systemic school reform coalitions. Rather, they highlight the senses in which civic mobilization must be sustained over time if key actors are to develop the links and sense of mutual trust that enable them to work cooperatively on issues of broad significance.

Parents are also a less significant force in school reform coalitions than would be anticipated either by normative theories or their sporadic visibility in popular accounts of school politics. One of the most consistent and seemingly uncontroversial findings in the education literature concerns the importance of parental involvement for children's learning and schools' success.[15] Parents, teachers, principals, and public officials readily subscribe to the premise that partnerships between parents and schools make a potent combination. This view has encouraged various reform efforts at the local level, including policies to improve communication from the schools to homes, to encourage teachers to make home visits, and to institute school-based decision-making teams comprised of principals, teachers, parents, and community representatives.

One out of every five of our respondents mentioned parents as an important education force, but as with school boards we found their visibility keyed to sporadic outbursts or school-specific initiatives rather than sustained involvement in systemic reform coalitions. With the heavy migration of the middle class from cities and city school systems, this pattern is unsurprising. Lower-SES parents have a long and continuing history of finding teachers and school administrators difficult to approach. Research indicates that the actions of school systems are an especially important factor in the degree to which parents become actively engaged. Yet among our eleven cities, only Pittsburgh made any systemwide effort to involve parents. Individual schools and pilot projects provided some involvement but it was not a matter of priority. Indeed, even when Baltimore and Washington, D.C., underwent mandated restructuring (subsequent to the period of intensive field interviewing), parental involvement received little attention. In D.C., parental involvement was simply not a consideration in that city's top-down initiation of reform. In the case of Baltimore, restructuring did create an official advisory role for parents, but the need for quick action took precedence over including them in the crucial early stages of planning and redesign.

Thus, despite vocal support for parental involvement from the U.S. Department of Education and many state departments of education as well, urban parents are scarcely visible as *active* stakeholders in the current school improvement movement. Among our eleven cities, the most likely source of a parent voice is the middle-class remnant that remains. Parents occasionally mobilize for school board elections, as was the case, for example, in key campaigns in Atlanta and Detroit. The Atlanta mobilization was not sustained and was not incorporated into an ongoing form of parent involvement, however, and many Detroit parents who initially supported the reform slate subsequently voted for their ouster.[16] Even though educators continue to voice complaints about the lack of parental engagement in the education of their children, educators remain largely inattentive to ways to provide avenues of parent involvement.

Variation in civic mobilization among the eleven cities occurs mainly in the involvement of teachers and of the business sector. In only three of the cities was the teachers' union a member of the reform coalition, and thereby in a position to put professional development on the table as an element of the improvement agenda. In another three, the teachers were active (if not always highly visible) opponents of reform. And in the remaining five they were largely nonplayers in broad school improvement efforts.

The involvement of the business sector also varied greatly. In the top three cities, business involvement was intensive and institutionalized at the time of our research. In the four intermediate cities business was significantly involved, but in Detroit that involvement was openly contested by a group of community activists who often framed their opposition in racial terms.[17] And in D.C. and in Baltimore that involvement was and remains guarded and has low visibility. In neither city did the business sector play a leading role in coalition building. On the other hand, in Los Angeles LEARN (the organized arm of school reform) was created by business initiative. In Houston, the business role was highly visible, but its leadership was tarnished in the Latino community by business involvement in the controversial selection of an African-American school superintendent at a time in which members of the Latino community felt that they had a strong claim to consideration for this office.

In the remaining four cities, the business role was quite small. All of these are cities in which business has, at least at some time, played a major role in development policy and related issues.[18] And in two of these cities, Atlanta and St. Louis, business has played a significant part in promoting or defending school desegregation. In community affairs overall, business leadership has been far from inconsequential in these four cities. But in education the business role is modest. And in Atlanta, where business did play an active part in replacing a discredited school board majority, the thrust of business leadership has been mainly toward promoting economy and efficiency rather than substantive educational policies for the improvement of human capital. It may be that the business stake in central-city public education is less compelling than some optimistic accounts suggest.[19]

A scattering of other actors (foundations, community-based organizations, nonprofits, and the office of mayor are among the major examples) have played a part in school improvement efforts, but in 1993–1994 they lacked the claim of being central stakeholders in the same way that educators, parents, and business were. Since then, the mayor's office has become more visible in national discourse, but local resistance to mayoral direction of the schools remains considerable, as evidenced in the recent debate about altering the governance of the D.C. school system.[20]

One major finding is the limited role that substantive educational reform can play when other issues demand immediate attention from community policy makers. The number of issues that can be seriously addressed by a community during any period is highly constrained by attention spans, resource limitations, and the time and energy necessary for civic mobilization. When mobilization is directed toward one set of issues, others must wait. Significantly, three of the four cities weakest in civic mobilization (Denver, San Francisco, and St. Louis) have been under broad desegregation orders, and some observers believed that court action has preempted local leadership. In addition, Denver has been subject to direct intervention by the governor of Colorado.

As one of the low-ranking cities in civic mobilization around education, Atlanta is a special case, but also bears in its own way the markings of federal court action. In the 1970s, controversy over busing took an important turn when a federal judge created a biracial committee to negotiate an agreement that came to be known as "the Atlanta Compromise."[21] African Americans agreed to relinquish their demand for busing in exchange for control of the top layer of school administration, which, up to that time, had been preponderantly white. School enrollment had become two-thirds African American, and that proportion was continuing to rise (it now exceeds 90 percent). After the agreement, the Atlanta schools were seen as the special province of the city's African-American population and business involvement in education declined.

Differences in degree of civic mobilization are only part of the picture. None of the eleven cities matches the ideal of a fully inclusive coalition, the members of which are engaged in an ongoing dialogue about educational improvement.

Instead, there are varying degrees of mobilization and a somewhat fragmented dialogue, hampered in some cities by deep-running conflicts. Moreover, the Baltimore case shows that even when a key figure like the mayor (Baltimore's school system at this time was a department of city government, not an independent authority as is often the case) is personally involved in the dialogue, he is constrained by a need to be attentive to the particular fears and concerns of his constituents. A dialogue among key elites is not the same as a dialogue among major groups.[22]

Even Pittsburgh—the foremost among our eleven cities in civic mobilization—had a disappointing experience with the Annie E. Casey Foundation's New Futures initiative for at-risk children and youth. Though chosen because of its record of civic collaboration, Pittsburgh's performance on New Futures was highly uneven. Turf battles were a major factor, and the school system was especially turf conscious. The collaboration that did occur was mainly at the elite level and involved minimal consultation with children and youth and those who worked most directly with them.[23] Thus, although Pittsburgh topped our eleven cities, even its civic mobilization had significant weaknesses. Moreover, continuing research indicates that Pittsburgh may have slipped some in degree of civic mobilization from the time when its education coalition was first put together in the 1970s.[24]

Assessing the level of civic mobilization across eleven cities, we see several general points to bear in mind. One is that there is substantial variation among cities. In particular, the role of business and the role of the teachers' union differ greatly from city to city. But there are also some general considerations that hold across all cities. School boards, appointed and elected alike, are not centers of institutional strength. That position is occupied by school superintendents and the administrative staffs they manage. School boards can hire and fire superintendents, but they have little mastery of the inner workings of the education bureaucracy and spend much of their energy on constituency service rather than matters of devising and overseeing policy direction. Professional expertise and command of operational detail give all bureaucracies some autonomy, but education bureaucracies have for many years enjoyed a higher degree of autonomy than most.

Parents, as the most directly affected constituency group for public schools, are a weak counterweight to professional autonomy. Citywide parent groups do exist across the eleven cities, but they are a modest force in school policy at best. Giving much less attention to oversight of general questions of school performance than to how particular schools are run, parents tend not to focus on systemic issues. Parental concerns are largely guided by the matters that most immediately affect their children, resulting in their practical, school-level focus. Because middle-class parents are much better positioned to play this game than their lower-class cohorts, parental oversight is less likely to deal with education problems related to concentrated poverty than to guard resources available to middle-class students. Because lower-income and minority parents often see government jobs, services, and community-based institutions as vehicles for upward mobility, they tend to be resistant to calls for school reform that have the prospect of leading to teacher cutbacks or school closures. Although more difficult to mobilize in general, ironically, when these parents *do* mobilize it is sometimes as an antireform counterforce.[25]

Overall, then, civic mobilization does not naturally occur in urban education politics, and it is unlikely to occur spontaneously simply because a need for educational improvement is felt. Business executives, parents, and various racial and community-based groups tend to have only selective engagement, hence they often have little voice in setting and overseeing school policy. Organized into unions of teachers and administrators, educators themselves are inclined politically to concentrate on "bread and butter" issues of compensation and job security. The commitment of some unions to the issue of professional development is, however, an indication of a potential for a wider role. The bottom line is a classic policy subsystem organizational structure in educational policy, with professionals setting policy subject to sporadic specific demands from issue-based groups.

If educational reform is to transcend the disjointed and piecemeal approach implied by the analysis above, civic mobilization is critical. Important as education is in the life of all communities, civic mobilization in the education arena is no easy process. Cross-sector collaboration is an intricate process to put together in the first place, and it is no small challenge to maintain it, once established.[26]

UNDERLYING SOURCES OF CIVIC MOBILIZATION

Given the substantial variation among our eleven cities, we might consider whether underlying conditions either facilitate or hinder civic mobilization. For example, is mobilization related to the socioeconomic character of a city? Another possibility, given the enormous importance of race and ethnicity in the education arena, is that civic capacity (or its lack) stems from the manner in which race plays out politically in school matters.

Socioeconomic factors have an important place in shaping political and policy responses, but social scientists differ in their interpretations of the independent strength and directness of the causal chain. During the 1970s, in particular, a number of visible and important studies concluded that such factors as wealth, education, and urbanization were the primary causes of variation in state and city policies, and that political institutions and political processes were of minor import.[27] These studies sparked an intense debate about which was more important—politics or economics—that probably generated more heat than light. Our interest in looking at socioeconomic factors and political factors as facilitators or obstacles to civic mobilization does not lie in declaring one or the other to be the "winner." It may be true in a simple sense that a socioeconomic factor such as community wealth can translate into a specific policy outcome (for example, per-pupil spending), but the link between socioeconomics and policy is always mediated through political processes that set goals, choose among alternative means, and authoritatively allocate public resources.

In exploring socioeconomic and political correlates of civic mobilization, our interest does not stem from the politics versus economic debate, but in two broader questions with meaningful policy implications. First, we are interested in assessing the extent to which local actors might indeed have maneuvering room to exert influence. If demographic factors are determinative, local actors may have little choice but to ride the winds of economic, social, and racial change. In particular, low-income central cities with heterogeneous populations may be doomed to political inefficacy and internal divisiveness. If, on the other hand, localities with similar socioeconomic profiles mount meaningfully different collective responses, there would be more room for leadership, initiative, and human agency to be asserted in progressive ways. Second, we are interested in identifying specific leverage points for policy intervention. Some school reform proponents argue that simple institutional changes—such as granting mayors authority to appoint school boards—can quickly and directly alter local dynamics in ways that are conducive to systemic education reform. If we find that civic mobilization is greater in cities with certain institutional or procedural characteristics, this might guide us toward specific recommendations for reform.

Demographics and Civic Mobilization

Civic mobilization does not appear to be the product of underlying socioeconomic conditions, at least in any straightforward sense. Table 4.3 summarizes the relationships between each city's demographic characteristics and our qualitative ranking of its degree of civic mobilization around education reform. Indicators of population change, in particular, show a complete lack of relationship with mobilization. Growing cities do not appear to have any advantage or disadvantage. Those with more stable white populations do not mount a more cohesive response, nor does the sharp loss of white residents spark a sharper reaction. The top three cities in civic mobilization include one each that is high, medium, and low in change in total population, change in youth population, and change in white population between 1960 and 1990. Nor is racial composition a reliable predictor. Two of the three cities that scored high in civic mobilization have relatively smaller African-American and Hispanic populations (Pittsburgh and Boston), but Denver and San Francisco rank seventh and last in percent African American and Hispanic, yet scored in the lowest category in mobilization.

There is a little more support for a relationship between civic mobilization and socioeconomic status, as measured by income and education. None of the cities that rank low on median household income, ratio of city to suburban income, or percent of college graduates are among the top three in civic mobilization. But neither is it the case that low-SES cities are destined to the bottom level of mobilization, and San Francisco is among our laggards in mobilization for education

Table 4.3. Civic Mobilization by Demographic Characteristics

Civic Mobilization	City	Population Change, 1960–1990			Racial Composition	Socioeconomic Status				White "Loyalty" to Public Schools
		Change 1960–1990 total pop.	Change 1960–1990 population age < 19	Change 1960–1990 white non-Hisp.	% white or Asian, 1990	Med. household income, 1990	Ratio/city to suburban income, 1990	Racial income equity (ratio of black/Hisp. income to white income)	% college educ. 1990	Ratio % wht. in pub sch. to % white pop.
High	Pittsburgh	L	L	H	H	M	H	M	M	H
	Boston	M	M	M	H	H	M	M	H	M
	Los Angeles	H	H	L	M	H	H	H	M	M
Medium	Baltimore	M	M	H	M	M	M	H	L	H
	Houston	H	H	L	M	M	H	L	M	M
	D.C.	M	L	L	L	H	M	H	H	L
	Detroit	L	M	H	L	L	L	M	L	M
Low	Atlanta	M	M	M	L	L	L	L	M	L
	Denver	H	H	M	H	M	M	H	H	H
	St. Louis	L	L	H	M	L	L	M	L	L
	San Francisco	H	H	M	H	H	H	H	H	L

reform, in spite of scoring high on every dimension of SES. We constructed a rough indicator of racial income equity by averaging the median income of black and Hispanic households and dividing that by the median household income for whites. We hypothesized that civic mobilization might be facilitated by a more equal distribution of income across the major racial/ethnic categories; here, again, the relationship is nonexistent.

Finally, Table 4.3 includes an indicator meant to capture some of the dynamic of white flight and public school exit discussed in Chapter 2. Census tabulations for school districts provide information on the percent of resident children attending that is white. We divided that figure by the percent of the total population in the district that is white. A score of 1 on this indicator would mean that the racial composition of the public school population reflects that of the overall population. Cities in which white households with children have been moving to the suburbs would score lower on this indicator, as would those in which white residents send their children to private schools. In theory, districts might score above 1 on this indicator, but in fact the range in our eleven cities ran from .18 to .69; in other words, white children were substantially underrepresented among the public school attendees in every case. If a district's ability to hold on to white families gives it a stronger foundation for political mobilization,[28] we would expect high scores on this indicator to correspond to higher levels of civic mobilization. The observed pattern is at least somewhat consistent with that expectation; in particular, a disproportionate loss of white children from the public schools does appear to be a fairly good predictor of low civic mobilization. A strong ability to hold on to white children, however, does not seem to be especially predictive of very high mobilization, and the case of Denver shows that even a public school system that does a fairly good job of holding on to its resident white children can mount a weak mobilization response.

Political Context and Civic Mobilization

Examining civic mobilization in relation to various political characteristics does not neatly isolate the facilitators and impediments, although it does provide us with a few more clues to the sources of civic mobilization.

As we discussed earlier, once the original set of case studies was completed it became apparent that the eleven cities did not vary along a single political dimension but rather that they displayed divergent dynamics. And these seem to correspond to interplay between politics and demography.

Black-led cities (Atlanta, Baltimore, Detroit, and Washington, D.C.) are black majority cities in which the student enrollment in the public schools is preponderantly African American and in which African Americans control all of the key institutional levers in the public sector: the superintendent's office, the school board, and city hall. Electoral control and the demography from which it rises give the black community a strong claim on major institutional positions and a means to enforce that claim. In short, these are cities in which there is a clearly identified education constituency of black children and their parents and the immediate control of schools is also in African-American hands. Hence there is a potential for concerted action.

At the same time, local electoral strength is only one base of power. City school districts are legal creatures of the state government (or in the case of D.C., the U.S. Congress), and these larger governmental bodies rest on a much different electoral base from those in the city. In addition, white business executives usually hold most of the levers of economic power. A black-white racial divide thus coincides with a division between those who hold immediate positions of authority in school matters and those who control more distant but nonetheless formidable leverage. Thus, racial division might stand as a formidable barrier to mobilization.[29]

Sunbelt cities (Denver, Houston, Los Angeles, and San Francisco) are multiracial cities in which the Hispanic population is both growing and becoming more politically conscious. San Francisco has the additional feature of a large and diverse Asian-American population. Overall, in the Sunbelt cities both the electorates and the student populations are diverse and changing. Political alignments are volatile and tensions abound between minorities as well as between whites and people of color. The racial complexity of these cities combined with their continuing demographic fluidity may provide a foundation from which civic mobilization would be especially difficult.

Machine-descendant cities (Boston, Pittsburgh, and St. Louis) were once dominated by patronage politics, and in an earlier era immigrant groups were politically mobilized mainly by ward bosses. In the post–World War II period, city leadership rested substantially on an accommodation between business executives who had an economic stake in the city and elected officials who commanded a largely working-class following. The politics of education is complicated in these cities by demography: Children of color—mainly African American—are a much larger segment of the public school enrollment than their parents are of the city electorate.[30] White students, though they are a minority in each of the three cities, are a significant presence in all. Thus the divergence between public school enrollment and electoral weight might work against civic mobilization, but might also broaden the base of concern with public education and thereby facilitate civic mobilization.

We found many similarities within these three clusters, and some clear differences across them, in the kinds of issues arising, the lines of conflict that tend to emerge, and the general tone and language of political discourse. Because the rallying of cross-sector support for education faces a different challenge in each of the three kinds of cities, we expected that levels of civic mobilization might differ systematically as well.[31] Yet, as indicated in the first column of Table 4.4, this typology was not a reliable predictor of community mobilization for educational reform. Two of the top cities—Pittsburgh and Boston—are in the machine-descendant category, but the third city in that category, St. Louis, is near the bottom

Table 4.4. Civic Mobilization by Political Context

Mobilization	City	Geopolitical context	Open system?	Number educated players	Cleavage–ethnic/racial	Cleavage–interest group vs. interest group	Cleavage–citizens versus local government/school board	Cleavage–city government versus school board
High	Pittsburgh	Machine	H	H	L	L	H	H
	Boston	Machine	M	L	H	L	L	L
	Los Angeles	Sunbelt	L	L	H	M	H	M
Medium	Baltimore	Black-led	M	L	M	M	M	M
	Houston	Sunbelt	H	M	M	H	L	H
	D.C.	Black-led	H	H	L	M	L	H
	Detroit	Black-led	H	M	L	H	M	L
Low	Atlanta	Black-led	L	L	M	M	H	M
	Denver	Sunbelt	M	M	M	M	H	H
	St. Louis	Machine	M	H	H	H	M	L
	San Francisco	Sunbelt	L	H	M	H	L	H

in civic mobilization. The Sunbelt cities are scattered among the three levels, and the black-led cities are also scattered.

The next several columns in the table are based on the coded interview transcripts. We asked respondents whether education decision making in their city was a specialized arena, dominated by education professionals, or an open arena in which multiple groups had access. If respondents indicated that the arena was open, we also asked what groups were key players in education decision making. According to the Progressives' vision, cohesive reform would be more feasible in a more circumscribed environment; an open arena, with many groups pursuing particularistic interest would be more likely to generate fragmentation and stalemate, according to this perspective. On the other hand, both public choice and pluralist theory suggest that closed arenas—dominated by educational professionals—would tend to become stagnant and isolated, presumably resistant to collaboration in a systemic reform coalition.

Columns two and three indicate that openness to interest-group influence may bear a complex relationship with civic mobilization. Although the relationship is not powerful, there is some indication that open systems are more conducive to civic mobilization; all four of the cities that scored high on this indicator also were either high or medium on our mobilization measure, and two of the three cities in which respondents indicated the system was a specialized arena scored low on our mobilization score. Among open systems, however, a higher number of education players was *not* especially conducive to the formation of a cohesive civic coalition around systemic reform. If anything, the pattern is the opposite; that is to say, there is some suggestion that an open system combined with fewer actors is more likely to result in strong civic mobilization.

We also asked respondents,"When there is conflict, what is its source?" Our coders identified thirteen different types of responses to this question; Table 4.4 highlights four that are particularly interesting. During the late 1960s and early 1970s, the combination of rapid racial change and the grassroots strength of the civil rights movement led many central-city education issues to be defined in racial and ethnic terms. The polarization and symbolic politics that resulted made collaboration difficult, even among groups traditionally allied around issues of equity and human capital investment.[32] At the same time some political scientists, such as Douglas Yates, were arguing that cities were becoming generally ungovernable owing to "street-fighting pluralism" and the excessive fragmentation that pitted interest group versus interest group in a draining battle for the benefits that government could provide.[33] Others at the time envisioned—even if they did not proclaim it to yet exist—a more populist political context in which cross-cutting cleavages like race, ethnicity, occupation, and neighborhood would be displaced by a general mobilization of the mass citizenry versus the elites who occupied the formal positions of governmental power.

Interestingly, by the early 1990s conflict along racial and ethnic lines was becoming much less common in some of the cities where it had raged two decades earlier. In any case, Table 4.4 provides little or no support for the notion that such lines of conflict are especially damaging to the prospects for civic mobilization. Nor is there support for the notion that conflict between citizens and elected officials either stimulates or undermines civic mobilization around education reform. There is, however, at least some support for the notion that hyperpluralism may have a corrosive effect; in none of the three cities with high mobilization were respondents likely to refer to generalized intergroup conflict, and such references were relatively common in two of the four cities that scored low on the mobilization scale.

Formal Decision-Making Structure and Mobilization

We might, then, turn to a third factor—the position of the school system in the formal structure of local governance. Some theories about school reform hold that structural changes introduced during the Progressive Era—changes designed to buffer school decision making from the patronage politics seen to permeate the general arena of city government—may have become part of the problem. These theories suggest that one way to stimulate a stronger systemic reform response is to bring school governance more formally into alignment with the institutions that govern funding and decision making across the rest of the local policy agenda. One way to do this is to give the mayor greater control over the membership of the school board. Another strategy is to increase the authority of the mayor and council to set school funding levels and review line-item allocations.

Perhaps civic mobilization is facilitated by the way the school system and general local government fit together. Institutionally, the connections between the local school system and city government vary, though the prevailing pattern among our eleven cities, as among school districts generally, is that of the school system as an independent taxing authority. As mentioned in Chapter 1, eight of our eleven cities are part of that pattern, as are seven out of ten of the other large, urban school districts that are members of the Council of Great City Schools. In Boston, Baltimore, and D.C., the schools depend on the cities' general taxing authority for their operating funds; these three then are scored high in formal connection between city and school district. In two of the remaining cases—Houston and Los Angeles—the divide between city and school district is further widened by the fact that their boundaries are not coterminous; these we categorize as "low" in formal connectedness.

But, as indicated in Table 4.5, this variation does not neatly correlate with mobilization rank. The two cities in which the mayors currently play the strongest role in selecting the school boards are Boston and Baltimore, and these two cities both score in the top half on our civic mobilization indicator. But the rest of the pattern is scattered at best. Moreover, Boston's high score on this indicator is largely attributable to an institutional shift from elected to appointed school board that did not occur until 1992; this shift was probably too recent to account for the

Table 4.5. Civic Mobilization by Political Structure

Mobilization	City	Formal connection city/school district	Federal judicial oversight?
High	Pittsburgh	M	No
	Boston	H	No
	Los Angeles	L	No
Medium	Baltimore	H	No
	Houston	L	No
	D.C.	M	No
	Detroit	M	No
Low	Atlanta	M	No
	Denver	M	Y
	St. Louis	M	Y
	San Francisco	M	Y

high levels of mobilization we encountered. Indeed, it is likely that the degree of cohesiveness and cooperation among key groups helps account for the structural change as the other way around.

The three cities highest in civic mobilization are scattered, one in each category of connection between school district and general city government. And none of the cities lowest in civic mobilization coincide with the weakest connection between schools and general city government. The broad features of governmental structure thus appear to be of no consequence in explaining civic mobilization. Nevertheless, it is true that education politics in the two cities in which there are mayoral-appointed school boards—Baltimore and Boston—have been significantly affected by mayoral leadership. Given its visibility in the urban mosaic of overlapping governments, the office of mayor can be a critical force to focus attention on school performance and to rally forces for improvement. Some of the impact of mayoral leadership in Boston and Baltimore has come after the period of field study (post-1994), but it is generally consistent with the Chicago experience, in which mayoral leadership has been a significant factor in school reform.[34] The Chicago experience, however, also points to the key role that business can play in creating a climate for school reform.[35]

The Limits of External Intervention

A different element of formal governance structure relates to the place of local school districts in the broader arrangement of our federalist system. A defining characteristic of our form of government is that it provides multiple venues within which groups may seek to promote their interests and the public good. This division of formal authority has the potential to exert a conservative drag on the system by in-creasing the strategic leverage of various "veto groups," with an interest in main-taining the status quo, but sometimes the availability of alternative venues can become the means by which groups can bring about nonincremental change.[36] Convinced that local political elites have too big a stake in protecting the existing ways of or-ganizing and running public schools, some education reformers have pinned their hopes on the prospect that reform can be jump-started through authoritative inter-vention by states or the national government. Such visions of external intervention take several forms. One form that has played an important historical role in U.S. education has been direct intervention by federal courts. The evolution of judicial involvement in bringing about equality of educational opportunity in America's schools has been a complex and controversial one, but both people who have fa-vored and those who have opposed aggressive judicial action have regarded it as a vehicle for superseding local political dynamics.[37]

The second column in Table 4.5 identifies school districts that were operat-ing under a federal court order related to school desegregation during the time of our field research. We find some compelling evidence that being subject to such external oversight may undermine the conditions for indigenous mobilization. Interviews in St. Louis, Denver, and San Francisco suggest that judicial involve-ment may lead some local actors to sidestep a sense of responsibility; resentment of—or even reliance on—oversight may in some senses replace an impetus for these groups to take things, collectively, into their own hands. This does not con-stitute an unambiguous argument against judicial intervention, however. Even if the court's role contributes to a slackened indigenous capacity, the substantive issues that prompted judicial intervention might carry greater weight. Moreover, in at least some instances, an aggressive judicial arm can serve as at least a partial and short-term *replacement* for locally generated reform action, as appears to have been the case in San Francisco.[38]

LOCAL HISTORY AS A CONDITIONING FORCE

Our examination of the roots of civic mobilization in this chapter has turned up a few suggestive relationships. We find some evidence that cities lower in socio-economic status have a more difficult time building working coalitions across important sectors, and some evidence that the ability to keep white families in-vested in the public schools may translate into advantages in civic mobilization. Our analysis indicates that more open educational arenas—in which decision making is not monopolized by educational professionals—may be more condu-cive to building links among stakeholders, but that there may be a point of dimin-ishing return associated with hyperpluralism, wherein additional actors might even begin to undermine mobilization. This may in part stem from the critical role that a shared understanding of educational issues plays in civic capacity, a topic we address in the next chapter. We also found a pattern consistent with the conclusion that federal judicial oversight might have the unanticipated side effect of eroding the motivations for indigenous mobilization.

Nevertheless, the kinds of demographic and political factors considered here seem to leave much variation unexplained. With only eleven cases to consider, it is not possible to carry out sophisticated multivariate analysis; it is certainly possible that the independent variables considered here would be found to be strong and reliable predictors of civic mobilization if we were able to undertake such analysis. But the weight of our findings suggests that the socioeconomic character of the city and the racial-political dynamic may be too remote from human problems and choices to be critical causal factors. They are not without consequence, of course, but their link to the motivations and actions of the major players is too indirect to account for very much. Population characteristics, population changes, racial distribution, dominant political cleavages, and formal structure do a poor job of predicting mobilization around education issues. Even the factors that do seem related to mobilization are not sufficient to account for some clear anomalies.

In attempting to account for anomalies, we find ourselves consistently drawn to elements of local political history to help us account for why factors that seem important in one context seem less so in others. Take, for example, the role of the teachers' union and of the business sector. These are in many ways an unlikely pair of partners, yet they are key elements in placing some cities high in the ranking on civic capacity. Political leadership and choice play a key part in the way some cities manage to forge links across these sectors that seem so naturally at odds in other settings. Yet the *kind* of leadership and choice that is important is not associated with the unique skills of particular individuals—in their vision, or resources, or force of will—so much as it is the accretion of habits and patterns of cooperation that have evolved over time.

Leadership and successful policy change do not arise in historical voids. Pittsburgh's education coalition did not emerge fully developed, like Minerva from the head of Jupiter. The earlier involvement of Pittsburgh's business sector in downtown redevelopment and community revitalization laid a foundation for subsequent involvement in education. But business engagement in downtown redevelopment by itself guarantees nothing. Both Atlanta and Denver have had business communities very active in economic development issues, but in neither city did this activity lead to a broad involvement in education.

Pittsburgh, Boston, and St. Louis provide an instructive comparison.[39] All three have generally similar backgrounds as cities in which immigrant groups were politically organized by patronage-oriented ward bosses. All three cities underwent major controversies over desegregation, but Pittsburgh managed to bring the various actors together to avoid lengthy conflict. Boston did not, and St. Louis also underwent a prolonged struggle over desegregation, though not as intense as the Boston conflict. The pattern of business engagement differs sharply across the three cities. In Pittsburgh, business was involved heavily early on. In St. Louis business leadership has taken a more ad hoc role than in Pittsburgh, and, although business took a part early in defending desegregation, the business involvement in education was much more shallow than in Pittsburgh. In Boston, deep business engagement in education came late—after the city's desegregation battle had been waged. But when it did come business participation was fully institutionalized through the Boston Compact. Thus, among three cities with similar political histories, the two high-mobilization cities differ clearly from the low-mobilization city in the nature of business involvement, especially the depth to which this engagement has been institutionalized.

Other cities represent varying patterns. In Los Angeles a business initiative brought together and institutionalized a school reform coalition. But this was done mainly in response to a perceived crisis, driven by a radically changing school demography. Houston's business leadership, which has a history of extensive participation in civic matters, increased its engagement at least partly in response to the issue of juvenile crime and disorder. However, a long-standing pattern of civic cooperation in Houston, especially in the field of education, centered on negotiation and connection between the business sector and leaders in the African-American community, with business elites as the linchpin in most forms of civic activity. Working from that top-down tradition, Houston's business sector inadvertently heightened tensions between the African-American and Latino communities. Thus, in that city a high level of intergroup tension limited the scope of civic mobilization.

Each city has a significantly different history of business engagement in education. In Detroit, when business leaders sought a high level of involvement in public education, they did so in a way that was politically inept and they navigated that city's racial divide poorly. Baltimore's business sector has displayed greater political skill in its relations with the African-American community, but for a time city hall operated with a tacit understanding that education was the special province of the black community. That tacit understanding was, however, overridden when a community-based organization (BUILD, an IAF affiliate) pressured the business sector into a more active form of engagement.

The role of history also helps to explain our finding about the sometimes perverse impact of judicial intervention. Especially important to the erosion of the conditions for civic mobilization may be the local business community. Stone and others have found that informal links between elected leaders and the business community can be critical determinants of civic capacity to undertake broad urban revitalization efforts.[40] Robert Crain's study of school desegregation in the 1960s also highlighted the role of city business elites. Crain found that, though the business sector did not dictate decisions about school desegregation and did not even necessarily take a direct part in the process, business did have an important influence in setting the political style of the community. Greater business involvement in public affairs helped to set a climate in which decision makers could be guided by broader concerns. Domination by political party leaders, by contrast, led to more narrow concerns.[41] Crain rejects a power-elite explanation in favor of a more diffuse form of class influence that stems from the personal skill, personal wealth, and interest in status that comes from personal involvement in broad civic matters. For Crain, then, the key is not business control over economic resources per se, but personal motivation and skill that become vehicles through which a group interest is expressed in the kind of city that business leaders want.[42]

With that as background, consider how the business role differs across our eleven cities, and we can see a dimension of business engagement beyond what Crain describes. Whereas school desegregation was a bounded policy decision, school reform is a more open-ended matter, requiring attention over a long period of time. Hence our research gives attention to institutionalization of engagement. Our eleven cities vary in the degree to which a business role is institutionalized and in the scope of that engagement.

In all but five of the cities, the business community was involved in a relatively visible, institutionalized "partnership" with the public education system during the period of our field research.[43] Such partnerships, which typically involved corporate pledges of support and jobs for graduates in return for school system guarantees about the quality of the education they were providing and the achievement of the students they graduated, were in place in Pittsburgh, Boston, Los Angeles, Baltimore, Houston, and Detroit. D.C. also mounted a serious business-led reform effort in the late 1980s, although its partnership arrangement was less institutionalized and—as matters proceeded—more ephemeral.[44] Although individual businesses and corporate leaders became involved in education reform efforts in Atlanta, St. Louis, and Denver, their role was considerably more limited, informal, and ad hoc.[45]

Significantly, each of the four cities with weak business involvement was subject to a form of external intervention that put the implementation of education policy in an arena outside the scope of local actors. In Denver, external intervention comprised both a federal court order and a substantial assertion by the office of the governor. In St. Louis and San Francisco, the court's intervention was especially forceful. In the case of Atlanta, the federal judiciary did not itself occupy a central place, but the judicially sanctioned agreement nevertheless eclipsed the business role and put responsibility in nonbusiness hands. In D.C., a mixed case of business involvement, the oversight of Congress, and the threat of its potential intervention plays an analogous role. External, especially judicial intervention, largely preempts the civic role of local actors, and it appears that business might be especially willing to move to the sidelines under such circumstances.

It is probable that business involvement will be more productively channeled in cities with general cultures of citizen involvement. Business engagement does not occur in a vacuum; it occurs in interaction with other stakeholders. Robert Crain directed our attention to the personal skill of business elites as players in city civic life. Civic skill may not be a generic quality, but one that is situationally bounded—hence, neighborhood political activism is potentially a significant part of the picture.

Two of the high-mobilization cities, Pittsburgh and Boston, have particularly strong traditions of neighborhood activism. Los Angeles has at least a moderately strong tradition of neighborhood political activism, as does Baltimore (at the upper end of the middle ranking on civic mobilization). What this suggests is that business actors *and their institutional representatives* may be more skillful in the art of coalition building where they have long experience in negotiating with other contenders for a civic voice. This experience may also give business a felt need to embrace a broad civic agenda.[46] The institutionalization of a business role in a broad agenda of civic affairs thus holds the possibility of engaging representatives of the business sector in coalition building and thereby providing a high level of skill. The importance of political skill gained explicit recognition in Los Angeles when the business-backed reform organization, LEARN, named as its executive director a state legislator rather than an educator with substantive expertise. In Pittsburgh, the longevity of the top staff of the ACCD is also consistent with the importance of the cumulative character of political skill in coalition building. By contrast, the ad hoc character of business engagement in St. Louis works against the cumulative sharpening of political skill in civic coalition building.[47] Political ineptness by business in Detroit and Houston also points to the importance of skill in dealing with diverse groups. In these two cities the scarcity of negotiating experience with neighborhood and community-based groups may have hampered business efforts.

From the evidence at hand, it seems that civic mobilization springs directly from neither the socioeconomic character of the city nor the racial-political dynamic rooted in a city's demography nor even from the formal structure of governing arrangements. The role of business appears crucial, but the extent of business effort seems to depend on whether external intervention has provided an alternative to the usual form of civic mobilization centered around business. Business, however, does not claim a central role simply by its economic importance to the community. Business has to organize and display skill in dealing with a broader array of players if it is to be a key facilitator of civic mobilization. The office of mayor provides another possible source of civic energy, but among our eleven cities the experience in this matter is quite limited. One piece still missing involves the way in which objective conditions are interpreted through subjective lenses. Civic mobilization under conditions of shared understandings is civic capacity. And this leads us to the issue of problem definition that we discuss next.

5

Conducting Policy in an Ill-Structured Problem Space

In the United States much of politics occurs in subsystems, out of the limelight of public opinion. Within policy subsystems, political actors having a stake make adjustments, but these adjustments almost never include major reforms. So long as policy is conducted at this subsystem level, radical change is precluded.

At times, however, collective attention is directed at a policy issue in a manner that makes "cozy" subsystem politics unfeasible. Groups mobilize; emotion intensifies; publicity increases. At such times of heightened mobilization, major change is feasible (although it may not occur for a variety of reasons).[1] In policy mobilizations, positive feedback, in which mobilization and attention beget more mobilization and attention, occurs. Even where policy making is pluralistic and decentralized, the policy ideas that underlie mobilization spill over from one policy venue to others, actually promoting rather than retarding change.

We have seen that our eleven cities differ in their levels of civic mobilization around the issue of systemic education reform. Here we examine the definition of issues harbored by elites in our eleven cities. We want to know the nature of the definitions of the problems our elite groups hold and their conceptions of the best solutions to those problems. In order to explore these and other aspects of civic involvement in education, we draw on the over 500 in-depth interviews our researchers conducted with three groups of community leaders: general influentials (politicians, business executives, and so on), community advocates, and program specialists.[2]

Education policy making is decentralized policy making. Most of the action is at the local and state levels. Policy subsystems form when there is a general lack of interest from community elites, and most school policy is in the hands of educational professionals—superintendents, board of education members, principals, teachers' unions, and parent-teacher organizations. Progressive Era theories about the separation of education from city politics and policy making inadvertently aided and abetted the insular nature of urban education. As important a policy arena as education is, this subsystem perspective holds for most of the time in most cities. As our analyses in Chapter 2 showed, local education subsystems are sporadically racked by demands, but those demands tend to be highly particularized—parents demanding resources for their school or demanding particular programs in their schools, teachers wanting better pay and working conditions, or businesses wanting economy and efficiency. Civic mobilization and serious educational reform are rare in urban America.

Civic capacity is civic mobilization under a common understanding of the educational problem. In this chapter, we examine the extent to which that common understanding exists among the varied groups concerned with educational policy in the city.

Because educational policy is decentralized policy making, different locales are better suited than others to take advantage of the winds of educational reform. Some cities have better developed civic capacities than others. We have shown earlier that the cities that served as the research sites for this work differ in the ability to mobilize diverse groups in pursuit of the common goal of improving education. In this chapter we argue that the capacity to mobilize to achieve collective ends is closely related to recognizing a problem and forging a shared understanding of the nature of that problem.

We explore in detail the in-depth interviews our field teams conducted with the community elites in the eleven cities. We examine differing understandings of the "education problem" and proposed solutions to the problem. Our major findings may be stated at the outset. First, *educational professionals see fewer problems in education than do community influentials and educational activists.* This is a classic, almost signature aspect of policy subsystems: Those involved are more attached to the status quo than critics from the outside. It is why civic mobilization is necessary to achieve substantial reform.

Second, *elite perception of educational problems and proposed solutions to those problems are both strongly related to the extent of civic mobilization in our eleven cities.* Other ways of grouping respondents—by type of city governing coalition or by the social location of respondents—do not relate to problem perception. Elites in high-mobilization cities are more likely to see educational problems, they are more likely to propose solutions, and the solutions they propose are more likely to involve cutting central bureaucracy, encouraging decentralization, and rejecting redistributive solutions.

Even if "improving education" were viewed as an important goal by most community elites (and we show below that it is), there is often an issue of how to bring about this desired end. Any consensus on collective ends tends to disappear when specifics are addressed. As a consequence, we focused a substantial part of our study toward assessing the manner in which community elites in our eleven cities perceived the problems that challenged local governments. We concentrated both on the general set of perceived problems that dominated the community agenda and we looked at the particular educational issues that our respondents thought that their communities faced. For general community problems, we queried our samples of general influentials and community advocates; for educational problems, we also asked our sample of educational program specialists to respond.

Herbert Simon has written, "Every problem-solving effort must begin with creating a representation for the problem—a problem space in which the search for a solution can take place."[3] In many problem situations, there exists no agreed-upon problem representation. Much of politics is about the defining of problems.[4] Do divergent understandings of problems in community education simply reflect differences in interests, or do they reflect serious issues in the understanding of the problem itself? It is not the case that everyone must share a common understanding of a problem to make progress. Divergent problem understandings, however, almost invariably lead to minor modifications of the status quo. Ascendance by any one faction might allow it to impose its problem definition and initiate reform efforts that seem appropriate, but in the face of slow or ambiguous results, groups holding alternative views of the problem will gain credibility that they can convert into countermobilizations. Since education reforms in urban settings are almost certain to generate slow and indirect payoffs, if any, the subsystem is especially vulnerable to backlash and reversal. Only where communities share a common perspective on the problem facing them is major reform likely to be put into place and kept in place. As a consequence, a common problem space is part and parcel of our notion of civic capacity.

ILL-STRUCTURED PROBLEM SPACES

Ill-structured problems are problems that involve open constraints: constraints on the problem are "generated from one transformation of the problem to the next."[5] Each attempt to solve the problem adds considerations that must be incorporated into the next attempt at a solution. Constraints that are added in the process of working toward a solution must themselves be considered in future attempts— and, indeed, can become obstacles to achieving a satisfactory solution. Because the problem space itself is not well specified, there can be competing notions of just how to represent the "problem." Ill-structured problems are characterized by differences of opinion about the importance of the various attributes, or components, of the problem.

Any problem may be represented as occurring within an "attribute space"; that is, the problem has a number of attributes or components that characterize it. Think for a moment of educating a child. Do children learn best when they are encouraged to explore? When they are drilled on the basics? When their mistakes are highlighted immediately? When they receive concrete incentives for performance? When each child's uniqueness is highlighted? When self-esteem is built? Each of these attributes of the learning process has been the basis for one or more major proposals for curricula change. Understanding a problem may be viewed as the assigning of weights to the attributes that characterize a problem. If teachers understand the learning problem as one of exploration, they may fail to offer the immediate feedback that can improve performance. If they focus mostly on feedback, they will doubtless downplay exploration and discovery. As a consequence, weighting attributes also has the effect of setting priorities for the components. That is, in a multiattribute problem space, assigning weights to components indicates the importance of the multiple components of the problem space.

Generally, the more numerous and conflicting the attributes that characterize a problem, the more confusion there will exist in defining the problem and relating it to a solution. In addition, differences of opinion on the relevance of an attribute to the problem are more likely to occur when various people address the issue. Many political problems are characterized by multiple sets of participants, with each set of participants imposing somewhat different constraints on the problem, which itself is both ill-structured and ongoing. In such situations, there is a tendency for participants to identify with subgoals rather than the overall goal of finding a satisfactory solution.[6] Participants in a process may identify with particular problem definitions or solution paths as they struggle to cope with difficult problems.

The politics of urban education takes place in an ill-structured problem space. That means that the attributes or components of the problem are not clearly related to the goal of providing educational services. Most will doubtless agree that schools are to educate the young. After that, agreement tends to break down. Are educational problems about equality of access? Financing? Quality? Insulation from political influence and corruption? Accountability? Efficiency? Integration? Discipline? Leadership? Each of these problem conceptions implies different solutions. Moreover, it is to be expected that participants identify with subgoals rather than the overall goal. Teachers may be expected to focus on resource adequacy—because they believe that with proper resources they can do the job. Businesses may think about high taxes and the need for efficiency, because they see the detrimental effects of taxes on economic development. At one time, minorities pressed for integrated schools, because serious violations of rights were involved. Each of these conceptions of the educational problem has the potential of focusing community attention to the exclusion of other components of the problem.

Multiple understandings of what characterizes urban educational challenges may be affected by selective attention. Similarly, different conceptions of the needs of the city compete with education as a major problem. At a more general level, community problems are similarly ill-structured.

Our focus on how community elites understand problems facing their cities and the solutions to those problems implies that an interest-based analysis of policy making will not tell the whole story. Even if community and educational interests did not differ, there could nevertheless exist fundamental differences about how to solve educational problems in communities. City business executives might see the major educational issue as one of economy and efficiency, as they tended to do in Atlanta, or they could view it as a problem in human capital development. Even if they viewed the issue as one of human capital, they very well could opt for different solutions to the challenge. Similarly, community groups, city school boards, teachers, and other stakeholders have adopted different conceptions of the problem of schools. In each case, the interests of the group are important, but so is the understanding of the problem to be addressed. Ill-structured problem spaces often generate different problem representations among participants even in the hypothetical absence of differences among potential beneficiaries of particular solutions. So the key questions for this analysis center on the nature of the problem definitions harbored by community leaders and the extent to which they are shared among different groups of leaders.

COMPONENTS OF THE PROBLEM SPACE

Because education issues may be represented by a number of different problem spaces, none of which is clearly right or wrong, we have tried in our interviews to map the major aspects of the problem representations in our samples of community elites. All problem representations involve simplification. The confusing complexity of reality must be represented in a form that allows understanding the essentials of the problem and addressing solutions to the problem. An overly simple problem space, however, may not yield robust policy solutions, in the sense that they may not be sensitive to side consequences or alternate problem representations.

As a starting point, we may distinguish between four separate components of elite problem spaces in politics. These are *content, complexity, elaboration,* and *appropriateness.* The *content* of the problem space is which substantive components of the problem are emphasized. We measure this by our coding of open-ended questions to our elite samples concerning the major problems or challenges facing the community. *Complexity* is the number of attributes that a problem solver uses in the process of representing the problem. It is measured by the number of components that the respondents used in representing the problem space to our interviewers. Because of limitations in attention spans and cognitive capacities of humans, limits on complexity exist. The more facets that a problem solver uses in problem representation, the more difficult it will be to manipulate these elements in thinking through a problem. In effect, the manner in which the various components interact quickly becomes overwhelming; the human mind demands simplification. On the other hand, too simple a problem representation yields an unrepresentative caricature of the issue.

Elaboration is the extent of knowledge participants hold concerning the components of the problem space; that is, how elaborate is their use of the concepts that they mention? Do they simply parrot the prevailing "hot" reform, or do they have some degree of understanding of the implications of the idea? *Appro-*

priateness is the "fit" between the simplified problem representation and the community problem itself. A final characteristic of collective problem solving (as opposed to individual problem solving) is *divergence*—the extent to which various participants stress a different problem representation.

Below we examine three of these four individual components of problem definition—complexity, elaboration, and content. Among the community elites we interviewed we find generally complex but weakly elaborated problem representations for general community issues. Simpler but more elaborated spaces characterize problems of children and youth (at least for community advocates; problem representations are less elaborated for the influentials). We also study the extent to which different sets of elites in different cities harbor divergent conceptions of educational problems. We find little divergence in perspective for general community problems, but considerable differences in regard to problems of children and youth.

COMMUNITY PROBLEMS: COMPLEXITY AND ELABORATION

From our open-ended interviews, we coded up to five community problems that respondents discussed in response to a question about the major problems facing the city. Taking a simple count of these mentions of problems is a rough indicator of problem space complexity. More mentions would indicate more complexity in the problem space. This question was asked only of general influentials and community advocates. These community leaders held moderately complex problem spaces: The modal category for each group was three mentions. General influentials tended to list more problems than community advocates. Figure 5.1 compares the number of community problems mentioned by position. More than a quarter of general influentials cited four or more community problems, whereas only about 15 percent of the advocates did so.

Our measures of *elaboration* come from the judgment of our expert interviewers. We asked our interviewers to judge how *specific* respondents were when asked about community problems, and how *spontaneous* they were in their responses. Both indicate familiarity and ease of use, and thus probably are linked to the knowledge the respondent has regarding the problems mentioned. Most of the community leaders responded spontaneously—without further probing—to our question, and there was no detectable difference in the spontaneity of their mentions (73 percent for general influentials versus 71 percent for community advocates).

Respondents were graded as to whether they were specific and discussed the problem with elaboration, or whether they mentioned the problem only vaguely. Our expert interviewers judged elaboration for the first three mentions of community problems. That allowed us to compare the specificity of mentions with the number of problems mentioned for the two groups of community leaders.

Almost all of the community leaders discussed the first problem they noted with considerable specificity, and there were no differences between the groups

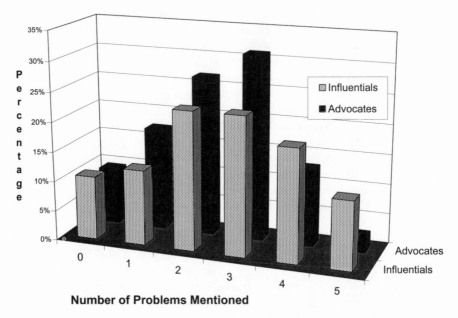

Number of Problems Mentioned

Figure 5.1. Number of problems mentioned by position

of leaders. About 90 percent of each group provided our interviewers detailed comments. For the second and subsequent problem, however, leaders were far less specific. For some reason, the second mention was judged as less specific, on average, than the third. On the third mention, a gap opens between our two groups of leaders, with a higher percentage of community advocates elaborating answers than general influentials.[7] Whereas community activists cite fewer community problems than general influentials, and there is no difference in elaboration for the first two mentions, community advocates are clearly more specific in their discussions of the third problem.

Comparing community influentials and advocates with respect to the complexity of their respective problem spaces suggests that the former tend to be attentive to more problems, but at a broader level of generalization. That is, they note more problems but know less about each problem they mention. In comparison to community advocates, the general influentials seem to hold more complex but less elaborated problem spaces. Community advocates tend to be problem specialists: They are concerned with fewer problems. Given that our sample of community advocates were active in the education area, it might be expected that these individuals concentrated on educational problems. As we show below, there is some support for this thesis, but community advocates do retain a more complex problem space than might be expected given their community positions, in comparison to the educational specialists that we interviewed.

CONTENT OF THE PROBLEM SPACE: COMMUNITY PROBLEMS

We now turn to the *content* of the problem spaces of community leaders. Figure 5.2 depicts the distribution of first mentions (of up to five coded) of community problems. If we assume that the first mention indicates something about the priority of the issue (this inference is supported by research into the accessibility bias by psychologists and political psychologists), then we may take Figure 5.2 as indicating the issues or problems with the highest priority among our respondents. Laboratory and survey research on the so-called "accessibility bias" indicates that people will mention the issue that they have thought about most or are most concerned with. Although first mentions may indicate a kind of "off-the-top-of-their-heads" response, they may also convey some notion of priorities, especially in the context of lengthy, in-person, in-depth interviews with community leaders.

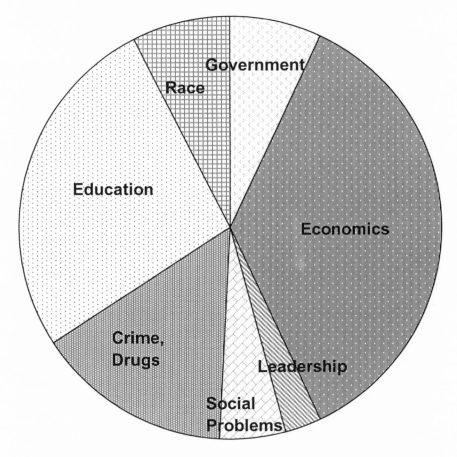

Figure 5.2. City problems, first mention (general influentials and community activists)

Economic development and education, with 36 percent and 27 percent of mentions respectively, dominate the community agenda in our eleven cities—at least in the minds of our samples of general influentials and community activists. And there were unsurprising differences in the first mentions of our two groups of respondents. For general influentials, economics was primary—36 percent mentioned some facet of economic issues as the first item in their discussions with our interviewers about community problems. Education was a clear second, at 26 percent. On the other hand, our community activists saw education as the most important problem in their communities—29 percent, versus 26 percent who cited the economy. On other matters the two groups generally agreed, except that community activists saw race as more central (9 percent versus 5 percent for the influentials).

We also examined differences among city types to see if citations of problems differed by geographic location. Although leaders in black-led cities tended to note economic difficulties at higher rates than the other cities (30 percent versus 24 percent for the Sunbelt cities and 28 percent for the machine-descendant cities), there were scant differences among the city types in their level of identification of education as a problem (18.5 percent for black-led cities, 16.5 percent for Sunbelt cities, and 19 percent for the machine-descendant cities). Leaders in machine-descendant cities cited race as an issue at higher rates than the other two types of cities (7.5 percent versus 6 percent for the Sunbelt cities and only 2.5 percent for the black-led cities).

Although there are some differences among the community leaders of the eleven large American cities we studied, more striking are the similarities. Economic development and education emerge as consensual priorities among community elites in these cities.

EDUCATIONAL PROBLEMS: COMPLEXITY

We now turn to an examination of the problem space representations of our samples of community leaders with respect to educational issues. We assessed our respondents' understanding of educational issues in a similar manner to the approach used for community problems more generally. Figure 5.3 indicates the number of problems mentioned in response to our query concerning the challenges to children and youth in the community. In this case we coded up to three mentions. Most of our community leaders could cite at least two problems, although more than a quarter noted but a single problem. On the other hand, about a third mentioned three problems (and some mentioned more, but we did not code these). Compare these figures to the responses to our more general question, where about half of our respondents mentioned three or more problems. This suggests that problem representation in the area of children and youth is simpler (less complex) than for general community problems.

It may not be surprising that the problem space for the general set of collective issues facing a community is more complex than the more specific problem space of issues facing youth. But it is surprising that general influentials hold more

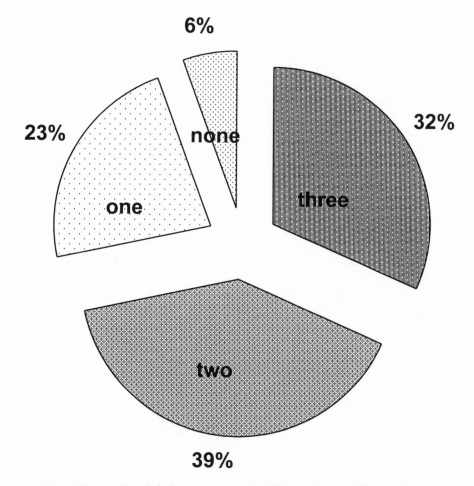

Figure 5.3. Number of challenges mentioned, children and youth (all respondents)

complex problem spaces with respect to youth and children than do community advocates or education specialists.

Figure 5.4 depicts these differences. In comparison to education specialists or community activists working in the educational area, general influentials note more problems in the educational arena. The finding, noted above, that general influentials are cognizant of more community problems than are community advocates holds for the specific area of education.[8] What is most striking, however, is the simplified problem space that educational specialists hold in comparison with the other two groups. Fully 10 percent of the educators fail to mention a single problem in the area of children and youth, and only about a fifth mention three problems. More than a third of advocates and influentials mention at least three problems.

Those working in the arena of education are far less cognizant of problems than those a little more removed from the issue. This is a signature finding from studies of policy subsystems: Those active in a policy arena are less critical of the prevailing system than outsiders. This lack of critical capacity has a strong cognitive and emotive component that goes far beyond simple self-interest: They identify with the organizations in which they are spending their working lives. This merger of identification and self-interest makes the educational policy subsystem a powerful bulwark against major change. It also indicates why nurturing civic capacity as a mechanism for overcoming the resistance to change inherent in educational policy subsystems is critical.

EDUCATIONAL PROBLEM SPACE: SIMPLE REPRESENTATIONS WITH LITTLE AGREEMENT

Figure 5.5 indicates the *content* of the educational problem space by depicting the topic of the first mention of all respondents. Unlike responses to general community problems, the education problem space is *diffracted*—consisting of many different problems and little agreement among the participants on priorities. No

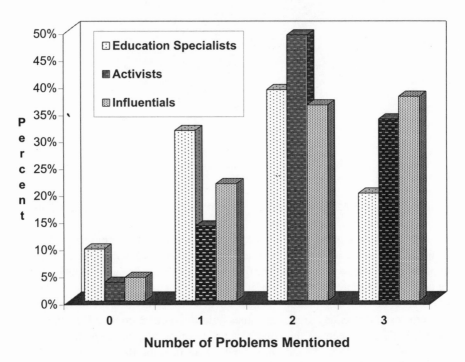

Figure 5.4. Number of challenges to youth mentioned by status of respondent

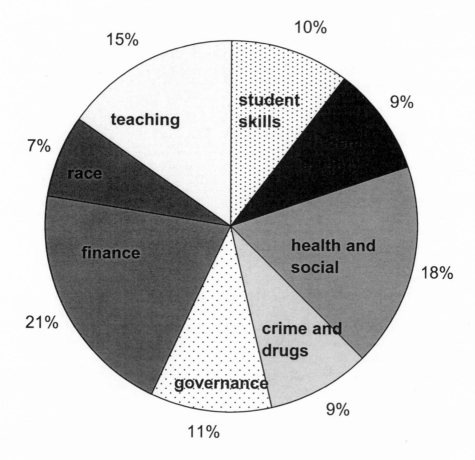

Figure 5.5. Challenges facing youth, first mention (all categories of respondent)

single problem or pair of problems dominate the problem space in the manner that economics and education dominate the more general community problem space (see Figure 5.2). Finance leads, with about 21 percent of respondents mentioning the issue first, but health and social problems are a close second at 18 percent. Fully seven different problems garner between 9 and 21 percent of first mentions among respondents. On the other hand, there are fewer mentions of problems overall. The implication is a simpler problem space, on average, but less agreement on its parameters among participants.

Examining the educational problem spaces of the three groups of leaders separately, we found only marginal differences. General influentials were more concerned with student skills, particularly problems in student skill preparation for the workplace (12 percent versus about 8 percent for the other two groups) and teaching (16.5 percent versus about 10 percent for educational specialists).

General influentials were also somewhat less likely to cite financing problems than the other two groups. Community advocates were substantially more likely to indicate that racial problems were a major issue for youth and children; educational specialists were notably unlikely to mention this issue at the onset (10 percent versus 4 percent).

DETERMINANTS OF COMPLEXITY

When we examined the potential determinants of complexity of the education-relevant problem space, we found that only status of the respondent (general influential, community advocate, or educational specialist) seemed to relate to problem-space complexity. In particular, we found that the nature of political arrangements and governing coalitions in a city was not related to complexity, nor was the extent to which respondents saw education as a specialized as opposed to a generalized domain. Governing arrangements were, however, related to the perception that education was a policy domain that was distinct and separate from other aspects of government.

Figure 5.6 indicates the strong influence that the type of governing structure has on the perception among participants that education is a separate and distinct domain of policy making. In the black-led and machine-descendant cities, most participants saw education as a general problem of community leadership. On the other hand, in Sunbelt cities, with their vigorous tradition of reform politics and "depoliticized" education systems, participants were equally divided in their perceptions concerning the distinctness of educational leadership.

It seems, however, that these structural characteristics do not affect the complexity of the problem spaces of participants. Recall that general influentials hold more complex understandings of the problem space, and that this holds for both community problems and for challenges facing youth and children. On the other hand, there exist no differences among the city types with respect to problem-space complexity. Problem space complexity is related to the status of the respondent within the city and the nature of the problem itself, but not to the particular governing arrangements in cities.

One of the prevailing ideas of educational governance, dating back to the Progressive Era, is that school boards ought to be insulated from partisan politics. The problem of partisan interference in educational governance for many years dominated the policy dialogue about these arrangements. Today, however, cities face different problems: Political influence in school policies was not on the radar screens of any of our respondents.

More common today is the view that separate school boards can facilitate educational subsystem politics and can make reform harder. The tendency of problems to span the type of political arrangement established to govern education suggests that all types of cities face similar educational problems, but have set up

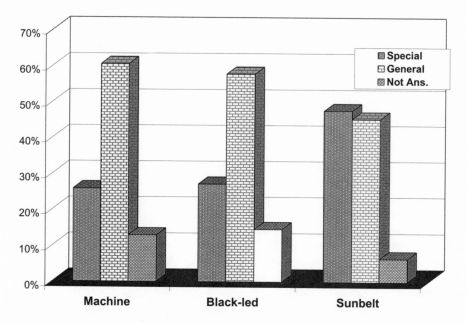

Figure 5.6. City type and education leadership specialization

structures that no longer reflect the nature of the problem. Three Midwest cities, Chicago, Cleveland, and Detroit, have experienced major political interventions into the separate school governing system, which was perceived as a large part of the problem.

The diffracted nature of the collective problem space held by our groups of community elites for education in comparison to generalized community problems creates difficulties in forging civic capacity. For education, in comparison to general community problems, fewer problems are mentioned but at the same time there is less agreement on problem priorities. The patterning of problem mentions among community elites implies a lack of consensus on the basic issues facing urban education. On the other hand, although there is little agreement on priorities concerning problems facing youth in our eleven cities, these concerns do not differ across positions. Educational specialists, community advocates, and general influentials all see a reasonably simple problem space, but there exists scant agreement on problem representation. Thus, there seems to be no direct connection between the interests of the participants and their characterizations of the problem. This implies considerable potential for forging civic capacity to address the issues. Moreover, it may be functional for communities to be able to isolate a panoply of problems, so long as they are able to prioritize solutions. As we show below, elites in cities characterized by higher levels of mobilization both suggest more problems and evidence more consensus on solutions.

ASPIRATION LEVELS

In unstructured and ongoing problems such as local education, *aspiration levels* of community elites are critical. Many potential problems crowd the community agenda, and elites must decide where to invest their time and energy. Setting priorities for investing in solving community problems requires a complex set of tradeoffs among competing demands. Participants are continually forced to "satisfice," or find adequate but not optimal solutions to the problems they detect. Problem identification and problem solving are mediated by aspiration levels—the extent to which people think there is a divergence between goals and performance.

The tendency of people to use aspiration levels facilitates the management of multiple goals in complex situations. In effect, aspiration levels allow rough comparisons between incommensurate attributes that characterize most difficult problems.[9] If a solution is adequately managing a problem, then it is likely that the aspiration levels of community elites will reflect this. If there is a deficit between aspirations and performance, then motive exists to direct effort at the problem, generally to the exclusion of other problems that might be addressed. As a consequence, community aspiration levels are critical components of problem understandings.

To assess aspiration levels in communities, we asked our sample of community elites if they felt that community effort was adequate in addressing the problems of education. In this case, there was a wide community dissatisfaction with current efforts—a large majority of respondents felt that the community was "falling short" in the area of education. Only about 25 percent of our respondents indicated any level of satisfaction at all in education—*fully 75 percent felt that community effort was falling short in education.* However, general influentials and community advocates did differ in their aspiration levels in the education policy sphere.

We also queried community leaders concerning what they thought the educational system was doing well. Again, the results were not encouraging. First, most did not respond to the question—only about 38 percent did so. Educators were particularly reluctant to comment (only about 11 percent did so), but 54 percent of the community activists and 46 percent of the general influentials commented. Of those who commented, however, some 20 percent explicitly responded that "nothing" was being done well.

Examining differences among leadership groups, we found that the general influentials were less likely to say that nothing was being done well in comparison with the community activists, and they noted more different areas of accomplishment. Particularly noteworthy was their citing of attempts to deal with social problems and to institute one form of school choice or another. Community activists, on the other hand, were more negative in general, and when they were positive, cited only attempts by educational professionals to encourage civic involvement.

Our examination of aspiration levels of community elites suggests widespread dissatisfaction with the current performance of community education. It afflicts general influentials and community advocates alike, but community advocates are

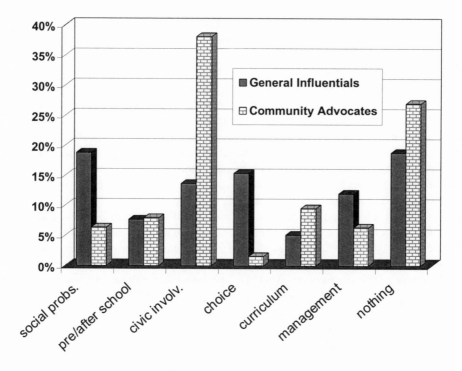

Figure 5.7. Leaders' judgments of accomplishments

even less sanguine about educational performance than are general influentials. The divergence between aspiration level and performance indicates a policy area ripe for change. This divergence helps explain the strong appeal of various major reform efforts in public education.

SOLUTIONS

Given the ill-structured and ongoing nature of the community education problem space, it is to be expected that recommended solutions differ among participants. We used several questions to probe the solutions that our community leaders saw as critical in solving the problems of education. We probed solutions by first asking what major changes community elites had seen "over the last several years." Our question on change was, as usual, coded from the extensive interview schedules. For the analysis here, we combined the issues that emerged from the discussions into those that implied that changes had been for the better (improvement in school quality, financing, social problems, crime and drugs, and school governance) and those that implied changes for the worse (declines in school quality, financing, social problems, crime, and school governance). We kept the separate categories of mentions of reform implementation and changes in the major actors relevant to educational policy.

Figure 5.8 graphs the results by position. The major change noted by all groups was the continual shifts in major players, presumably making educational reform efforts more difficult. Changes in relevant actors particularly disturbed community advocates. Although many of our respondents applauded the implementation of education reform, more leaders saw the general education situation as deteriorating than improving. Community advocates were considerably less sanguine about the implementation of educational reforms. The educators were quicker to cite the implementation of major reforms but were actually more likely to see most other changes as negative.

When we probed the content of the solution space held by our samples of community leaders, we found a general consensus on the direction of reform, but a consensus that itself could mask major difficulties. Figure 5.9 presents a distribution of the proposed solutions that our respondents mentioned first in their discussions with our interviewers. Two proposed solutions dominate: the redistribution of resources, generally from taxpayers in other regions of the state (33 percent), and the improvement of the educational bureaucracy (30 percent,

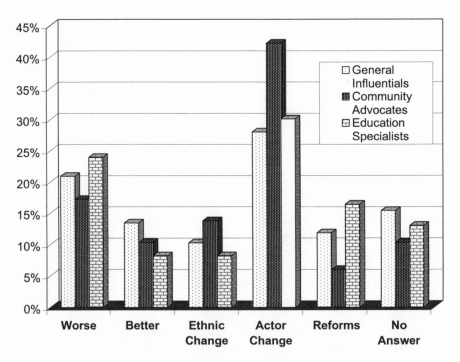

Figure 5.8. Perceived change by status of respondent

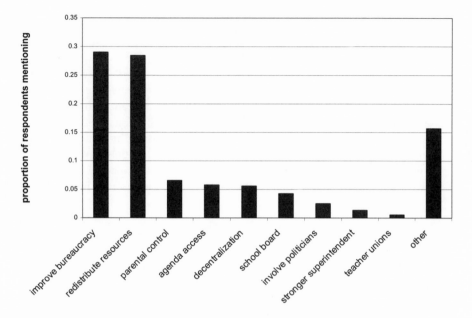

Figure 5.9. Solutions proposed by community elites

plus 4 percent suggesting a cut in bureaucracy). Also noted, but far less promi-
nently, were parental involvement and control (third in mentioned solutions at
6 percent), decentralization (5 percent), and a set of answers that implicated community leadership (including a better formulated agenda, a stronger superintendent, more involvement of political leaders, and a stronger school board). These
leadership concerns accounted together for 15 percent of the respondents' prof-
fered solutions. Other solutions—such as privatization or charter schools—were
endorsed by almost none of our respondents.[10] An examination of proposed solutions by the social location of leaders indicated scant differences, although general
influentials were somewhat more prone to endorse the redistribution of resources
as a solution than community advocates.

The consensual solutions that community leaders propose in the eleven cities we studied are incrementalist, centering on improving the existing service
delivery system and garnering more financial resources from outside the city. There
are few mentions of imaginative and internally generated approaches, with the
minor exceptions of accountability and decentralization, and almost no voices are
raised on behalf of more radical reforms.

It would seem that the solutions harbored by our sample of leaders are not
commensurate with the complexity of the problem space or the divergence between the performance of the existing system and the aspiration levels of the elites.
The solutions they propose imply the collaboration of actors outside the city, who
may well see the problem space as different, or involve bureaucratic adjustments

within the city. Although these remedies are doubtless badly needed, such solutions are likely to be seen as "more of the same"—incremental reforms plus demands for more resources. Moreover, we are struck by the lack of creative or nonincremental proposals proposed in our discussions with community leaders. The high dissatisfaction levels with the current system would suggest a more imaginative and innovative set of proposals. Ironically, among our groups of leaders, high levels of dissatisfaction coexist with a paucity of creative and viable solutions.

Finally, we studied the distribution of proposed solutions by leadership group. No striking differences emerged, although the general influentials were more likely to suggest that redistribution of resources was necessary, whereas community advocates and educational specialists tended to suggest bureaucratic improvement.

CIVIC MOBILIZATION AND PROBLEM DEFINITION

We now turn to the relationship between the civic mobilization in cities and the problem understandings of elites in those cities. In Chapter 4 we saw that civic mobilization is not a straightforward consequence of preexisting demographic attributes or reigning governmental institutions. Rather than a direct causal relationship, it is possible that objective elements of the local environment affect civic mobilization and capacity via mediation through subjective factors, such as the way problems are perceived and solutions evaluated. If that is the case, we should find substantial and important differences in the problems seen by elites in high-mobilization cities and the solutions they propose in comparison to lower-mobilization cities. And we do.

When asked about general community problems, the elite respondents in high-mobilization cities did not differ significantly in their responses from those in medium- or low-mobilization cities. But we encountered a very different pattern when our questions focused specifically on children and youth.

There are no substantial differences among the respondents grouped by civic mobilization of their cities and the number of general community problems they perceive. There are some differences among cities in the type of problems perceived, but they do not vary systematically with mobilization. There was a difference in the number of mentions of education as the most important problem (importance is measured as the first problem mentioned among the up to five we coded): low civic mobilization: 25 percent; medium civic mobilization: 30 percent; high mobilization: 23 percent. There is no difference among cities categorized with respect to civic mobilization and the sophistication of the problem spaces that they used (as judged by our interviewers).

On the other hand, important differences emerge when we look at elite perceptions of problems affecting children and youth. Elites in cities characterized by high civic mobilization are less likely to say that there are no educational problems; they are also more likely to cite three or more problems concerning youth and children (see Figure 5.10). There also are some interesting differences on problem perception (Figure 5.11). Elites in the high-mobilization cities are more likely to perceive problems existing in teaching and in governance than in the other two groups. They are less likely to cite financing and social problems (health and crime) as school problems.

The differences across the types of cities are even more pronounced when we look at elite perceptions of proposed solutions. Elites in high-mobilization cities are considerably more likely to propose solutions themselves. Nine out of ten of our respondents in high-mobilization cities used the occasion of the interview to outline possible solutions to problems affecting children and youth; this was a significantly higher rate than in either medium- (85 percent) or low-mobilization cities (80 percent).

The type of solution proposed also differs markedly across the city types. Elites in cities characterized by high civic mobilization were more likely to want to cut central bureaucracy and build a better bureaucratic system, and were far less likely to advocate redistributing resources and to encourage parental control.

Perhaps most remarkable are the differences in recourse to a redistributive orientation in framing the discussion of possible solutions. Considerable research in urban policy has established that local government is especially constrained when policies are framed in redistributive terms.[11] Because local boundaries are permeable and advantaged businesses and taxpayers have the option to relocate when policies work against their interests, public officials have a strong incentive to emphasize developmental or allocational policies over those that would take from the richer to give to the poorer. We find evidence here that cities may be

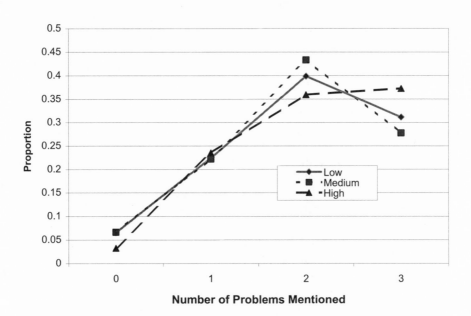

Figure 5.10. Number of problems for children and youth cited by level of civic mobilization

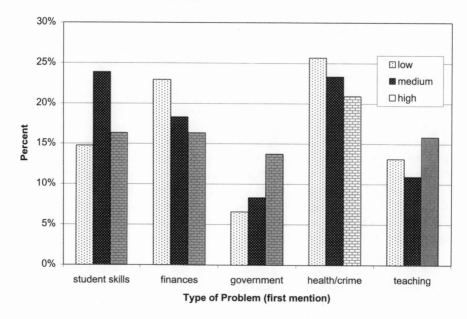

Figure 5.11. Civic mobilization and type of problem perceived

better able to build cross-sectoral coalitions around education reform when they manage to frame solutions in ways that do not immediately pit one group against others (Figure 5.12). The strategies for change in low- and medium-mobilized cities are clearly other-directed: They are oriented toward attaining more resources for the ongoing educational approach. In sharp contrast, elites in high-mobilization cities clearly focus more on internal problem solving: improving and streamlining the educational bureaucracy.

The definition of civic capacity we have been using here stresses a general consensus among community elites on the nature of the problem. Some evidence of this can be gleaned by calculating the variability in the solutions suggested by community elites. We calculated the standard deviation in the proportion of our respondents in each of the thirteen categories of solutions as an inverse indicator of consensus on solutions. For low-mobilization cities, the standard deviation across solution categories was 0.67; for medium-mobilization cities, 0.59; for high-mobilization cities, 0.51. Elites in high-mobilization communities hone in on a more limited number of solutions than those in cities characterized by lower mobilization.

Calculating similar standard deviations across problem categories yields an inverse ranking among the groups of cities. The high-mobilization cities had higher variability across categories (SD = 0.124) than either cities with medium levels (SD = 0.112) or low-mobilized cities (SD = 0.106).

Elites in higher-mobilization cities spontaneously cite more problems than those in lower-capacity cities and suggest a richer variety of problems, yet hone in on fewer

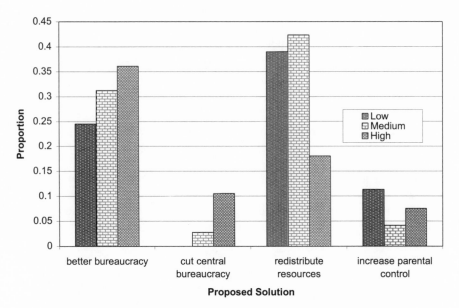

Figure 5.12. Civic mobilization and proposed solutions

potential solutions. High mobilization is associated both with the capacity to detect more problems in the environment and prioritize solutions that might be employed.

Elites in cities with high civic mobilization are able to articulate more problems facing youth in their cities. They tend to focus on school performance as the premiere problem in this policy domain. They are far more aggressive in proposing solutions, and their solutions are focused on solving the immediate problem of delivering educational services. They aren't interested in redistributing resources, and they are not particularly interested in more parental involvement. They *are* interested in solving educational delivery problems using a professional, service-delivery model. They seem to be saying: Schools are for *education*. Schools are a local *responsibility*. Make them better by cutting central control and improving the direct system of delivery.

CONCLUSIONS

Educational policy making is characterized by a fundamental ambiguity about the representation of the problem that policy is supposed to solve. In this chapter, we have used our comprehensive coding of open-ended questions to map the problem spaces and recommended solutions harbored by our samples of three groups of community leaders.

Even if the interests of participants could be fixed, there would nevertheless be considerable differences of opinion about how to represent the problem. We find that our elite samples hold complex but not well-elaborated representations of community problems, and that they hold simple but better elaborated representations of the problems facing children and youth. In particular, we find the following:

1. Education and economic development are consensual priorities for community elites.
2. There is widespread and consensual dissatisfaction with the educational performance and efforts at improvement among general influentials and educational activists. Educational professionals display considerably less dissatisfaction.
3. Many educational problems are cited by elites with little agreement on their priorities.
4. Problem perception is not related to the type of city governing coalition (black-led, machine-descendant, or Sunbelt), nor to political arrangement (whether education is a separate governmental function).
5. Problem perception is related to city civic mobilization, with elites in highly mobilized cities more sensitive to educational problems. They are also more likely to focus on teaching and governance issues and less likely to cite financing and crime.
6. Solutions in general tend to be incrementalist (improving the bureaucratic delivery system) or externally directed (redistribute state-level resources to urban school districts).
7. Elites in highly mobilized cities are more likely to propose solutions and the solutions they propose are different from those in low or medium cities. They are far less likely to advocate redistribution as a solution and far more likely to focus on cutting and improving the school bureaucracy.

Two findings from this analysis bear emphasizing. First, educational professionals are less critical of the educational establishment than are community advocates or general influentials. Educational specialists are part and parcel of an ongoing policy subsystem; they are also more cognizant of the difficulties in reforming education. They are more likely to see the incremental reforms as effective, less likely to cite problems in education, but also more likely to see the circumstances in which they do their jobs as deteriorating.

Second, a yawning gap opens in issue definition between elites in highly mobilized cities and those in cities with lower rates of mobilization. Elites in highly mobilized cities are much more in tune with the prevailing winds of educational reform. Although they are more likely to see problems, they are nevertheless more attuned to solving educational problems internally, with the existing resources available.

There is, then, a relationship between civic mobilization and the understanding of educational problems in the cities we studied. This connectivity between the problem understandings among groups in the city and the mobilization of those groups is civic capacity.

6

Civic Mobilization and Policy Effort

At the core of the concept of civic capacity is a pragmatic orientation toward power and government. Rather than looking at power as the leverage that one group exerts over another group, we look at power in terms of the capacity to produce results. Rather than looking at government as a crystallization of resources to be captured by one group or another, we look at government as an institution through which diverse interests can coordinate their efforts to pursue collective goals. But what does that mean in the complex arena of urban education? Does the mobilization of a cross-sectoral coalition oriented around discrete and feasible educational objectives actually make a difference in the nature of the educational initiatives that school systems provide?

In this chapter we turn from the issue of how civic mobilization around education issues arises to the questions of whether and how civic mobilization can lead to better education for inner-city youth. To address these questions, we need first to have some way to distinguish better school systems from those that are not as good, and that turns out to be no simple task. In spite of the seeming consensus that we are in the midst of an education crisis, one of the ironies in the public debate about education reform is that there is little agreement about what an effective education system looks like.

In place of a consensual measure of an effective education system, urban school reformers tend to offer various surrogates, none of which are totally satisfactory. The approach that we take involves a focus on collective effort as distinct from specific outcomes and broad and systemic effort as distinct from episodic and ephemeral initiatives. To complement indicators of priority based on budgetary commitment and subjective indicators of success, we offer a rough measure of systemic reform effort based on the qualitative analysis of our case studies. We find that this indicator of systemic reform effort is closely related to our measure of civic mobilization. This underscores our central contention that the key to bringing about broad change in urban education lies in politics, not the pursuit of particular pedagogies or programs. More than thirty years ago, sociologist Morris Janowitz called for abandoning the "specialization model" in favor of a broader, that is, holistic, approach.[1] As Janowitz argues, school systems do not operate in a vacuum. Their ability to change and the direction they move in are shaped by their environment. Building on Janowitz, we find that schools are open systems, shaped by their environments.

SYSTEMIC REFORM EFFORT AS DEPENDENT VARIABLE

Americans have diverse and often conflicting visions of what schools ought to do. For some, the focus should be primarily on stimulating creativity and higher-order reasoning; for others, the true measure lies in instilling good work habits and the provision of basic skills. For some, a good school system should teach children the facts and values that define Americanism; for others, the test is whether schools prepare children to deal with a global economy and to understand other languages and cultures. For some, the mark of a good school system would be its ability to find and nurture each child's strongest interests and talents; for others, a good system is one that finds and addresses the weaknesses all children carry with them into the schooling years. For some the test is identifying and rewarding performance; for others, it is narrowing the inequalities that society and the economy allow to grow.

A national resolution of these conflicting visions seems unlikely. American education has a long tradition of local autonomy, rooted partly in federalism and partly in the experience of settlement along a moving frontier. American local governments generally, and especially local school districts, are also products of a system of growth and incorporation in which income stratification and racial separation have played major parts.[2] In a highly fragmented system, issue conflicts can go unresolved and particular localities may lay claim to value choices distinct even from neighboring jurisdictions in the same state. Hence, historically each community has been relatively free to adopt its preferred curricula and pedagogic preferences, and relatively free to adopt its own ways of measuring its failures or success.

But this traditional sidestepping of the need to identify common national goals becomes problematic when poor educational performance propels school reform onto the national agenda. Both reform advocates and policy analysts share the difficulty. For reform advocates, the challenge is to find a common and objective standard that allows them to declare some systems deficient, even if the citizens and officials of those jurisdictions appear indifferent or satisfied. For analysts like ourselves, the challenge is to find some common indicators of success so that we may empirically test various theories about what factors facilitate or inhibit effective educational reform.

One characteristic of the contemporary reform movement has been its insistence that measurements of educational outcomes, especially standardized tests of educational achievement, should be preferred to measures of effort, such as the amount of public revenue that communities are willing to target toward educational spending. This focus on outcomes rather than inputs makes sense to us in theory, although it can create some nettlesome problems in practice. Some of the impetus to the movement has evolved out of the important debate over "does money matter?" As we discussed in Chapter 3, higher levels of spending do not automatically translate into better education; if dollars ensured learning, the eleven cities in our study would be among the leaders in education in their states.

But switching to student outcomes—particularly as measured by standardized test scores—raises its own nest of difficulties. One problem with this as a surrogate for system performance is a simple one of data availability. Since school systems are free to pick and choose among available standardized measures, there is no common metric for comparing performance across systems. Some of the school systems we studied use the Comprehensive Test of Basic Skills to evaluate their students; some use the Iowa Test of Basic Skills; some use the California Achievement Tests; some use the Stanford 9; and some rely on state-specific tests that are linked to the content of their curriculums. At the time we conducted our field research, only four of the eleven used a common test, and since then at least two of those four have switched to other assessment mechanisms. Some high school students in every district take tests like the SATs, but the sample of those who take that examination is far from representative, and the proportion of students who take it can vary substantially from place to place. Tests like the National Assessment of Educational Progress are designed to eliminate this selection bias, but they are taken by a sample of students in the participating states, and those samples are not designed to provide reliable estimates of performance at the district level.

Two other problems with relying on test scores as an indicator of system performance are more fundamental. First, standardized tests tend to be one-dimensional indicators, whereas educational goals are multidimensional. The choice of a particular style of examination and its content implicitly elevates one or two goals over others, with the result that some things that some citizens care about deeply may be pushed into the background. The second problem is that the causal links are loose and unmapped between what schools do and what children know. This can lead us to jump to the conclusion that a school district that scores well on standardized tests is a "good" one, even though we know very well that various family background factors have more to do with test performance than what goes on in the classroom. Defining effective school districts by student outcomes, in other words, might lead us to characterize a system as a success simply because it is fortunate enough to draw its student body from among those already educationally advantaged.

Partly because of problems such as these, we turn in this chapter to several indicators of public sector *educational effort* as our dependent variable. This is largely a practical decision, dictated by the lack of consistent and valid outcome measures, but it also reflects our belief that collective and systemic effort is a meaningful focus in its own right. Successful educational reform ultimately depends on a combination of motivation, sound ideas, and the capacity to put those ideas into place. Based on our research, we are convinced that the eleven cities we studied lack neither motivation to change nor openness to proven ideas. In no city that we studied was poor educational performance the result of indifference toward education as a collective responsibility. A broad sector of the community in every district placed a high priority on education, and the history of education in each city revealed numerous instances in which citizens and public officials mobilized in the name of systemic school reform. Nor did we find evidence of simple resistance to new ideas about teaching, curriculum, or school organization.

Our researchers entered the field with a checklist of reform ideas that were commonly mentioned in the national school reform literature. To our surprise, we quickly discovered that, despite their reputations for bureaucratic sluggishness, in each of the eleven cities a full range of reform notions was being considered and most cities had working examples of most reform ideas in place in at least some schools for at least some period of time.

Since the seeming lack of progress in reforming urban education is rooted neither in lack of motivation nor blanket resistance to new ideas, we are drawn to the conclusion that the key stumbling block is translating desire and ideas into cohesive, sustained, collective effort. In focusing on effort, however, we are drawing a sharp qualitative distinction between initiatives that are comprehensive and oriented toward systemic change and those that are disjointed and without clear direction. The evidence is clear that much of the activity that occurs in American school systems amounts to little more than policy "churn"—a frenetic but undirected process of spinning wheels.[3] To distinguish mere activity from systemic reform effort we offer three broad measures. First, we look at respondents' assessments of how well their system is doing. Second, we look at some indicators of budgetary commitment chosen to distinguish undifferentiated overall spending from specific local commitment systemic reform effort. Third, we develop and make use of an original index of scope of reform effort.

CIVIC MOBILIZATION AND PERCEPTIONS OF SYSTEM PERFORMANCE

We asked respondents in each of our cities the following question: "Recognizing that no city can do everything that it would like to do in education, how would you generally characterize the effort in City X?" We asked them to select among the following four choices:

1. Doing everything that can be done.
2. Doing fairly well.
3. Falling short of what we could be doing.
4. Not doing well at all.[4]

The results are presented in Figure 6.1. By and large, respondents were highly critical. Overall, fewer than one in five thought their local system was doing a good job and only a little more than one out of four thought they were even doing a fair job. Although the overall assessment is negative for all cities, there are meaningful differences in degree.

Figure 6.2 arrays the eleven cities according to their level of civic mobilization and the percentage of respondents who characterized the local educational effort as not doing well at all. There is a slight tendency for cities with low civic mobilization to have a higher percentage of respondents who characterize the local effort as failing, but this is primarily attributable to the case of St. Louis. Generally speaking, our measure of civic mobilization appears to be a rather poor predictor of how local elites view school system effort.

In light of our discussion in Chapter 5, however, the absence of a stronger relationship should not be surprising. We saw that problem definition varies by community and by level of civic mobilization. Elites in high-mobilization cities seem to view education through more discerning lenses. That Boston respondents are more likely to express extreme dissatisfaction than those in Baltimore, and be

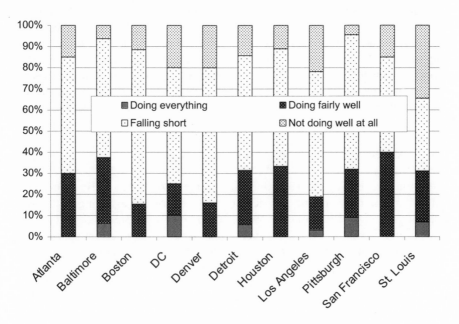

Figure 6.1. Respondent assessment of system effort

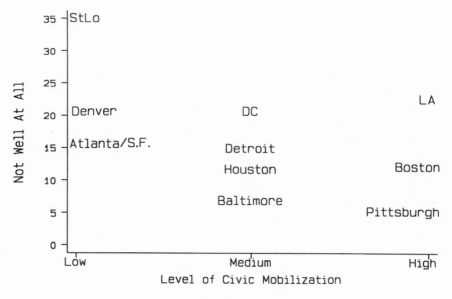

Figure 6.2. Level of civic mobilization

only a bit less likely to do so than those in San Francisco or Atlanta, may reflect their higher expectations rather than actual levels of performance. A phenomenon similar to this has been found in other settings. For example, surveys have found that lower-income respondents often evince levels of satisfaction with their housing and neighborhood conditions that are quite comparable to those expressed by upper-income households, even though the objective conditions in which they live appear to be much worse.[5] To get a better handle on whether effort relates to civic mobilization, then, we need more objective indicators of local educational effort.

CIVIC MOBILIZATION AND LOCAL FISCAL EFFORT

Educational spending can be an indicator of the priority that a district places on education and its willingness to devote resources toward investing in the long-term human capital represented by the community's children and youth. There are several problems with using spending as a surrogate of effectiveness, however. One technical problem involves accounting for different costs of living in different parts of the country, especially as that is related to the cost of hiring teachers. Another technical problem is that local school spending levels can be dramatically affected by state financing policies and local property wealth, making simple comparisons across districts problematic. Still another problem results from the fact that districts may vary in their budgetary practices, following different procedures, for example, in defining revenue sources or in allocating expenditures to specific line items.

Some of these technical problems can be partially adjusted for and others cannot. In this section we use multiple indicators as a way to reduce our reliance on any single flawed indicator. Table 6.1 presents, for each level of civic mobilization, the average total per-pupil expenditures, measure of local revenue effort adjusted for local income levels, the ratio of per-pupil city expenditures to expenditures in their surrounding suburban districts, and the percentage of expenditures for instructional purposes. High-mobilization cities spend more per pupil, and this is neither simply a factor of their receiving greater state or federal aid nor of their being located in high-cost areas. The local revenue effort indicator is calculated by dividing the local per-pupil revenue raised for elementary and secondary education by the city's per-capita income. Thus, we can see that high-mobilization cities expend about 25 percent more revenue effort than low- and medium-mobilization cities. High-capacity districts also appear to spend more for instructional purposes. Only the relationship with spending in proportion to surrounding jurisdictions does not appear to relate to civic mobilization in any coherent way.

Although this provides support for our hypothesis that civic mobilization provides a launching pad for more substantial educational efforts, there remains a challenge to the use of financial measures that is more telling than the technical problems discussed above. As we explained in Chapter 3, there is a large body of literature that challenges the notion that higher levels of spending make a difference in student learning. Using spending or revenue raising as an indicator of system effort, according to this perspective, risks mistaking waste and patronage for effort and efficiency. We accept the warning that money *alone* is not the answer. Money can be frittered away in any number of ways. Nonetheless, it is clear to us that local citizens and public officials strongly believe that money is *very* important. It seems most reasonable, therefore, to regard the commitment to raise and spend public funds as a necessary but not sufficient precursor to effective education. And high-mobilization cities spend more of their own resources to educate their youth. In order to add a sense of what systems actually *do* with the money, we devised a specific index of systemic educational reform.

Table 6.1. Civic Mobilization and Fiscal Effort

Civic mobilization	Total expenditures per pupil (1992–1993)	Local revenue effort (1992–1993)	Expenditures per pupil as percent of suburban expeditures (1989–1990)	Percent of expenditures going for instructional purposes (1992–1993)
High	$7,061	26.1	126.9	59.3
Medium	$5,746	20.6	90.1	55.7
Low	$5,749	21.2	130.0	54.8

CIVIC MOBILIZATION AND SYSTEMIC REFORM EFFORT

In addition to perceptions of system effort and to objective indicators of financial commitment, it is important to look at what systems are doing. In doing so it is important to distinguish directed, sustained efforts from simple counts of new undertakings.

Most school systems do lots of things, but few are selective and focused, and few institutionalize meaningful reforms.[6] Though today's educational scene teems with new ideas, pilot projects, demonstration programs, and experimental schools, initiatives rarely scale up into broad and sustained systemic change. Ultimately, then, it is important to distinguish between ornamental policy and deeper implementation.

Shortly after they completed their fieldwork, each research team filled out a questionnaire about reform efforts in their district. Each district was scored on the degree to which it had undertaken ten distinct strategies that were, at that time, core elements being promoted by national proponents of systemic education reform. Four of the items fall under what has been called an "infrastructure of support."[7] These types of reforms seek to bridge the gap between the K–12 school system and other group institutions that also play a role in nurturing and developing youth. The reform activities we considered involve extraschool efforts to enhance the readiness of students to learn and heighten their motivation to achieve academically through preschool, parent involvement, and school-to-work programs plus the provision of school-linked services.[8] Four of the items relate to efforts to alter internal school operations through site-based management, parent participation in school improvement teams and kindred bodies, the extent of the school system's reliance on research and evaluation for informing educational decisions, and the system's use of assessment measures to encourage active learning. Two of the items relate to efforts to increase reliance on market forces as a way to stimulate school reform. Hence, the index spans governance as well as other internal moves.

Coding of the individual cities was based on assessments by the field researchers after they had engaged in the full range of interviews and documentary analysis. To increase reliability, we did not ask our researchers to make fine distinctions or draw risky inferences. The primary distinctions had to do with whether particular reforms were on the local agenda, whether they had been implemented at all, and, if so, whether they were limited to just a few schools or were found generally throughout the system.[9] Some of the items were coded on a scale from 1 to 4 and some on a scale from 1 to 3. To compare across these we have included an adjusted mean that converts all items to a 4-point scale.[10] For the most part, though, we are interested in overall systemic reform effort. Our index for that is simply the sum of the scores for the ten items.

In using this approach we have minimized the possibility that our estimates of civic mobilization and the assessment of structural reform are confounded.

Table 6.2. Systemic Educational Improvement Efforts

Type of reform initiative	Internal moves	Infrastructure of support	Market reforms	Potential range	Actual mean	Adjusted mean	Rank (adjusted)
School-linked social services		x		1–3	2.14	2.81	1
Postschool transition (school-to-work; school-to-college)		x		1–4	2.77	2.77	2
Parent involvement in school governance	x			1–4	2.59	2.59	3
Administrative decentralization and school based	x			1–4	2.55	2.55	4
School choice			x	1–4	2.50	2.50	5
Preschool and early childhood development		x		1–4	2.36	2.36	8
Use of systematic evaluation research	x			1–3	1.82	2.33	6
Innovative testing and assessment practices	x			1–3	1.82	2.27	7
Parent involvement in the education of their own children		x		1–4	1.91	1.91	9
Privatization through contracting out			x	1–3	1.24	1.39	10

Note: Adjusted mean standardizes the 3- and 4-point scales

Reform assessments are based on the direct knowledge of our field researchers. Civic mobilization was judged from a reading of the case materials by the authors of this volume, focusing only on the networks among groups in the cities, prior to the development and analysis of the policy measures.

Considering, for a moment, the individual items, there are a few observations worth mentioning. First, the eleven districts were more aggressive in undertaking internal reforms that involved reorganization (parental involvement in governance, school-site management) than internal reforms that involve the systematic use of research or innovative student testing procedures, such as individualized portfolios. Second, when it comes to developing an infrastructure of support, there was less activity at the "front end" involving preschool and parents than at the "back end" involving school-to-work and transition to college. Third, although there was much public attention to the idea of contracting out the management of public schools to private firms, at the time we conducted our field research such efforts at privatization were very much the exception.

Figure 6.3 shows the relationship between civic mobilization and each district's aggregate systemic reform effort. The results indicate that greater civic mobilization is directly associated with various efforts to improve education. Pittsburgh, Boston, and Los Angeles, with the highest ranking on civic mobilization, score much higher than the other eight cities on the cumulative indicator of effort to promote educational improvement. Medium-mobilization cities average only a slightly higher level of systemic reform effort than low-mobilization cities.

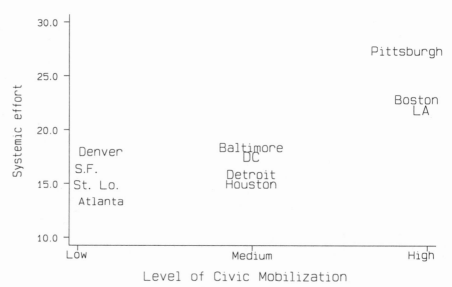

Figure 6.3. Systemic effort by mobilization level

If we examine the cases of weak mobilization a little more closely, however, we see that in Denver, San Francisco, and St. Louis important external forces were at work that probably boosted reform activities beyond what would have occurred based on indigenous levels of mobilization. The only area in which St. Louis received the maximum possible school reform was the extent of school choice; its extensive network of magnet schools and a cross-district public choice arrangement that enables some city residents to attend school in the suburbs and some suburban youth to transfer to city schools owe less to local reform coalitions than to judicial intervention following a desegregation lawsuit. Similarly, in San Francisco the significant factor was a consent decree under a desegregation order by the federal district court.[11] Working with the school superintendent, the court's panel of experts has moved beyond numerical racial balance to the issue of school performance for minorities. A targeted set of schools has thus been reconstituted, and the authority of the federal court perhaps provided a substitute for civic mobilization in providing a context in which innovation can occur. The court decree, for example, overrode the teachers' union contract in the targeted schools. In Denver, a teachers' strike enabled the governor to intervene and impose a contract settlement, which included an ambitious set of school reforms. So, again, a powerful external force was at work, providing an alternative to local civic mobilization.

The correlation between civic mobilization and overall systemic reform effort is high ($r = .80$; $p < .003$). This reinforces our assertion that broad and sustained reform is more possible when various stakeholders inside and outside the education bureaucracy develop habits and routines of cooperation.

But differences among the eleven cities are only part of the story. By stepping back a bit and looking at the broader picture, we can identify two important ways in which all eleven cities respond in common to the strong national winds of educational reform. The first is the fact that not even the districts with the least reform orientation show complete resistance to the kinds of initiatives promoted by advocates of systemic reform. All eleven of our cities engaged in a panoply of small-scale, partial, disjointed attempts to introduce change.

Critics of public education in urban America have painted a very bleak portrait, some even arguing that urban public school systems, as presently constituted, are fundamentally incapable of undertaking meaningful reforms.[12] Each of the eleven districts we studied has been charged with being rigid and inflexible by local media and by many of our respondents. Yet even in the cities that scored lowest on our systemic reform scale we found that respondents were aware of reform notions and that many of the ideas promoted by advocates of systemic reform were being actively debated or tentatively put into place. It is not clear to us if urban education bureaucracies ever were as insular and uniformly resistant to change as their critics contend, but, in any case, the image of total impenetrability certainly does not apply today. In its place the current pattern is one of piecemeal efforts. These exist in great abundance in most of the eleven cities, indicating a high level of policy ferment and a widespread search for a new systemic arrangement.

The cities are similar in that they all have at least some reform efforts under way, but they are also similar in the ultimate inadequacy of their efforts to date. Civic mobilization is unimpressive in all the cities save perhaps Pittsburgh and is well short of complete mobilization even there. Particularly noteworthy is the feeble part played by local school boards and the limited contributions local educators have made. A few superintendents have had an impact, but without the vigorous support of the local education establishment, action and implementation at the systemwide level are enormously handicapped.

WHY IS CHANGE SO DIFFICULT?

Why is it so difficult for urban school systems to undertake comprehensive efforts at systemic education reform? The answer comes in several parts. One part has to do with why it is hard to initiate and sustain a broad coalition. Divisions of race and ethnicity run deep, and the centrifugal force of functional specialization is strong. Trust, especially across the urban racial divide, is difficult to establish, and, once tentatively initiated, requires continued nurturing.[13] Existing ways of doing things have a life of their own and require sustained and coordinated effort to change.

One place to begin is with how the education task in cities is organized politically. Education reformers too often focus on the ideal to be realized and give little heed to the social and political context in which that ideal is to be advanced. Education is not a set of technical activities that take place in a detached organizational structure. Altering that organization or rearranging and modifying its activities do not take place in a vacuum. If change is to be genuine, it must involve revamping an underlying set of relationships. So we have to ask, How are schools connected to the communities they serve? What relationships drive the politics of urban education?

Functional autonomy. One of the most widely recognized features of urban school systems is their functional autonomy. Most school districts are independent taxing authorities and therefore not subject to any formal control from the city or other general local government. Eight of our eleven cities enjoy this formal independence and that is in line with the proportion for all members in the Council of Great City Schools. Beyond this formal independence, there is a long history of educators struggling to gain and maintain acceptance of their standing as professionals entitled to deference as experts in their subject matter. The last few decades have seen that standing erode. Nevertheless, it is a central feature of public education in the twentieth century, and much practice is built around the idea of "keeping politics out of the schools." Even over the past few decades, the major battles in urban education have been mainly over attendance boundaries and related issues of desegregation.

The question of community control generated a spurt of activity in New York City and a few other places, but for the most part internal issues of school structure and classroom practice have not been political targets in big-city systems.

Professional autonomy was less an achievement of classroom teachers than of education administrators. The twentieth century saw the development of the superintendent's office and the growth of substantial central office bureaucracies. Schools became centrally administered operations with career ladders that moved talent, energy, and resources from the local school site to the central office. Recent research shows, for example, that in the Baltimore and St. Louis school systems scarcely more than half of their resources are deployed in the classroom as opposed to various administrative and service operations.[14] The presence of a large central staff has enormous consequences for the running of schools and their potential to resist efforts to bring about fundamental change. At the same time, because administrative reputations can be enhanced by a record of innovation, narrow gauge initiatives, which do not threaten the position of others, are a likely product of a large central staff. A large staff with highly differentiated roles, then, appears to be just the setting that gives rise to the "policy churn" described earlier or what Chicago reformers know as "Christmas tree" schools.[15] This pattern has the added feature of meeting external demands for change by piecemeal, and therefore internally unthreatening, initiatives.

Thus, functional autonomy becomes a muffler of reform impulses when the professional education community develops its own problem definition—one that is either overly sanguine about the need for fundamental change or one that is also perhaps too inclined to attribute the problem to broad societal forces outside their ability to control. Research by the Public Agenda Foundation indicates why internally generated reform is relatively rare (see Table 6.3). Superintendents seem to see schools as much less problem-ridden than business leaders do, in fact even less so than teachers. Moreover, superintendents are much less inclined to see bureau-

Table 6.3. Contrasting Views: Business versus Educators

	Business leaders	Teachers	Superintendents
Schools are seriously on wrong track	79%	55%	32%
Outsiders who criticize schools underestimate the good things happening	13%	68%	75%
Schools doing poor job on:			
English skills	56%	14%	10%
Math and science	66%	15%	9%
Flexible learning	43%	16%	14%
Very serious problems facing schools:			
Overburdened with societal problems	49%	74%	71%
Bureaucracy and waste in administration	66%	60%	21%

Source: Public Agenda Foundation

Table 6.4. St. Louis Public Schools: Characteristics of Top-Ten School Administrators

Position	Race and Gender	Years in Education	Years in Current System
Superintendent	White M	36	36
Chief of Staff	Black M	34	33
Associate Superintendent of Schools	Black M	33	33
Associate Superintendent Curriculum and Programs	Black M	42	42
Associate Superintendent Personnel	Black F	24	11
Executive Assistant to the Superintendent	Black M	42	42
Executive Director Curriculum Services	Black M	40	40
Executive Director State and Federal Programs	Black M	25	25
Executive Director Community Relations	Black M	29	29
Treasurer	White M	24	11

cracy as a problem than either business leaders or teachers. Societal problems are widely recognized but are given greater weight by educators than business leaders. Our research uncovered a somewhat similar pattern to that found by Public Agenda. When asked the same question about local educational effort that we discussed earlier in this chapter, 41.5 percent of our respondents who worked in the education community said their district was "doing everything that can be done," or "doing fairly well"; this compared to 24.4 percent of all other respondents.

In the last chapter, we presented evidence that differences in the formal institutions that reinforce functional autonomy are not strongly associated with variation in civic mobilization. The insularity of the education community, however, rests on more than just the formal structures that buffer it from direct political control. Let us consider the St. Louis school district, one recognized to be performing poorly. The St. Louis schools operated in the midst of a great deal of legal and political turmoil around the issue of who sits in the classroom with whom. Yet the central administration of the school system was a remarkably stable group. The median years

Table 6.5 Detroit, Michigan: Ten Largest Employers by Number of Employees

Firm	Nature of Business	Number of Employees
Detroit Public Schools	Public School System	18,822
City of Detroit	City/Municipal Govt.	16,200
Chrysler Corp.	Automotive Manufacturer	13,659
The Detroit Medical Ctr.	Health Care	12,858
General Motors Corp.	Automotive Manufacturer	11,542
U.S. Government	Federal Govt.	10,611
State of Michigan	State Govt.	8,065
Henry Ford Health System	Health Care	7,425
Wayne State University	Higher Education	4,426
St. John Health System	Health Care	3,443

served in the St. Louis system was 33, and the mean was 30.2. One might argue that the St. Louis figures are atypical, and in some sense they are. At the time of the field research, the superintendent was an up-through-the-ranks appointee who had been in the St. Louis system for 36 years. Subsequently, he retired and was replaced by an external appointee, but few of the other top positions changed. This is a general pattern, rotation at the peak but great stability just below the peak. For example, Baltimore, which has had considerable turnover in the superintendent's post, nevertheless looks not very different from St. Louis. In Baltimore, the median number of years for top administrators was 25 and the mean 21.8.

Though turnover is no guarantee of able and change-minded officeholders, stagnant administration and a staff strongly inclined toward mutual protection of common problems were identified in management studies of both the Baltimore and St. Louis systems.[16] These are features that contribute to the widely held view that the problems of schools are attributable to bureaucracy and they are features that work against internally generated reform. It is reasonable, then, to expect that only a substantial external intervention is likely to alter urban schools as they have operated. But what are the barriers to outside intervention?

Employment regimes. As some observers see it, education politics revolves around the clash of ideas. School politics, they argue, is about unresolvable value differences. Indeed, at the national and state levels, ideological battles are much in evidence. Yet at the local level politics takes on an additional dimension. To understand how schools are related politically to the urban community, it is important to see them as bundles of material benefits—jobs, contracts, and career ladders occupy a major place in the city economy.

Particularly since manufacturing has diminished as a source of jobs in the city, schools have occupied one of the top spots as employers. Consider the example of Detroit. Detroit still stands in the national psyche as a center of manufacturing and blue-collar employment. Yet the Detroit public schools have emerged as the biggest single employer in the city, followed by the Municipality of Detroit. Only Chrysler at third and General Motors at fifth remain as remnants of the once-dominant place of manufacturing in the Motor City. The pattern across the other ten cities is not greatly different. When the city school system is not the largest single source of jobs, it is never below fourth in size as an employer. In today's job-scarce cities, schools thus hold a prominent economic position.

The number of school jobs is only a partial indicator of their importance. Schools also provide in high proportion middle-class jobs with strong employment security attached to them. Tenure often comes with three years of employment, and administrative positions in these complex organizations provide comfortable salaries with, at least until recently, limited accountability. A management study of Baltimore found no case in which a principal had been dismissed for poor performance.[17]

For African Americans, once excluded from other business and professional positions, school employment holds an especially valued place.[18] Perhaps for related reasons, superintendencies and other high-level administrative posts are greatly prized, and these positions have become objects of substantial conflict between minorities.

Unionization of teachers and other school employees added a dimension to schools as employers. It involves more than collective bargaining. Unionization organizes workers politically around their material concerns—level of pay, job security, and hours of labor. To be effective, unionization requires worker solidarity. Hence, union contracts tend to emphasize seniority and other measures that encourage worker unity and avoid divisions among the workers. All in all, unionization relies on the lowest common denominator, and it is not in itself a means toward professional fulfillment or a force to encourage greater cultivation of intrinsic rewards.

With unionization, teachers have become significant electoral forces in a number of localities.[19] The particulars of how they operate politically vary from city to city. In Baltimore, for example, the black clergy are major channels for teacher influence.[20] In Chicago for many years the Democratic speaker of the Illinois House of Representatives served that role.[21] Typically, "bread-and-butter" issues rather than professional fulfillment make up the focal concern. For example, when Chicago teachers gained collective bargaining rights, almost all of the union effort went into salary increases and little more than lip service was paid to educational improvement.[22] Electoral activity by teachers' unions thus tends to fit the mold of distributive politics and resemble the standard version of pluralism, at least on the surface. This means that those with immediate interests, though perhaps not a numerical majority, usually carry the day. Immediate objectives, such as salary and job security, are powerful and dependable motivators. More diffuse concerns and nonspecific goals, like good schools, often prove politically weak. Even when such general aims rally supporters, their fervor tends to be short-lived. In this vein, Plunkitt of Tammany Hall characterized reformers as "mornin' glories," unable to hold up through the heat of the political day.

Board of education members are often focused on constituency service in small, more easily achieved aims, so there is little about the local politics of education that lends itself to organization around large issues of education policy and reform. One might argue that the weak performance of urban schools would make them prime targets for reform, and the disappointing level of academic achievement might be a spur to action. But it seems more common for educators to reconcile themselves to poor results and buffer themselves against external demands. John Goodlad reports that in schools perceived as less effective, parent-teacher contact is lower than in schools regarded as more effective.[23] Former U.S. commissioner of education Francis Keppel once talked about the "fortress" character of inner-city schools.[24] Early warriors against poverty identified "bureaucratic introversion" as a major problem, and the schools as a leading example of this problem.[25]

Many educators emphasize the culture of schools, and schools enrolling mostly low-income students are often characterized as having a culture of low expectations or a psychology of defeat. James Comer talks about his initial experience in New Haven in a school "where you could feel the hand of hopelessness."[26] Others talk about "the depth of division and frustration."[27] In Baltimore a management study cited a "culture of complacency" and concluded that: "Of all the barriers to change . . . , the most difficult is that of entrenched employee attitudes."[28]

Not all reports from the field are bleak. In Goodlad's study, schools regarded as more effective were also "perceived by teachers to be more gratifying work places," and teachers in these schools "tended to score somewhat higher on the indices of teacher professionalism."[29] Thus, as we put the pieces together, we see that educators in schools and systems in a better position to be effective academically are more likely to have their professional aspirations flourish and become part of the work environment. Where the possibilities are weaker, where student poverty is more concentrated, the intrinsic motivation of teachers and administrators is also likely to be weaker—leaving the political ground to be occupied mainly by "bread-and-butter" issues. In short, in big cities where a large proportion of the student body is at or near the poverty level there is little in the school system itself to counter the tendency for education politics to be organized around employment issues and other bread-and-butter matters, such as contracting for new buildings and remodeling old ones. When educational matters reach the agenda, they tend to focus on the specifics of particular programs at specific schools. As an organizing goal, academic performance occupies a very weak position unless strong and deliberate efforts are made to build a special base of support for such a purpose.

CONCLUSIONS

The primary obstacles to systemic school reform are not a lack of clever ideas, indifference to education, or a lack of willingness to try new things. The primary obstacles are political in nature; they are rooted in the fact that various groups have distinct interests that often lead them to work against one another in ways that dissipate energies and blunt reform efforts. Substantial resistance to centrally initiated change occurs at the level of the individual school site.[30] With a few exceptions, district-level forces add to rather than overcome resistance. As a consequence, reform—not in state capitals and not in national rhetoric, but at the ground level in local school districts—is more a matter of scattered skirmishes than of sustained mobilization. Fragmented activities form the central story line for urban school reform. Tentative starts and weak follow-through on more far-reaching proposals are the usual story.

The experience across our eleven cities manifests this typical pattern of partial efforts and limited mobilization. Even in the cities that seemed most capable of generating cross-sector alliances, systemic reform initiatives lacked the breadth and sustained momentum that we had hoped to see. Yet there are variations among the cities we studied, and more extensive efforts are associated with a higher level of civic mobilization. In the next and final chapter, we consider the implications of this finding for the design and orientation of more successful efforts at systemic urban school reform.

7
Implications and Recommendations

Everyone in America seems to agree that education reform is an extremely high priority. Public opinion polls show that the public wants better schools, and politicians running at all levels of government have discovered that they need to be able to offer a plan for school improvement to be credible candidates. In spite of that seeming consensus, progress on bringing about systemic education reform seems sluggish, especially in the large, central-city districts where the need, arguably, is most evident and severe. This book and the project that gave rise to it were designed to explore that apparent contradiction and to identify leverage points for initiating more comprehensive, effective, and sustained collective efforts to engage in social reconstruction.

Although our research affirms that school systems have accomplished little in the way of substantial systemic reform, we have also found that this is not for lack of trying. Even in the cities with the least successful efforts, tremendous energies and resources have been—and continue to be—mounted by parents, educators, leaders, community, and government. It is not that these efforts have not been useful and productive; in many cases they have. But many innovations have turned out to be fads with little lasting effect on school performance.

A major problem in educational reform has been the certainty with which policy entrepreneurs have pushed their desired solutions. This has led to disjointed and unfocused change as the system rushes from one magic bullet to the next. Civic capacity and collective problem solving require not only committed entrepreneurs pushing favored solutions, but also serious open discussion within a public forum about the problems and potentials of educational change. In this chapter, we highlight why simple answers do not work and why the solutions they engender can distract communities from more fruitful undertakings.

Contemporary school reform panaceas typically fall into one of two broad categories. The first category comprises *programmatic reforms.* Programmatic changes emphasize specific new ways for schools to go about their traditional responsibilities; they include new ideas about curriculum, teaching methods, professional development, school calendars, and the like. The second broad category of one-shot reforms involves *institutional changes.* These reform approaches focus less on what happens in the classroom and more on the way that decision making about such matters is structured. Institutional approaches to reform come in several flavors: some emphasize shifting emphasis to market forces (for example, vouchers, charter schools); some emphasize moving responsibility horizontally within the public sector from one decision-making venue (such as school boards) to another (mayors); some emphasize decentralizing authority within the public sector (for example, school-based decision making); and some emphasize centralizing accountability and authority (like instituting and aggressively enforcing state standards, backed by threat of state takeover of nonperforming districts or schools).

One-shot approaches are unlikely to suffice as a means of instituting sustained and systemic reform, and under some conditions may actually make things worse. Some of the policies associated with the programmatic and institutional approaches can play a valuable role in setting the ball of reform rolling, but reform is not self-sustaining, and reform efforts that overinvest in these approaches frequently falter and lose steam. The very same programmatic and institutional reforms that work in one school district may fail to take root in another district or stimulate a powerful backlash.

Bringing about systemic education reform is like kicking a stone uphill: A swift swing of a strong leg is enough to get it going, but keeping it going may call for something else entirely. Our analysis suggests that a necessary, if not fully sufficient, condition is the development of local civic capacity, including an ability to frame issues so that they present a series of winnable challenges, an informal pattern of accommodation and cooperation among a range of stakeholders, and sufficient formal authority to make local elected leaders credible and reliable bargaining partners. These are conditions that emerge from a history of collective efforts; they cannot be instantaneously injected or fashioned out of whole cloth.

Although our most confident conclusions are about what will *not* work, and though our sharpest message is about why genuine reform will not come easily, our findings also point toward a positive agenda for change. But the route we prescribe looks different from the reform maps typically provided within the education policy literature. Rather than a focus on specific programs or institutional reforms, our policy orientation is built around attention to the relationships among groups and the conditions under which it is possible for disparate groups to find and build upon common ground. Realigning relationships takes time, and in some ways our policy proposals stand in contrast to various "big bang" proposals that imply that a short burst of attention can build and institutionalize radical change. But, as we shall elaborate, this should not be taken as an argument for incrementalism, at least as incrementalism is commonly understood.

The orientation we propose can be seen as a union between two evolving lines of intellectual development about the conditions for effective reform. One of these has progressed primarily within the education policy community; the other has been situated within the broader social sciences and has focused on education only peripherally. Within the education arena, the intellectual tradition is marked by conflict between two paradigms, one placing primacy on the role of information, knowledge, and ideas, and the other emphasizing bureaucratic self-interest. Within the broader social sciences, the key theoretical evolution has involved a movement away from a preoccupation with fixed and independent interests to a new appreciation for the importance of ideas, culture, and social capital. Progressive dissatisfaction with both the information paradigm and the bureaucratic resistance paradigm has led some of the more progressive thinkers within the education arena to begin to shape a new vision that situates education policy in a broader social context. This vision—captured in shorthand by the slogan "it takes a village" to educate a child—has drawn the education debate into close juxtaposition with more general theorizing about social capital. This is a step in the right direction. Both the new "village" metaphor and the reigning conceptions of social capital, however, suffer from an overeagerness to wish or think away some issues related to interests, power, government, and politics that, although messy and problematic, ultimately hold the key to the challenge of sustaining meaningful social change.

CONVENTIONAL DIAGNOSES OF NONREFORM

Responsible proponents of reform need to do more than paint a rosy picture of a better world. To devise a workable plan for introducing the changes they advocate, reformers need some understanding of the obstacles to adoption and implementation of their proposals. And to sway others to ally with their efforts, they must be able to convey their diagnosis of nonreform in a manner that is understandable and credible to potential partners.[1] In education, as in most policy arenas, building a formidable coalition requires winning the attention and commitment of third parties for whom education is not necessarily the highest priority; because these potential allies have other interests and other demands on their time and resources, it is especially important to convince them that the reform venture has a reasonably good chance to succeed.

The pressure to offer compelling diagnoses of nonreform is especially strong when proponents suggest that they are offering a simple one-shot solution. The more simple and certain the benefits touted for this or that reform—whether programmatic or institutional in design—the more critical it is to be able to explain why no one has done this before.

In this section we briefly review two major competing perspectives for understanding the lack of reform that have emerged within the education policy debate. We label these the information and bureaucratic resistance paradigms. We argue that each of these perspectives on nonreform is linked to a broad solution set of policy approaches intended to work through or around the perceived obstacles. Much of the political and intellectual history in the arena has consisted of competition between these two perspectives, but we suggest that there also has been an internal dynamic, driven largely by frustration with sparse results, that has led each paradigm to move progressively from an emphasis on particular reforms to a more systemic posture. Continued frustration has prepared the ground for a third perspective, characterized by a much greater willingness to understand the education arena as an open system, integrally knitted into the broader social and political context.

Insufficient Information

Advocates of specific programmatic reforms frequently rely on an information paradigm to explain why reform is difficult. The information paradigm suggests that the primary obstacle to school reform is either lack of convincing evidence about what works or, where there is such evidence, failure to disseminate adequately that information to practitioners in the field. In highlighting ideas and knowledge as the primary lubricators of reform, the information paradigm nests nicely within the Progressive vision, in which education professionals are to be given substantial autonomy and support. It is not surprising, then, that education professionals are often its most enthusiastic proponents.

It is possible to discern three distinct levels within the informational paradigm. The first level focuses on disseminating information about particular pedagogical reforms that are presumed to hold the key to making students learn better and more quickly. Historically, there have been any number of pedagogical innovations that have been hailed as the pathway to better learning—if only teachers and principals could be made to see their advantages. These have included whole language instruction, various iterations of "new math," open education, computer-assisted learning, and more. In the continuing search for the right combination of programs and institutional devices, the notion in favor currently is to try highly programmed instruction combined with high-stakes testing.

Difficulty in realizing this vision led to the development of another iteration of the information paradigm, characterized by an organizational focus on a broader institution—the profession in place of the school or classroom—and an intellectual focus on the testing of ideas rather than the promotion of one or another favored innovation. This intermediate version emphasizes the need to invest in professional development as a vehicle for creating an education community that is simultaneously more open-minded and discerning. It also emphasizes the need for more systematic evaluation of educational programs and the systematic dissemination of information about those that have been proven to work.

Failure of this intermediate set of approaches to break the logjam blocking broad school reform played a major role in fueling the bureaucratic resistance perspective as a distinct alternative to the information paradigm. Rather than blame the failure on close-mindedness, self-interest, or resistance among educators, however, some hold on to the core precepts of the information paradigm and point the finger instead at aspects of the broad institutional structure that limit and constrain the pursuit of knowledge and implementation of new ideas. This more structural perspective is in some ways a revitalization of the traditional Progressive view, holding that the key to instituting reform is providing even more independence and resources to educators, freed from political meddling. Rather than specific ideas about pedagogy, the emphasis of this more structural perspective is on institutional forms that encourage and reward expertise in organizational innovations, such as career ladders, merit pay, master teachers, site-based decision making, and criterion-based testing.

A number of policy prescriptions follow logically from a diagnosis of insufficient information at one level or another. At the state or national level, they can include funding "demonstration programs" and helping to develop networks of information dissemination. At the district level, they include reforming teacher training, setting tough standards for teacher recertification, rewarding and expanding the responsibilities of master teachers who can help to bring others along, encouraging district representatives to visit and "learn from" a few model school administrations around the country, and hiring top administrators who have proven their knowledge of cutting-edge techniques by successfully implementing reform strategies in other jurisdictions. What links these disparate emphases is an assumption that most stakeholders share common values and interests about education, so that consensus and cooperation can be expected once ignorance, misinformation, and misperceptions are overcome.

Bureaucratic Resistance

In contrast to the information paradigm, the "bureaucratic resistance" paradigm presumes that we already have a good idea what needs to be done, but that self-interested education professionals, wielding disproportionate power, scuttle or emasculate any efforts that interfere with their comfortable routines. Self-interest, according to this perspective, propels bureaucracies to resist reforms that would increase workloads, make existing skills obsolete, interfere with habits and routines, or impinge on discretion and control. Moreover, stressful working conditions and conflicting messages about social priorities can induce even well-meaning and unselfish educators to adopt self-protective habits and routines that work against the interests of their students.

In addition to arguing that bureaucracies have an *interest* in deflecting reforms, the bureaucratic resistance paradigm asserts that bureaucracies have the *power* to block reforms, even when those reforms have popular support and the endorsement of elected leaders. That power is presumed to rest partially in the bureaucracy's monopoly over information and its reputation for expertise; these advantages presumably help bureaucracies to define issues in terms favorable to them and are most likely to accrue at the agenda-setting and implementation stages when overall levels of attention are lower than they are at the policy formulation stage.[2] But the power also comes from more conventional sources such as resources and the motivation to use them. Educational bureaucracies can bring to bear such resources as a large and readily mobilized constituency, the threat of work stoppages, and political contributions and campaign support, making them formidable players in the open battles over policy formulation. Education professionals also have a clear, substantial, and immediate stake in education policies, whereas other groups and the general public have a more diffuse interest. Small but intensely motivated groups often carry the day over larger and less intensely motivated groups.[3]

The bureaucratic resistance paradigm appeals to the impatient public, at least in part because it dismisses the view that reform is complicated and that it is necessary to defer to experts; it also appeals because it identifies a villain. Asked about a series of possible steps states could take to reduce educational expenditures in tight budget times, a vast majority (73 percent) favors reductions in the number of administrators.[4] Business leaders, an important constituency when education reform is under consideration, are especially likely to subscribe to the view that educators are an obstacle to progress. In one survey, 86 percent of business executives agreed (49 percent strongly) with the statement "usually, educational reforms are resisted by unions and administrators who like to keep things the way they are."[5]

The bureaucratic resistance perspective leads to a different type of policy proposal from those associated with information deficits. Rather than gathering and disseminating information about specific programs, it suggests that reformers need to restructure institutions in order to reallocate decision-making power. These institutional approaches share an emphasis on wresting power from those who traditionally have called the shots, particularly elected school boards and the more permanent elements of the central school administrations. They differ—often dramatically—in where they propose to place that reassigned authority.

As with the information paradigm, internal differences within the bureaucratic resistance school can be seen as constituting three levels. Level one, an emphasis on particular reforms, engenders such proposals as ending principal tenure and making union contracts less invasive of management prerogatives. An intermediate level of analysis zeroes in on the organization of the education bureaucracy and offers proposals to make bureaucracies less resistant to change and more responsive to parents, for example, through decentralization to school-based decision making. Finally, there is a more structural orientation, based on the premise that the power of educators to scuttle school reform is hard-wired into the broad institutions of public school governance. This version generates proposals to end the public school monopoly and replace it with a marketlike system.[6]

The Failure of Both the Information and Bureaucratic Resistance Perspectives

The information shortage and bureaucratic resistance perspectives help fuel the debate that still dominates the education policy arena: whether the route to reform lies in handing power to the professionals or blasting them out of their positions of power. But a sense is growing within many quarters that both the debate and its intellectual armaments are missing key points. Both the information and bureaucratic resistance perspectives oversimplify the nature of the problem in ways that may ultimately lead to misdirected political and policy responses. Rather than lack of ideas or blanket resistance to new ideas, urban school districts, at any point in time, are undertaking multiple initiatives. Moreover, our research suggests that problems associated with concentrated poverty introduce special challenges to education reform that make both programmatic and institutional change more problematic than either the information or resistance perspectives fully comprehend.

When we set out to do our research, we developed a long checklist of the kinds of reforms that were being discussed in public debates and in the education literature. We expected that some cities would be trying many of these reforms, and that others would be trying few or none. Even though most of the cities we were studying did not have reputations as innovators, we found, instead, that almost every city has at least some examples of almost every type of reform.

In each of the eleven districts that we considered, school officials and school district publications highlight an impressive array of innovative efforts. In Denver, for example, some elementary schools are including Montessori programs, some middle schools are building a core knowledge curriculum, and high schools have adopted numerous curricula, including baccalaureate high schools emphasizing a European-style approach and alternative high schools for students who have failed to learn through traditional approaches.[7] In Detroit, seven African-centered academies were established; the Academy of the Americas offers a curriculum that emphasizes the language and culture of the Latino community; and the Tech Prep Partnership 2000 Consortium is attempting to refashion vocational education.[8] Most of the eleven districts boast of some special magnet programs, education for the gifted, "school-to-work" programs, and special initiatives in using computers and technology. Several have instituted, or plan to institute, Comer schools or other efforts to incorporate families into the learning process. St. Louis, in 1994, began an initiative to establish fourteen community education centers that would offer nontraditional programming, invite participation by the adjacent neighborhoods, and emphasize a holistic approach to education.[9] Boston alone has at least three pilot projects that emphasize parental involvement, although all three rely on external funding and are vulnerable to cutbacks.[10] In Detroit, four professional development schools have been established, making it possible for teachers to receive technical training and support from Michigan universities.

The District of Columbia offers an interesting case illustrating how a school system that is widely viewed as a dismal failure and resistant to systemic reform can simultaneously be the setting for numerous, uncoordinated reforms. As early as 1989, the Committee on Public Education (COPE) listed characteristics of the system: far too many employees; a "confused and unwieldy budget"; a nonresponsive central administration; major problems with facilities attributable to deferred maintenance; an obsolete curriculum; a tendency of many teachers to overemphasize rote learning and standardized tests; and evidence that poor principals sometimes were simply transferred to the central office.[11] Then, in November 1996, the control board appointed by Congress to address the city's fiscal crisis issued its analysis, descriptively titled "Children in Crisis: A Report on the Failure of D.C.'s Public Schools." Charging that "too many children have suffered as a result of mismanagement, uninspired leadership, and institutional disregard . . . ," the board used that report as the launching pad for firing Superintendent Smith and hiring General Becton. In February 1997, a series of articles in the *Washington Post* underscored the breadth and depth of the system's failures.[12]

Yet the D.C. public schools, even prior to the congressional intervention, were hosts to numerous pedagogical reforms. As part of a decentralization effort, every school had been required to establish a Local School Restructuring Team, and over forty "enterprise" and "renaissance" schools had been given special discretion to shape their own policies at the school level. Many schools offered specialized programs that had developed loyal constituencies. These included an elementary school with dual language (English and Spanish) immersion, another elementary school with an Afrocentric curriculum, and special "academies" designed to provide high school students with career-relevant education (including a Health and Human Services Academy, a Public Service Academy, and a Trans Tech Academy). Public/private partnerships were in place in dozens of schools; many of these provided enriched career-related training, including separate programs in Culinary Arts, Interior Design and Landscape Architecture, International Studies, Pre-Engineering, Business and Finance, Travel and Tourism, and COMSAT's computer and science partnership with Jefferson Junior High. In addition, during the early 1990s, an aggressive deputy superintendent spearheaded the expansion of the District's Early Learning Years program, which involves a more child-friendly curriculum and a heavy emphasis on making certain that teachers and principals receive the training and support they need to put the curriculum into place. The District is perhaps the only large urban school district to offer a full-day early childhood education program in every elementary school, and the program has been expanding to incorporate many three-year-olds. In 1995 Congress passed legislation initiating a major charter school program in D.C., but even before Congress acted, the public system had experimented with "School-within-School Charters," including a Montessori school, a Nongraded School, and a Media Technology Social Research School.

To conclude that the problem is neither lack of new ideas nor blanket resistance to new ideas, however, is not the same as concluding that there is no problem at all. We encountered lots of evidence of programmatic initiatives and even broad spasms of systemic institutional reform, but there is little evidence that all this scattered activity has added up to systemic reform. Many of the initiatives are at the individual school level. It is very rare indeed for there to be any formal evaluation of these programs. Not only are central administrators not in a position to offer data about what works and what does not, often the central administration lacks the capacity even to identify all the initiatives that are under way. In some cases, reforms may be superficial or exist in name only. In other cases they may be working and working well. The sad fact is that we simply do not know. We found this pattern of multiple but undigested reforms fairly typical among the eleven cities in our study, and it has been noted in other places as well. Farkas, as we noted earlier, refers to this as the tendency toward a "reform du jour."[13] Hess calls it "policy churn."[14] Thus, concluding that the problem is neither a lack of ideas nor blanket resistance to new ideas is not the same as concluding that there is no problem at all.

TOWARD A NEW PERSPECTIVE

Although differing in very major respects, both the information paradigm and the bureaucratic resistance paradigm look primarily inside the school system to account for nonreform. More recently, a new line of thinking has begun to emerge. This perspective recognizes that the ephemeral nature of school reform is not simply attributable to failures within the education community, but relates also to the way competing demands within the broader community can sap energy and resources from education initiatives. For school reform really to take root, this perspective holds that school systems must shed the buffers they once built deliberately to shield themselves from outside "interference" and build lasting linkages with other important stakeholders in the broader community.

It Takes a City

A useful illustration of the intellectual evolution leading toward a new perspective can be found, in microcosm, by looking at the evolution of ideas in a series of works coauthored by Paul Hill. In *Reinventing Public Education,* Hill and his coauthors emphasized the need for a radical restructuring of the governance institutions that traditionally frame public education and argued that a specific organizational initiative—contracting with private corporations or nonprofits to run public schools—held the best prospect for catalyzing the necessary changes.[15] Avoiding simplistic bureaucracy bashing, *Reinventing* largely reflected the bureaucratic resistance paradigm and settled on a particular institutional end-run around that bureaucracy as the key to its policy message. By 1998, in *Fixing Urban Schools,* Hill, with Mary Beth Celio, had broadened his line of vision. *Fixing* considered a broader range of policy options and concluded that no single strategy would suffice.[16]

By 2000, writing now with Christine Campbell and James Harvey, Hill had refined his argument further, in ways that have important parallels to the themes that we have articulated in this book. *It Takes a City* begins by noting the frequent failure of reforms to take root, even when they appear to have strong stakeholder support and even when school districts take the preliminary steps to put the reform initiatives into place. The book identifies implementation and sustained effort as the core challenges, and concludes that "leadership must come from a longer-lasting source and one that is both more deeply rooted in the community than a superintendent and less protective of the status quo than a school board or district office."[17] They propose a "community partnership" arrangement in which different responsibilities for monitoring schools and ensuring educational quality are allocated across a wide range of actors, including private investors, churches, community groups, a civic oversight board, and market forces.

A similar new emphasis on the need for educators to broaden their links can be found in other recent works. Several of these have direct or indirect ties to foundations that have found it more difficult than they initially expected to leverage their dollars into progressive change.[18] Attempting to account for the disappointing progress of school reform, for example, David Mathews, president of the Charles F. Kettering Foundation and a former secretary of health, education, and welfare during the Ford administration, observes that school systems "appear to be walled off as formal, quasi-governmental institutions rather than public agencies embedded in a rich civic network."[19] Rather than any single reform, since "there isn't any single reform that will do for all time," he argues that schools must make improvement habitual. This, in turn, requires that school systems develop "an enduring capacity . . . rooted in the communities that surround them."[20]

The Link to Social Capital

As education reformers have begun thinking seriously about the linkage between school systems and communities, their ideas and images have drawn closer to theories that had independently been percolating more broadly in the social sciences. The concept of social capital, as others have noted, is slack enough to have meant rather different things to different analysts. One important strain of theorizing about social capital, in fact, has its own roots in the education sphere. James Coleman turned to the idea of social capital as a network of relationships built on trust and norms of reciprocity to account for his finding that Catholic schools tend to have greater success than public schools in educating children even when the socioeconomic background of the students is taken into account.[21] Others have continued to build on that base.[22]

But it is Robert Putnam's development of the concept of social capital that has done the most to put the concept at center stage in contemporary discussions about community and civic life.[23] The link between Putnam's ideas and the evolving new ideas among education reformers has enriched the latter in several ways. Because Putnam's work is framed in terms of a much more general debate about the nature of democracy and social progress, the linkage has broadened the range of ideas and evidence from which education analysts can draw. Simultaneously, this has given the same analysts a much larger potential audience to which to speak. Putnam's ideas can be understood, moreover, in the context of a general backlash against the one-dimensional portrayal of individual and group interests that had begun to play a dominating role within political science and public policy studies. The idea of social capital, as he evoked it, demands that we take seriously the ways in which culture, social networks, and institutions shape and channel the ways in which individuals and groups conceive and pursue their perceived interests. School reform analysts who had been *feeling* a sense of frustration and *intuiting* that this was a sign of limitations in the reigning perspectives could draw from Putnam and the surrounding debates a more self-conscious and theoretically rich basis for understanding that neither ideas nor bureaucratic interests alone could tell the whole story of nonreform.

Joined with the concept of social capital, the emerging new perspective on education reform properly begins to shine the spotlight on elements of the social and political context beyond the school system. In this context, calls for "systemic reform" take on a greater weight than when the system that needed changing was a relatively closed and defined bureaucracy. A system perspective of the kind now being proposed means looking beyond the surface facts of an abysmal performance and, instead, searching for underlying reasons. A school district may be performing badly despite the good intentions and hard work of many people.[24] Angela Blackwell, architect of the Urban Strategies Council in Oakland, California, talks about the insight that led her to change approaches. After considerable experience as a public interest lawyer suing public agencies on behalf of low-income clients, she reports that, one day, "I saw that most of these agency people were basically good people who wanted to do right for their clients, but they truly don't know how."[25] The Urban Strategies Council represents an attempt to create "a whole new way of doing community business."[26] In short, Blackwell's aim was systemic change—at the city level.

Small, much less individual, efforts are not the answer. To be sure, pockets of strong performance can be and have been created, but there is risk that the resources and exceptional staff required to sustain these efforts only make the situation more hopeless elsewhere. The reform challenge is indeed systemic. Piecemeal change will not turn around a set of mutually augmenting weaknesses.

Embodied in the recent efforts of several foundations, such as the New Futures initiative of the Annie E. Casey Foundation, is a theory of social change. As explained in one report, it was assumed that "involving a city's 'movers and shakers'—mayor, CEOs, school superintendent, along with corporate leaders and public agency heads—would create a shared picture of problems and lead to a common vision about what to do about them."[27] Some education reformers hold a similar idea in talking about getting stakeholders together. In both instances the idea is to mobilize a powerful constituency behind reform.

But what does it mean to mobilize? Part of the research reported here does support the idea that civic mobilization creates a favorable climate for school improvement, but we also have tried to go further. As we survey the state of the study of urban education, we see a need not simply to add another voice to the call for reconnecting school and community but to explore the conditions under which the reconnection can take place.

From Social Capital to Civic Capacity

Contemporary voices recognize the need for systemic reform but they can identify no obvious point of leverage for change. The vision of a unified village or city that animates the emerging new perspectives on systemic reform has become too divorced from the forces and institutions that have the capacity to convert nice dreams into lasting practice. It is true that shared norms, trust, and habits of reciprocity can be the tissue and sinew that hold together the communal body, but to exert force they need to be integrated into an infrastructure including muscle and bone. In turning to the concept of civic capacity, we have tried to highlight the need to consider both political power and formal institutions of governance as critical components in any strategy to lead America into a serious grappling with the problems of central-city school reform.

We believe the findings and perspective we have developed in this book hold some promise for continuing the evolution in the way that school reform is being approached in the United States. At the same time, the emerging understanding of school reform can contribute something to debates about social capital, policy change, and democracy that have occupied social scientists in the broader scholarly community. School reform, in important respects, can be seen as a window into a larger and enduring set of questions relating to collective problem solving. In particular, this case sheds some light on the special dynamics that characterize what we have labeled "high-reverberation" subsystems: policy subsystems characterized by frequent reshuffling of mobilized stakeholders, multiple and deeply held competing value and belief systems, and ambiguous boundaries, making the prospects for establishing a new equilibrium more problematic than is normally the case.

We conclude by highlighting two related sets of implications. First, we offer some conclusions that we think will interest social scientists concerned with the broad phenomena of collective problem solving and democratic change. Following that we present some more specific applications to contemporary debates about education policy.

LESSONS FOR COLLECTIVE PROBLEM SOLVING

Public Arenas as Leverage Points

Civic capacity implies the vigorous involvement of community influentials, but it cannot involve solely a narrow stratum of elite players. Without the involvement of business and other broad-based urban interests, the educational policy-making subsystem will be allowed to continue with "business as usual." We saw this pattern in Atlanta, where an unstated bargain allowed businesses to concentrate on physical renewal and the attraction of capital, whereas the black community held sway over school politics. The involvement of broader interests is crucial, and, of all urban actors, elected politicians stand out as the ones who have the incentives and the resources to construct broad coalitions capable of action in education.

On the other hand, the involvement of politicians does not guarantee success. To the extent that civic action rests on a narrow foundation of elite cooperation, it is vulnerable to quick collapse. Having a few key actors embrace a reform idea may only invite opposition from those not part of the deliberation and fearful of its consequences. For a mayor or teachers' union president to get out of line with important constituencies may thus set back the whole process of moving toward fundamental reform.

Baltimore's experience with a pilot project—contracting out the management of nine schools to Education Alternative, Inc.—illustrates the problem.[28] When Kurt Schmoke was elected mayor, he was eager to turn around the performance of Baltimore city schools but found the central school bureaucracy to be a formidable force of resistance. Even though BUILD, a community-based organization, and the Greater Baltimore Committee, an organization of major businesses, had already done groundwork for school reform, there was little forward momentum. With a new school superintendent of his choosing in place, Mayor Schmoke sought an innovative way to move the school system toward greater decentralization and improved academic performance. With encouragement and support from a local foundation, the mayor had the school superintendent and union officials make site visits and consider a private company, Education Alternatives, Inc., for a pilot project of managing nine of the city schools. The teachers and principals in these schools would be kept in place if they so chose or they could transfer to other positions in the system. The teachers' union president endorsed the idea. However, once the project was put in place and the company transferred teacher's aides out of the nine pilot schools and replaced them with college-educated interns, apprehensions about job security rose. This transfer of teacher's aides helped foster unease within the African-American community about privatization and contracting out. It set off alarm bells about a potential threat to the school system as a source of employment for the city's African-American community. The school system was the city's largest employer, and over 70 percent of the jobs in the system were held by African Americans.

As the contracting-out pilot moved to implementation, BUILD and the city's black clergy criticized Mayor Schmoke for acting without consultation, and the president of the teachers' union shifted from support to opposition. Limited consultation was a major hindrance to continued momentum toward school reform, but it is also significant that an initial focus on what was "good for kids" (as phrased by the teachers' union president) gave way to concerns about race and employment as the proposal became public and a wider array of players added their voices.[29] Whether Education Alternatives, Inc. was a sound project to pursue is not the issue. The point is that agreement among a small number of individuals, even though they held key institutional positions and even though they enjoyed support from the newspaper and the Greater Baltimore community, did not constitute strong civic capacity. The larger racial context asserted itself, reversed momentum toward school reform, weakened the mayor's standing as a leader in education, and heightened community tensions. Civic capacity proved highly fragile and earlier experiences of working together quickly lost their weight. A wider form of deliberation might have maintained momentum behind reform, but in the mayor's judgment it would simply have cut off a chance to pursue an experiment and left him still stymied by an uncooperative school bureaucracy. Subsequently, a reform alliance has been reassembled, but it is more narrowly based than the earlier coalition. As a result, civic capacity in Baltimore remains at an intermediate level, loosely coupled in form, and still hampered by the city's racial divide.

The role of race in eroding civic capacity in Baltimore needs to be properly understood. Though it could be a rallying force behind the cause of inner-city children, race often fails to take on that role. Instead, race remains a potent force of division in American cities, even when the transition of those cities to majority-minority is no longer a fresh trauma.[30] This, along with the various socioeconomic characteristics reviewed in Chapter 3, is one of the important ways in which big-city school reform can present more difficult challenges than those found in other settings. It turns out that race too often is a factor that introduces damaging stereotypes, mistrust, suspiciousness, wariness, and volatility into the political arena, and it is the latter forces that are the more direct threats to civic capacity. Moreover, regardless of a city's racial composition or history, we need to acknowledge that civic capacity is a fragile tool, especially when put into play in a high-reverberation arena like urban school reform.

To withstand the corrosive power of public contention, civic capacity needs strong pillars of support. Informal alliances are relatively weak pillars; formal and fully staffed collaboration is stronger. Voluntary and cooperative mechanisms for coordinating activity do not suffice when there is a need to override narrower interests that hold an effective power to veto; in these instances the official word of law and flexing of government's legitimate coercive authority may be required.

Institutionalization, involving but not limited to government, plays an important role in distinguishing among our eleven cases between higher-capacity cities like Pittsburgh and Boston and others that mimicked elements of those cities' strategies but depended on spontaneous convergence of goodwill to keep the alliances in place over time.[31]

Civic capacity in Pittsburgh's education arena grew out of the desegregation struggles of the 1960s and 1970s. Key leaders came together around the idea of school improvement as a way to transcend battles over racial balance. The Allegheny Conference on Community Development (ACCD), the business sector's voice on major civic issues, made some vital moves. First, it created the Allegheny Conference Education Fund to support innovative projects within the school system, and it brought in national experts to foster school-business partnerships. Second, ACCD provided leadership for a Citizen's Advisory Committee formed in 1980 and that committee developed a school improvement plan as well as launched a "community dialogue" to engage neighborhood leaders. The committee also sponsored a public information campaign along with a series of troubleshooting meetings to emphasize the strengths of the school system.

The president of the teachers' union was an important member of the school improvement coalition, providing a critical base of support for the reform process. In 1980, Richard Wallace was hired as superintendent, and he further shaped reform around an "excellence agenda" and brought the education-research community in as participants in reform. During his twelve years as superintendent, Pittsburgh acquired a reputation as "a national model of urban educational reform."[32] Wallace's successor, Louise Brennan, continued an activist's agenda. Moving in the new direction of decentralization, she used a series of broad-based task forces to develop a strategic plan of action. The plan provided for an expanded and formally recognized role for parent and community involvement, and she also inaugurated a program of training for parent involvement in the new structure. Thus, Pittsburgh established and made strong use of a tradition of civic collaboration in education. Yet ongoing events show that even such a tradition may rest on a tenuous basis, as a financial squeeze, the redirection of business attention to issues of regional economic decline, and continuing tensions over racial balance versus neighborhood schools have taken a toll on civic cooperation. The ACCD provided crucial institutional support for collaboration around education, and, with that organization now less focused on city issues than regional ones, civic cooperation is today less firmly anchored than at any time since the 1960s and 1970s.

All of this is a difficult set of arrangements to maintain, and if these arrangements break down at some point or never quite gel, then there is a risk that misunderstanding and mistrust will carry the day. That civic capacity centers on community problem solving means that major *public* issues are considered, and these are matters always apt to become contentious. Any civic consensus is far from stable, and therefore the process of building support for a program of action around one problem is not easily transferred to (or borrowed from) another exercise in problem solving.

Civic capacity is therefore not akin to the microlevel social capital described by Putnam and others. That kind of social capital is largely the unconscious byproduct of everyday interactions. Civic capacity is the conscious creation of actors seeking to establish a context in which extraordinary problem solving can occur. As such, it is always across the grain of what Hannah Arendt calls "automatic processes" and therefore subject to erosion.[33] Civic capacity is neither easy to establish nor easy to maintain once it is set in motion. For that reason, institutionalization is a surer foundation than informal understandings among select individuals.

In this institutionalization there is no substitute for government—the general-purpose government of the municipality. Heads of general government—that is, mayors—have access to the media in a way that narrow-purpose governments do not. One reason that school superintendents are seldom involved in major reform efforts is that they do not command the attention that the mayor does. Even when it comes to reforming their own arenas, school superintendents are mostly failures. They sit at the top of a vast, but very narrow, policy arena. Mayors are generalists, and as a consequence, must be involved in the promotion of broad-scale civic action.

Government is not simply one among many equal social entities. It is the unit best suited to generate a collective sense of purpose when one is missing, to coordinate or coerce action when interests remain disparate, and to provide a vehicle for democratic control.

How Collective Cognition Matters

Neither the traditional interest group model that long dominated political science nor the social capital model that some see as the antidote has much to say about collective cognition. The interest group model put rational calculation front and center, but sidestepped cognition as a variable through assumptions about perfect information. Moreover, its zealous focus on individuals left little room for concepts such as public ideas or broadly shared perceptions, other than as the simple aggregation of the personal thoughts of autonomous actors. Reaction against this reductionism was not limited to theorists of social capital.[34] But social capital's emphasis on norms, values, and trust clearly fit into this intellectual backlash.

Putnam's idea of social capital, however—particularly as picked up and reified within the popular media—gives cognition a backseat to emotion and socially ingrained instinct. Our finding that problem definition and assessment of solution sets are key elements in civic capacity suggests a need to reconsider this assignment of status. The point we want to stress is that understanding of a need to act, that is to say *cognition,* can and often does alter as actors come together *in a civic role.* When a mayor convenes an education summit or when various community leaders form a civic entity, such as the Boston Compact or the El Paso Collaborative for Educational Excellence, they are acting in a special capacity. In such a setting, the president of the teachers' union is in a different role from that when bargaining over a new union contract. A special civic perspective is expected. Similarly, there is a difference between a business executive thinking and acting in the capacity of president of the company (or voice of the trade association) and thinking and acting as a civic leader. The civic arena operates under norms and expectations different from a business or electoral arena.[35] Cognition is affected accordingly. The arena shapes the questions asked and the information elicited. The civic arena also creates an expectation of wide representation in problem solving, not in the form of advocates of partial interests, but as voices to diversify the considerations encompassed. In such a setting, collective cognition may develop because of the dynamic of deliberation.

A set of simulation exercises illustrates. As recounted by Hill, Campbell, and Harvey, seven sessions were conducted over three different cities. Participants came together to recommend school reform strategies. In each session, participants started from an individual perspective. They drew on their personal experiences and training. However, as the sessions progressed, they began to *exchange* ideas and thoughts and to consider the perspectives of their fellow participants. In the end, "they ultimately considered a much broader array of strategies than they had anticipated. They attributed their expansive thinking to the ideas of other panelists who brought a variety of perspectives to the table."[36] Of course, a simulation is missing tensions that would be present in an actual decision situation, but the exercise shows how deliberation can remain focused and still expand the perspectives of participants and give them a wider understanding of the issue than they started with individually. Collective cognition is a real process that can take place in the right circumstances.

In our eleven-city study, we did not fully anticipate the finding that elites in high-mobilization cities simultaneously see more problems and focus on fewer solutions, but we have come to see it as provocative and significant. Recognizing the world's richness and complexity without becoming paralyzed by that recognition is a challenge that many of us wrestle with on personal terms. Key stakeholders in high-capacity cities appear to scan the environment better and be more realistic about the extent to which broad social factors constrain deliberate interventions within a modest range. But in focusing on fewer and more feasible actions, it appears that they may be better able to maintain a steady state of reform. That this is not an argument for simplistic incrementalism or for ignoring structural inequities is a point to which we will return.

Our study of collective problem solving in education points to conscious creation of both networks of action and a general sense of purpose among the actors involved. That sense of purpose includes both a realistic idea of the problems facing the city and a general consensus on the priorities of the proposed solutions to the problem. The notion of social capital is passive, because there is no theory of activation via collective problem-solving activities. Waiting for social capital to be deployed may be akin to "waiting for Godot."

Subsystem Breakup Is Not Enough

Accumulated frustration with the difficulty of reforming public education has led some policy activists to adopt a "break-up-the-system" stance in which bulldozing the existing institutional framework becomes the dominating theme. Implicit is the assumption that some combination of individual interests and social networks will coalesce into a new working arrangement once the old obstacles are out of the way. A similar leap of faith can be seen in some of the political science literature on subsystem change. Conventional pluralism takes it for granted that the ongoing interplay among fluid interests gravitates toward an equilibrium solution even after external shocks.

Recent work on stability and instability within policy subsystems has made it clear that aggregated elite advantages can enforce an extended period of relative stability, but that such arrangements are ultimately vulnerable to challengers armed with powerful ideas. The result is a pattern of "punctuated equilibria," in which pent-up discontent erupts in a compressed period of sharp change, as one monopoly is displaced and another takes its place.[37] This perspective appropriately recognizes that political equlibria, where they occur, are not spontaneous and natural but created and defended. Power, institutions, and problem definitions are the building material and glue.

A general lesson to be drawn from the education policy arena, however, is that the transitional period between equilibrium periods can be extended and that, indeed, there is no assurance that a transition will occur. Subsystem breakup is not enough; one needs a political settlement to impose a new policy regime. The prospects for sustained turmoil are greater where formal power is fragmented, symbolic politics potent, problem definitions contested, causal linkages uncertain, and the public interest ill-defined. That, we have suggested, is why generating civic capacity is more difficult when applied to social reconstruction than to the physical reconstruction of urban downtowns. And it is why we believe it is useful to distinguish high-reverberation subsystems from others, where the ground is more stable and the consequences of initiatives are more assured.

APPLICATIONS TO CONTEMPORARY EDUCATION DEBATES

The U.S. educational landscape is littered with the carcasses of reform efforts that have been tried and failed. Many of these have been pedagogical reform initiatives, germinated and disseminated within the education community, then launched with high hopes and good intentions, only to falter in the face of spotty implementation, underfunding, disappointing progress, political backlash, or simply displacement by the next new idea. Generalized frustration with the lack of progress associated with such pedagogical initiatives has set the stage for an array of more institutional approaches. Some of these have been top-down approaches, intended to force reform by the authoritative application of clear standards, mandated procedures, and clear penalties and rewards. Often these involve centralizing authority at a higher level of government, or at least one somehow external to the local education agency that has been judged to have tried and come up short. Judicial intervention and high stakes–testing regimes with the threat of state takeovers are examples of these external institutional approaches. Other institutional approaches have had more of a bottom-up orientation. These include efforts to decentralize decision making to the school level, as well as charter school and voucher plans that envision harnessing market forces as an alternative to governmental authority.

That most of these institutional approaches have proven problematic also might occasion a new wave of frustration and fatalism. The lesson some have chosen to learn is that public education cannot be saved, and that only much more radical alternatives are worthy of consideration and support.

Although broad forces may impose powerful limits on local communities, we find that there are, nonetheless, meaningful differences in the way the eleven cities we studied have responded. Even more significant, we find that these differences are not strictly determined by demography. The two cities in our study that had the highest median family income—San Francisco and the District of Columbia—have not shown much capacity to mobilize around systemic school reform, while Pittsburgh, the highest scorer on our civic capacity index, had lower incomes than all but Atlanta, Detroit, and St. Louis. In building capacity for systemic school reform there is room for human agency and room for deliberate intervention organized at the local level. But civic capacity requires more than good ideas or conducive institutions. Ideas and institutions must be embedded within, and augmented by, a supportive array of relationships. Without those relationships, even the best ideas and most appropriate institutional reforms are like good seeds spread on barren ground.

Currently, the most popular approaches to school reform involve institutional rearrangements intended to reassign responsibility for assessing and directing educational change. Almost all these approaches envision reducing the authority of local school boards and educational professionals, although they differ substantially in their notions of where that responsibility ought to be relocated.

We find only modest support for the optimistic vision that institutional tinkering will suffice to unlock the potential for nonincremental reform. Our wariness is not toward the general strategy of using institutional change as leverage for reform. Sometimes the institutional status quo is simply unacceptable and external intervention is mandated, on either constitutional or moral grounds. Even when the consequences of changes in formal institutions may be minor—when compared to those that might follow from broad shifts in culture, power, or economic resources—governing institutions make appealing leverage points because their formal status makes them more readily identifiable and more susceptible to deliberate and democratic intervention. Rather, our wariness is toward the notion of the sufficiency of institutional change as a catalyst. Injecting new institutional arrangements into the boiling pot of educational politics may or may not be necessary—it certainly will not suffice.

Currently popular institutional fixes are arrayed in hierarchy based on how far the formal decision-making impetus is distanced from its traditional site in the local school board and education agencies. Less radical changes involve horizontal shifting within the local public sector, for example, from superintendents and school boards to mayors and city councils. Somewhat less incremental, but still retaining a local commitment to control, are formal shifts in power from central agencies to local school-based communities. More extreme versions shift authority out of local hands altogether—to state and federal actors in the judicial, legislative, or executive branches.

Perhaps the most promising institutional reform that is currently in favor involves bringing responsibility for the schools more directly under the auspices of the same elected leaders who are responsible for other public services. In popular parlance this seems often to be presented as the "Chicago solution." In 1995, the Illinois legislature passed legislation that reconstituted the Chicago school board and put it under the direct control of Mayor Richard Daley. Quite apart from their substantive merits, such strategies have some appeal because they are politically feasible ("other cities have done it, so can we") and at the very least can be counted upon to shake things up. Given the political obstacles that end up frustrating many other reform impulses (and the corroding impact that failed efforts can have), the trait of feasibility has some value in its own right. Further, the seeming implacability and immovability of the status quo system give more than an ounce of attraction to anything that promises change. Movement in this direction, moreover, is quite consistent with our findings about the positive role of politics and our normative allegiance to the idea of democratic control. Yet our own research reminds us that the empirical evidence in support of such institutional solutions is slight. Pittsburgh, our most highly ranked city in civic capacity, provides the mayor no special formal role in the education process. Second-ranked Boston does, but its move in this direction is too recent to have accounted fully for the degree of collaboration and focus that we found during our field research. Baltimore, with the longest tradition of formal mayoral authority, is mired in the middle of our cities on the capacity index, and its trajectory is not promising.

Our skepticism toward another set of institutional "solutions"—those involving reorganization to radically decentralize decision making or to replace bureaucratic control with sensitivity to market forces—is based on a somewhat different foundation. Efforts to spark reform through decentralization have diffused rapidly, and nearly every one of our eleven cases exhibited at least some movement toward school-based decision making. In some cases the new arrangements were more symbol than substance, but in some the initiatives were quite serious. Among the latter cases, early enthusiasms have faded in most cases, as the effort proves more demanding and the results less dramatic than proponents had supposed. As yet, there is little empirical evidence that decentralization generates measurable improvements on the conventional indicators of educational achievement. Proposals for vouchers and contracting with private education providers tell a different tale. With very few exceptions, these ideas have encountered deep resistance. In Baltimore, where a contract arrangement *was* put in place, the most apparent legacy was increased racial polarization and the dissipation of the short-lived alliance among churches, community, labor, and the mayor. Civic capacity, we conclude, may be a prerequisite for the formation and implementation of some types of institutional reforms rather than a probable consequence.

Reforms for Coalitions versus Coalitions for Reforms

In contrast with much of the work on educational reform, a focus on civic capacity translates into less concern with prescribing a particular program of reform or making evaluations of initiatives in progress and more serious attention to the politics of reform. We have been more concerned in this book to make discoveries about process, that is, about the conditions that facilitate or hamper diverse elements in urban communities coming together around an agenda of educational improvement.

In keeping with the Progressive tradition, many contemporary advocates of school reform, if they acknowledge the process of politics as a potentially positive force at all, think of it as a necessary unpleasantry. Politics and coalition building are what might be needed to get their desired programmatic or institutional reform into place, but then it should be relegated to the background while the reforms take effect. In contrast, our analysis suggests that reforms without sustaining politics are ineffectual. Sometimes a new reform idea, though, can be a helpful catalyst to mounting an assault on the status quo. Therefore, we reverse the priority: Programmatic and institutional reforms are something that might be important as one of the tools necessary for putting together a sustainable political coalition, but there is a risk to letting any fixed strategy become the defining essence of a reform coalition.

One very important consequence of this reformulation is that it can save a superintendent or a city from overinvestment in any particular strategy. Overinvestment in a particular strategy can fuel resistance and backlash, as Kurt Schmoke discovered in Baltimore, and can restrain key stakeholders from making pragmatic accommodations that might broaden their constituency.

That does not mean that we are indifferent to the substance of reform. Instead, we believe that the challenge is to launch a broadly based move toward fundamental reform. Once that occurs, it matters little what particular reforms receive initial consideration so long as the drive is toward comprehensive and coherent change. As communities seek fundamental reform, their concerns will go deeper and extend in scope. In that process, as reform agendas evolve and mature, we believe they will inevitably overlap to a high degree. What is likely to emerge may be termed "hybrid reforms."[38] The executive director of Parents United, a school reform organization in Washington, D.C., commented that her organization had started years earlier as an advocate of increased funding for the city's schools, but that members quickly concluded that they had to take on a wide range of interconnected issues.[39] So it is with any effort to achieve fundamental reform.

Often the beginning point is outcome accountability. It quickly links into recruitment and professional development for teachers and principals. Concerns about raising performance frequently direct attention to early childhood development and preschool programs. After-school programs and the motivating force in structured transitions to work and college are also likely to receive attention. Parent and community involvement emerge as important in virtually all discussions about school improvement. Nor does it take most reformers long to conclude that family and social supports are important, hence social services for families and children are useful as well.

Because the particulars requiring attention and eliciting support vary from place to place, decentralization in most operations is a logical complement to outcome accountability. In addition, decentralization is congenial to parent and community involvement. Whether the reform drive is on the state level or the local level, the measures considered cover much the same range of issues.[40]

Fundamental reform, however, is not simply an aggregation of particular actions.[41] If reform is to be genuinely systemic, then attention must center on academic performance. And the agents of change need to be mindful of how reforms affect one another, they need to monitor their impacts, and they need to make *combinations of moves* that heighten expectations and create an environment of change.[42]

The points of greatest friction are likely to be around seniority and tenure for faculty and administrators. How these issues are resolved and the extent to which they are dealt with vary from place to place, and may determine whether reform momentum builds or is stymied. But that is why it may be critically important to have teachers and principals as well as higher-level administrators as part of the reform coalition.[43] As Hill and others observe, "Important civic leaders must become engaged in building and sustaining a reform strategy over a long time. Legitimate representatives of affected groups, especially parents and grandparents and leaders of churches and community groups in the neighborhoods most burdened by bad schools, must also be committed and influential participants"[44]

Of such stuff is civic capacity made. Once a reform coalition gives agency to this capacity, an open rather than a closed agenda is in order. A reform coalition needs an ongoing process of observing, learning, making adjustments, and pursuing new avenues.[45] The reform process needs to move beyond the conventional lines through which official responsibilities are defined and turf is divided.

Starting with a prescribed set of reforms may simply encourage key players to raise their defenses. All things considered, process holds more promise than a prescribed set of initiatives. With that in mind, we urge a *process* of community consultation that goes beyond "rounding up the usual suspects." Consultation needs to encompass those often left out, as Hill, Campbell, and Harvey suggest—the parents, grandparents, and community-based institutions in those neighborhoods long treated as marginal. The "usual suspects" among civic elites have a part to play as do educators themselves, but fundamental reform in education also requires a depth of community engagement far greater than is the case with most policy areas.

With teachers and administrators inclined to varying degrees and forms of resistance,[46] fundamental reform is likely to be stymied unless a clear and authoritative signal is given that "business as usual" is not the order of the day. Planned change acquires needed acceptance only under extraordinary circumstances when the locality speaks through its civic voice and backs that voice with active involvement. A one-shot "summit" will not do it. Fundamental reform turns on sustained engagement by a wide array of actors who see themselves as stakeholders in the community's education system.

Rethinking Mayoral Leadership

One institutional reform that has begun to receive substantial attention is the idea of increasing the mayoral role in education decision making. Chicago is the case that has received the most attention, but the phenomenon is much more widespread. Among the eleven cities we studied, Boston, Detroit, and the District of Columbia have moved aggressively in this direction. Baltimore had long assigned the mayor a major role in selecting the school board. In many respects, this movement can be seen as a reaction against the Progressive reformers' early-twentieth-century efforts to buffer schools from political meddling. During that era, elected mayors were regarded skeptically by reformers, who saw them as machine-based practitioners of patronage and cronyism.[47] Today the image of the urban mayor is on the upswing, and contemporary reformers see these pragmatic and tough-minded leaders as likely allies in their effort to bring the education bureaucracy to heel.

Opponents of this new emphasis on mayoral leadership portray it as an attack on elected school boards and suggest that it constitutes an assault on democracy. This was the case, for example, in the June 2000 special referendum in the District of Columbia, which abolished the existing ward-based school board for a smaller body in which nearly half of the members were to be mayoral appointments. Although the reform passed, it did so narrowly, and voting patterns revealed a stark polarization of the vote along racial lines. African Americans saw the proposal as an outgrowth of congressional efforts to diminish local home rule and voted accordingly.

We are in general sympathetic to the new emphasis on mayoral leadership. It is ironic that separately elected school boards, which were put into place as a way to insulate schools from politics, are now sometimes seen as the seedbed for democracy. In reality, school boards are often highly politicized, with the seats used as "stepping stones" to higher office. The result is that school boards can come to reflect the most narrow forms of politics—casework that caters to individual parent wants or concessions to highly organized interests such as teachers' unions. In our research, we found very little indication that school boards were serving as an effective focal point for shaping a broad public agenda. And, as we have emphasized, we believe that civic capacity demands a central place for politics and formal governmental authority.

Nonetheless, we think that it can be a mistake to invest too much in the role of a particular leader or formal position of authority, just as it can be a mistake to invest too much in any particular substantive reform. As we see it, the question is not mayoral leadership or not. The real question is whether the mayor's leadership is part of a substantial civic coalition. If it is not, there are dangers that the mayor may be more interested in the school system as a source of patronage or a useful screen upon which to project an image of activism. Even if a mayor is sincerely committed to investment and improvement in city schools, translating good intentions into stable initiatives will be problematic without a civic base. Hence, mayoral leadership is not a quick managerial fix, nor is it necessarily a means to impose accountability. The mayor's potential contribution depends on the larger picture. Indeed, in settings like Washington, D.C., where the local community history invests institutions with added meaning and potent symbolism, it is easy to imagine a campaign to restructure local governance wrenching the very social fabric upon which rests the long-term prospects for reform.

The Limits of Extraordinary Interventions

We find reasons, also, to resist the notion that long-lasting reforms can be forcefully injected into local communities by powerful outside actors like state legislatures, federal courts, or Congress. The impetus to turn authoritative external intervention is an understandable outgrowth of frustration with local bureaucracy and its seeming insistence on meeting demands for change with incrementalism and symbolic posturing. Although much in vogue, both the historical record and our own research suggest that such initiatives have a spotty track record.

First, many external interventions fail to generate results that are as speedy and substantial as the rhetoric with which they were announced led the public to anticipate. *Brown v. Board of Education* was arguably the single most dramatic example of federal judicial intervention in local school affairs, but for nearly ten years after the decision virtually no integration took place in the eleven southern states that were the primary target.[48] The New Jersey Supreme Court issued its *Robinson v. Cahill* decision calling for greater fiscal equity in 1973; more than twenty years later the state is still struggling to deal with a system in which spending per pupil across the state's districts ranges from $5,000 to $16,000.[49] Five years after the inauguration of the nation's first publicly funded program to send children to private schools, analyses of test scores leave it debatable whether there has been any impact at all on student achievement.[50]

Second, even among those that are implemented aggressively, initially celebrated, and for which early results are encouraging, some external interventions tend to lose steam or to stimulate a reconsideration or backlash that leads to their unraveling. For example, Prince George's County, Maryland, was frequently cited as a national innovator in the use of magnet schools as a tool for integration and educational improvement; Prince George's County initiated the magnet program in 1985 as part of a court-ordered settlement of a lawsuit originally filed by the NAACP. In January 1988, President Reagan declared them "one of the great success stories of the educational reform movement."[51] Two years after that, the *Washington Post* editorialized: "Test scores are up. The specialized magnet programs are of generally high quality, and their presence has sparked a new influx of interest and investment in the schools."[52] But by 1991, the superintendent who had been celebrated for fashioning the magnets had left, dissatisfied with the support he was receiving. By 1993, a prestigious panel appointed to review the system declared, "Our schools are failing, our children are falling behind. . . , " and, by the following year, the *Post* observed that the "business community in the county, which only a few years ago was so enamored of the county schools that it paid for an advertising campaign on their behalf, is now openly critical of the school system's leadership."[53] In 1996, the local school board pulled the plug on some key aspects of the program, voting to soften some of the regulations intended to ensure that magnets desegregate, in spite of some concerns that this risked losing state financial support and could eventually lead to the program's total demise.[54]

Others have noted such limitations on the courts as effective instigators of social change.[55] Kirp, looking specifically at the role of courts in dealing with school desegregation, notes that courts "necessarily depend on the collaboration—or at least the acquiescence—of a great many people inside and outside the school system if a remedy is to work."[56]

Although the challenge can be especially great for the courts—because they lack formal powers to directly implement policy and because, as the least political among the branches of government, they often lack the tactical savvy and experience to mobilize their own constituencies—some of the same constraints apply when reforms are externally imposed by legislators or executive agencies at the state or national levels. New Jersey's late-1980s' implementation of laws permitting state takeover of failing local districts was roundly applauded and, in the subsequent years, a number of states have passed similar legislation. These vary in specifics, including whether whole districts are targeted (as in New Jersey) or only individual schools (as, for example, in Maryland), whether the trig-ger for state involvement is explicit and automatic (for example, triggered by low performance on standardized tests), and the extent to which the state offers vari-ous carrots and rewards in addition to the threatened stick of intervention. Yet, in the spring of 1995, about six years after its takeover in Jersey City and four years after its takeover of the Paterson schools, New Jersey's commissioner of educa-tion told a state senate committee that the improvement in test scores in Jersey City and Paterson "is not as high as we hoped."[57] In June 1999, the state announced plans to return Jersey City to local control. In doing so, state officials declared victory, claiming that there had been improvements in many areas. But other observers suggested that test score improvements were only marginal and came at a high financial and political cost.[58] Reflecting on the original motivation for the Jersey City takeover, the commissioner of education observed: "There was a vague assumption on our part that if we fixed the central office, and replaced the people who were there with good people, those good people would solve the prob-lems of urban education." By the spring of 1999 he had concluded, "It turns out to be not that simple."[59]

When, on June 8, 1989, the Kentucky Supreme Court declared that the exist-ing system failed to meet constitutional standards and would have to be funda-mentally redesigned, the state superintendent celebrated: "Today the court has propelled us from the 19th century to the 21st," he said.[60] Former assistant secre-tary of education Chester Finn declared that, on paper, the state plan designed in response to the judicial mandate "represents the greatest advance toward a public education system designed around student outcomes and institutional accountabil-ity that I've seen on American shores."[61] But more than five years later, the effort is beset by political and implementation problems that may or may not prove crip-pling in the long run. According to one Kentucky official, "the question is, are we going to throw this out and start something else, or are we going to maintain this? And it's a real touch and go issue."[62]

Finally, as we have found in the Civic Capacity and Urban Education Project, there is some evidence that external interventions, under some circumstances, can erode indigenous forces for systemic reform by encouraging a collective tendency to pass the buck to the more powerful external actors, as well as by providing local defenders of the status quo with a convenient foil for rallying resistance to reform initiatives. The Kentucky experience suggests the importance of continuing mo-bilization and for mobilization at the local as well as the state level.

Final Observations: On Incrementalism, Focus, and the "Big Picture"

Much of the rhetoric of school reform has emphasized "crisis" and the need for immediate and radical institutional reform.[63] Probably the most famous statement is that contained in *A Nation at Risk;* "the educational foundations of our society are presently being eroded by a rising tide of mediocrity," the National Commission on Excellence in Education declared in that 1983 report. "To those who want to see real improvement in American education," then-president George Bush declared in April 1991, "I say: There will be no renaissance without revolution." Even more recently, New York City mayor Rudolph Giuliani touched off a war of words with that city's school superintendent when he pronounced that the entire public school system should be scrapped and rebuilt from scratch.[64]

Compared with such dramatic proposals, our recommendations may seem mild and incremental, and too "soft" when compared to the specific and guaranteed solutions of many policy entrepreneurs. Maybe so, but our comprehensive studies have raised serious doubts about institutional quick fixes. Without a process of coalition building that requires attention and nurturing over an extended time, serious reform efforts tend to fail. Civic capacity ultimately rests on the relationships among groups, and these, in turn, rest on shared understandings, feelings of trust and mutuality, and a pragmatic orientation toward give and take. We have found that working coalitions do not flow automatically from a convergence of contemporary interests; they are often dependent on a set of groups having a previous history of working together successfully. Civic capacity also is easier to nurture when governmental institutions are responsive and effective. When communities lack such relationships and institutions, even the greatest of policy notions is likely to fizzle. Building such relationships and institutions, where the foundation does not already exist, cannot be done overnight. Finally, and critically, civic capacity appears to be related to a particular way of looking at the problem environment—one that recognizes multiple and complex causes and yet zeroes in on a smaller and more immediately feasible set of policy options.

The "quick-fix" mentality of many educational privatizers relies on idealized conceptions of markets rather than serious study of real firms in real markets. The prospects for serious public sector reform in education cannot be compared to some idealized notions of how economies work. Economies, just like political systems, are made up of organizations, and those organizations differ enormously in their capacities for change. Educational reform is more like changing Boeing or General Electric than changing today's new biotechnology firm. Economies are dynamic and nimble because they encourage the creation of new firms to take advantage of new opportunities, not because older, settled businesses are particularly daring or nimble. For settled businesses, the short-term environment is not that threatening, and, just like governments, they tend to do things based on standard operating procedures and past successes. As a consequence, they face many of the same problems in reform that city school bureaucracies do.

One could learn much more about how to change vast educational bureaucracies by studying Boeing or General Electric than by relying on loose analogies drawn from economic theory. Indeed, CEO John Welch and the management of GE emphasize the "social architecture" and "cultural transformation" of the company, writing that the objective is to "involve everyone in the game; to leave no one—and no good idea—out."[65] The terms of GE's business are not the traditional economic terms of command, control, and incentive, but "boundarylessness," "informal, intense reviews," and unimpeded learning and problem solving. There is little doubt that Welch's words are not window dressing, but that they are the key philosophical underpinning of managing a huge and diverse company.

In a way, then, the approach we propose does indeed reflect the best of the private sector. Indeed, it is doubtless the case that many large companies could benefit from an understanding of the politics of civic capacity in America's large cities.

It is indeed important to align incentives for participants—teachers, principals, and school administrators—with desired performance. But that is not enough. People are not just selfish maximizers following the dictates of incentive. They are—or at least can be—collectively oriented problem solvers. Although people bring ideas to the table that are colored by self-interest, they can nevertheless learn about the perspectives of others and often can agree on the nature of collective problems. But they can do so only in the proper forum.

We believe that the conditions for children and youth in American inner cities are unforgivable, and the imperative for public action is powerful. We believe, too, that a fully effective response to the educational needs of urban youth will require addressing the broad institutional parameters that reinforce socioeconomic inequalities and that entice those inequalities into a spatial pattern that leaves central cities sorely disadvantaged. But the fact that there are broad and important injustices ought not become an indirect excuse for failure to make real gains that are within our reach. In an era of limited government, it might well be that those who will be successful (in the sense of getting something done) will be those who focus on the doable.

A heroic demand that the community solve broader problems before it tackles smaller ones is not the answer. Educators who do nothing more than complain about insufficient resources or the fact that children enter their schools already severely disadvantaged may be speaking truths. But they are losing potential allies, who read this as a recipe for futility or a direct assault on their pocketbooks. That leaves open the question of whether leaders who take this charge seriously thereby consign themselves to small-potatoes projects. We think not. Rather, this can be seen as an additional argument for educators to seek out coalitional partners. If they *do* hope to have real success (to improve prospects for children and not simply to achieve community mobilization), they will need to alter the broader political environment, but that is something they certainly cannot do alone.

Successful action calls for a marathon, not a sprint. Marathoners engage in careful preparation and lengthy training before moving to the starting line. Marathoners set an ambitious goal, but break down the overall course into many shorter segments and discipline themselves to maintain a sustainable pace. Similarly, to prepare for a radical improvement in social investment in our youth, we can settle in for the long run without shaving down our goals; we can accept small advances without limiting ourselves to baby steps.

Notes

INTRODUCTION

1. The term is from Jeffrey L. Pressman and Aaron B. Wildavsky, *Implementation* (Berkeley, Calif.: University of California Press, 1973). In our view, their portrayal of institutional inertia in the implementation process is overly pessimistic, in large measure because they fail to consider fully the role that political entrepreneurs can play in building momentum for change.

2. James S. Coleman, *Foundations of Social Theory* (Cambridge, Mass.: Harvard University Press, 1990): 304.

3. Robert D. Putnam, "Bowling Alone: America's Declining Social Capital," *Journal of Democracy* 6:1 (January 1995): 65–78.

4. Clarence N. Stone, "Civic Capacity and Urban School Reform," in *Changing Urban Education,* ed. Clarence N. Stone (Lawrence, Kans.: University Press of Kansas, 1998): 250–76.

5. Norton E. Long, "The Local Community as an Ecology of Games," *American Journal of Sociology* 64 (November 1958): 251–61.

6. Frank R. Baumgartner and Bryan D. Jones, *Agendas and Instability in American Politics* (Chicago: University of Chicago Press, 1993).

7. Ibid.

8. Wilbur C. Rich, *Black Mayors and School Politics* (New York: Garland, 1996).

9. Norton Long, "Aristotle and the Study of Local Politics," *Social Research* 24 (1957): 287–310.

CHAPTER 1. THE SCOPE OF THE PROBLEM

1. There have been numerous articles, books, and reports declaring that American education is in crisis. Most famous and influential among these was *A Nation at Risk,* the report by the National Commission on Excellence in Education (Washington, D.C.: U.S.

Government Printing Office, 1983), which vividly charged that "the educational foundations of our society are presently being eroded by a rising tide of mediocrity that threatens our very survival as a Nation and a people." For reviews of that literature and an argument that some of this concern has been overstated for political purposes, see Jeffrey R. Henig, *Rethinking School Choice: Limits of the Market Metaphor* (Princeton, N.J.: Princeton University Press, 1994): chap. 2; David C. Berliner and Bruce J. Biddle, *The Manufactured Crisis: Myths, Fraud, and the Attack on America's Public Schools* (Reading, Mass.: Addison-Wesley, 1995); Richard Rothstein, *The Way We Were? The Myths and Realities of America's Student Achievement* (New York: Century Foundation Press, 1998). Whether the broader system has failed as dramatically as the dominant rhetoric suggests, there is no question that the plight of many large, central-city school systems is severe.

2. Lynn Olson and Craig Jerald, *Quality Counts '98: The Urban Challenge,* an *Education Week* and Pew Charitable Trusts report (January 8, 1998): 9, 12.

3. John Kasarda, "Urban Industrial Transitions," *Annals* (January 1989).

4. E.g., Maryann Haggerty, "Momentum Is Building in Downtown Revival," *Washington Post* (November 22, 1998): A-1; "Phoenix Rising: Baseball Brings Downtown Revival," *Arizona Republic* (March 26, 1998): 4; editorial desk, "Transformation in the Bronx," *New York Times* (December 12, 1997): A-34; "Downtown Is Making a Comeback," commentary column, *St. Louis Post-Dispatch* (July 12, 1998): B-3; Patricia Johnson, "Art's New Horizon: Galleries Add Richness to Downtown Revitalization," *Houston Chronicle* (February 14, 1999): 8.

5. Chester Finn, *We Must Take Charge* (New York: Free Press, 1991): 111. Finn attributes this complacency to a combination of feel-good rationalization and misleading information disseminated by the education community.

6. Frederick M. Hess, *Spinning Wheels: The Politics of Urban School Reform* (Washington, D.C.: Brookings, 1999): 5.

7. Steve Farkas, *Educational Reform: The Players and the Politics* (New York: Public Agenda Foundation for the Charles F. Kettering Foundation, 1992): 4.

8. Robert Holmes, *The Status of Black Atlanta* (Atlanta: Southern Center for Studies in Public Policy, 1993).

9. Douglas Brinkley, *The Unfinished Presidency* (New York: Viking, 1998).

10. On the Atlanta Compromise and its impact see Barbara L. Jackson, "Desegregation: Atlanta Style," *Theory into Practice* 17:1 (1978): 43–53; Clarence N. Stone, *Regime Politics* (Lawrence, Kans.: University Press of Kansas, 1989).

11. Anthony S. Bryk, Penny Bender Sebring, David Kerbrow, Sharon Rollow, and John Q. Easton, *Charting Chicago School Reform: Democratic Localism as a Lever for Change* (Boulder, Colo.: Westview, 1998).

12. Maribeth Vander Weele, *Reclaiming Our Schools: The Struggle for School Reform* (Chicago: Loyola University Press, 1994): 3.

13. Dorothy Shipps, "Corporate Influence on Chicago School Reform," in *Changing Urban Education,* ed. Clarence N. Stone (Lawrence, Kans.: University Press of Kansas, 1998).

14. Bryk et al., *Charting Chicago School Reform,* 19.

15. Significantly, however, the creation of the local school councils had the unintended effect of focusing attention on individual neighborhood schools to the detri-

ment of citizen concerns about citywide education policies and issues—Shipps, 1998, 179.

16. M. Susana Navarro and Diana S. Natalicio, "Closing the Achievement Gap in El Paso," *Phi Delta Kappan* 80 (April 1999): 597–601. See also El Paso Collaborative for Academic Excellence, *El Paso Education Summit Briefing Book,* February 18–19, 2000.

17. Ibid., 599.

18. The Education Trust, *Good Teaching Matters* (summer 1998): 4.

19. El Paso Summit Briefing Book.

20. On the importance of external organizations as sources of ideas and support for local staff people, see Lisbeth Shorr, *Common Purpose* (New York: Anchor Books, 1997).

21. V. O. Key and Frank Munger, "Social Determinism and Electoral Decisions," in *American Voting Behavior,* ed. Eugene Burdick and Arthur J. Brodbeck (Glencoe, Ill.: Free Press, 1959): 299.

22. Dennis Shirley, *Community Organizing for Urban School Reform* (Austin, Tex.: University of Texas Press, 1997). See also Morris Janowitz, *On Social Organization and Social Control,* ed. James Burk (Chicago: University of Chicago Press, 1991), on the difference between the "specialization model" and the "aggregation model."

23. Marilyn J. Gittell, ed., *Strategies for School Equity: Creating Productive Schools in a Just Society* (New Haven, Conn.: Yale University Press, 1998).

24. Gary Burtless, ed., *Does Money Matter?* (Washington, D.C.: Brookings, 1996).

25. Christopher Jencks and Meredith Phillips, eds., *The Black-White Test Score Gap* (Washington, D.C.: Brookings, 1998).

26. Frank R. Baumgartner and Bryan D. Jones, *Agendas and Instability in American Politics* (Chicago: University of Chicago Press, 1993); Mark Moore, "What Sort of Ideas Become Public Ideas," in *The Power of Public Ideas,* ed. Robert B. Reich (Cambridge, Mass.: Harvard University Press, 1988).

27. Cheryl L. Jones and Connie Hill, "Strategy and Tactics in Subsystem Protection: The Politics of Education Reform in Montgomery County, Maryland," in *Changing Urban Education,* ed. Clarence N. Stone (Lawrence, Kans.: University Press of Kansas, 1998): 139–57.

28. Robert L. Lineberry, "Reformism and Public Policies in American Cities," *American Political Science Review* 61 (September 1967): 707.

29. Susan Clarke and Gary Gaile, *The Work of Cities* (Minneapolis: University of Minnesota Press, 1998), is a worthy exception. Although less attentive than Clarke and Gaile to the broader global context, meriting attention here, too, are a small cluster of urbanists who studied school politics while it was not especially fashionable to do so, including but not limited to: Marilyn Gittell, Jennifer Hochschild, Gary Orfield, Wilbur Rich, Frederick Wirt, and Ken Wong.

30. National Commission on Excellence in Education, *A Nation at Risk.*

31. Tim L. Mazzoni, "State Policymaking and School Reform," in *The Study of Educational Politics,* ed. Jay D. Scribner and Donald H. Layton (Washington, D.C.: Falmer Press, 1995).

32. Local institutional structure includes whether the school board is elected or appointed, and, if the former, whether by ward or at-large. Such structural parameters *can* be significant, and indeed we give them serious consideration in this study. But

disconnected from less formal political factors they provide a one-dimensional picture at best.

33. The team leaders were: Atlanta: John Hutcheson (Georgia State University), Carol Pierannunzi (Kennesaw State College), and Desiree Pedescleaux (Spelman College); Baltimore: Marion Orr (Brown University); Boston: John Portz (Northeastern University); Denver: Susan Clarke, Rodney Hero, and Mara Sidney (University of Colorado); Detroit: Richard Hula (Michigan State University); Houston: Thomas Longoria (University of Texas at El Paso); Los Angeles: Fernando Guerra (Loyola Marymount University); Pittsburgh: Robin Jones (University of Pittsburgh); St. Louis: Lana Stein (University of Missouri– St. Louis); San Francisco: Luis Fraga (Stanford University) and Bari Anhalt Erlichson (Rutgers); Washington, D.C.: Jeffrey Henig (George Washington University).

34. Researchers were instructed to attempt interviews with the following individuals or their representatives: the mayor; two city council members (if mixed at-large/district one from each category); city manager or chief administrative officer; two school board members; president or executive director of the chamber of commerce or other major business organization; CEO or personnel director of large private employers or officer of a local bank or utility; minority business executive; Private Industry Council (PIC) chair; head of education committee of chamber of commerce or counterpart in another business organization; member of city future commission or strategic planning body; head of teachers' union/organization; executive director of United Way; board chair of Black United Fund or other minority charity; board chair or executive director of local foundation; editor/publisher of local newspaper or reporter who covers city hall or education; state legislator from city, preferably on education committee; judge or attorney on desegregation case/issue. Here, as elsewhere, each research team was given considerable discretion in adapting its research quota to the idiosyncrasies of its city.

35. Researchers were instructed to attempt interviews with the following individuals or their representatives: head of community-based organization with some concern in area of education and children's issues, preferably from an umbrella organization; two influential religious leaders, at least one of whom should be from a coalition or alliance of religious groups; systemwide PTA officer; head of another parent advocacy group or, if there is no such group, a second PTA officer; education committee chair or other specialist from a good government group (such as the League of Women Voters); three minority organization representatives, spread as appropriate to the city's demographic base, and should include at least one nonmainline organization; two heads of children's advocacy organization or day care advocacy groups.

36. Researchers were instructed to attempt interviews with the following individuals or their representatives: the superintendent; two assistant school superintendents or equivalents; Headstart administrator; Chapter One administrator; police department official with responsibility to address school violence; social services individual who liaisons with schools (e.g., JOBS or preschool); two principals in innovative school or heads of innovative education programs; economic development administrator with education portfolio; school board staff member, preferably someone with institutional memory; education compact administrator or counterpart for school/business partnerships; PIC staff member with education responsibilities; United Way or similar staff member (with preschool or youth development responsibilities); lobbyist for school district in city hall or state capitol.

37. As noted earlier, the interview schedules used for the three types of respondents differed in some respects. Overlap of questions was greatest for the general influentials and community advocates. Interviews with program specialists were intended to get detailed information on decision making and policies *within* the education community; the interview schedule employed for the specialists, as a result, did not include as many questions about the broader political and policy environment. Most of the quantitative analyses of survey results presented in this book draw from responses to questions that overlapped in the general influential and community advocate interviews, but not all the questions were asked of program specialists. This is the major explanation for the different number of responses from question to question. In addition, although interviewers tried to make certain that they covered the core material in each interview, the need to follow lines of inquiry and the fact that they were dealing with strong-minded individuals who often had their own sense of what needed to be said inevitably resulted in some questions not being asked of some respondents.

38. Whitney Grace and Heather Strickland carried out the coding, under the supervision of Bryan Jones. A handful of respondents requested that the interviews not be taped. In those cases, interviewers took as detailed a set of notes as possible, and coding was carried out using those notes.

39. Paul T. Hill, Christine Campbell, and James Harvey, *It Takes a City: Getting Serious about Urban School Reform* (Washington, D.C.: Brookings, 2000): ix.

40. Ibid., 107.

41. Baumgartner and Jones, *Agendas.*

42. Hannah Arendt, *Between Past and Future* (New York: Penguin Books, 1968).

43. Robert D. Putnam, *Making Democracy Work* (Princeton, N.J.: Princeton University Press, 1993).

44. Bryk et al., *Charting Chicago School Reform;* Susan H. Fuhrman, ed., *Designing Coherent Education Policy* (San Francisco, Calif.: Jossey-Bass, 1993); and Marshall S. Smith and Jennifer A. O'Day, "Systemic School Reform," in *The Politics of Curriculum and Testing,* ed. S. Fuhman and B. Malen (Bristol, Pa.: Falmer Press, 1991).

45. Compare with Bryk et al., *Charting Chicago School Reform.* See also Paul Hill and others, *Educational Progress* (Santa Monica, Calif.: Rand Corporation, 1989).

46. Gary Orfield and Susan E. Eaton, *Dismantling Desegregation: The Quiet Reversal of Brown vs. Board of Education* (New York: New Press, 1996).

47. James P. Comer, *Waiting for a Miracle: Why Schools Can't Solve Our Problems—And How We Can* (New York: Plume, 1997).

48. Joan Walsh, *The Eye of the Storm* (Baltimore, Md.: Annie E. Casey Foundation, 1998).

49. Ibid., 31. See also Bryk et al., *Charting Chicago School Reform.*

50. Daniel Bell, *The End of Ideology* (New York: Collier Books, 1961).

51. Ibid., 346–47; Robert Darnton, "What Was Revolutionary about the French Revolution?" *NY Review of Books,* January 19, 1989, 3 ff.

52. Philip Abrams, *Historical Sociology* (Ithaca, N.Y.: Cornell University Press, 1982); and William J. Sewell Jr., "A Theory of Structure," *American Journal of Sociology* 98:1 (July 1992): 1–29.

53. Barrington Moore Jr., *Injustice: The Social Bases of Obedience and Revolt* (White Plains, N.Y.: M. E. Sharpe, 1978): 376–81.

CHAPTER 2. THE CHALLENGE OF CHANGE
IN COMPLEX POLICY SUBSYSTEMS

1. The seeming consensus masked considerable disagreement that bubbled beneath the surface. For one view of the political nature of this disagreement and how the conflict was kept latent, see Ira Katznelson and Margaret Weir, *Schooling for All: Class, Race, and the Decline of the Democratic Ideal* (New York: Basic Books, 1985).

2. Edward C. Banfield, *The Unheavenly City Revisited* (Boston: Little, Brown, 1970).

3. Clarence N. Stone, "Systemic Power in Community Decision-Making," *American Political Science Review* 74 (December 1980).

4. Compare with Clarke and Gaile, *Work of Cities.*

5. Robert A. Caro, *The Power Broker: Robert Moses and the Fall of New York* (New York: Alfred A. Knopf, 1974): 713.

6. Paul E. Peterson, in *City Limits* (Chicago: University of Chicago Press, 1981), notes the somewhat ambiguous status of education in terms of his threefold typology (developmental, redistributive, allocative).

7. Thomas J. Anton and Alison R. Flaum, "Theory into Practice: The Rise of New Anti-Poverty Strategies in American Cities," *Urban News* 5 (winter 1992): 1 ff; Joan Walsh, *Stories of Renewal* (New York: Rockefeller Foundation, 1997); and Clarence N. Stone, "Poverty and the Continuing Campaign for Urban Social Reform," *Urban Affairs Review* 34:6 (July 1999): 843–56.

8. Benjamin Barber, *Strong Democracy* (Berkeley, Calif.: University of California Press, 1984).

9. Jane J. Mansbridge, *Beyond Adversary Democracy* (New York: Basic Books, 1980); Peter Marris and Martin Rein, *Dilemmas of Social Reform; Poverty and Community Action in the United States* (Chicago: Aldine, 1973).

10. Compare with Dennis Chong, *Collective Action and the Civil Rights Movement* (Chicago: University of Chicago Press, 1991).

11. Charles E. Bidwell, "Toward Improved Knowledge and Policy on Urban Education," *Politics of Education Association Yearbook* (1991): 193–99.

12. Kenneth K. Wong, "The Politics of Urban Education as a Field of Study," *Politics of Education Yearbook* (1991): 3–26.

13. Edward Pauley, *The Classroom Crucible* (New York: Basic Books, 1991).

14. Betty Malen, "The Micropolitics of Education," in *The Study of Educational Politics,* ed. Jay D. Scribner and Donald H. Layton (Washington, D.C.: Falmer Press, 1995).

15. Bryk et al., *Charting Chicago School Reform,* 10.

16. Paul Peterson, *School Politics, Chicago Style* (Chicago: University of Chicago Press, 1976); and Wong, "The Politics of Urban Education as a Field of Study."

17. David Cohen, "What Is the Systemic in Systemic Reform?" *Educational Researcher* 24:9 (December 1995).

18. James G. Cibulka and Frederick I. Olson, "The Organization and Politics of the Milwaukee Public School System, 1920–1986," in *Seeds of Crisis,* ed. John L. Rury and Frank A. Cassell (Madison, Wis.: University of Wisconsin Press, 1993): 73–109.

19. U.S. Department of Education, National Center for Education Statistics, Statistics of State School Systems; Revenues and Expenditures for Public Elementary and Secondary Education; and Common Core of Data surveys.

20. Margaret Weir, "Central Cities' Loss of Power in State Politics," *Cityscape* 2:2 (May 1996): 23–40.

21. Jeffrey Henig, Richard Hula, Marion Orr, and Desiree Pedescleaux, *The Color of School Reform: Race, Politics, and the Challenge of Urban Education* (Princeton, N.J.: Princeton University Press, 1999): chap. 6.

22. See especially the political history of the Detroit schools by Jeffrey Mirel, *The Rise and Fall of an Urban School System* (Ann Arbor, Mich.: University of Michigan Press, 1993). Also see Rury and Cassells, eds., *Seeds of Crisis.* On revenue producers versus service users, see Wallace S. Sayre and Herbert Kaufman, *Governing New York City* (New York: W. W. Norton, 1965).

23. Bidwell, "Toward Improved Knowledge and Policy on Urban Education."

24. On Chicago, see Vander Weele, *Reclaiming Our Schools;* on Washington, D.C., see Sari Horwitz and Valerie Strauss, "A Well-Financed Failure," *Washington Post,* February 16, 1997.

25. Guilbert C. Hentschke, "Radical Reform Versus Professional Reform in American Schools," in *Rethinking Los Angeles,* ed. Michael J. Dear, H. Eric Schokman, and Greg Hise (Thousand Oaks, Calif.: Sage, 1996).

26. Margaret Weir, "Central Cities' Loss of Power in State Politics," 23–40; Marion Orr, Clarence Stone, and Circe Stumbo, "Five Princes and a Pauper," paper given at the Annual Meeting of the Urban Affairs Association, April 15–17, 1999, Louisville, Kentucky.

27. Hentschke, "Radical Reform Versus Professional Reform in American Schools."

28. Gary Orfield, "Metropolitan School Desegregation," *Minnesota Law Review* 80 (April 1996): 825–73.

29. U.S. Department of Education, National Center for Education Statistics, *The Condition of Education 1998,* Supplemental Table 43-3.

30. Ibid.

31. Jeannie Oakes, *Keeping Track* (New Haven, Conn.: Yale University Press, 1985). But see Tom Loveless, *The Tracking Wars: State Reform Meets School Policy* (Washington, D.C.: Brookings, 1999), for a contrasting perspective.

32. The United States separates students into tracks earlier and more heavily than many other advanced industrial societies. Gerald Grant and Christine E. Murray, *Teaching in America* (Cambridge, Mass.: Harvard University Press, 1999): 26.

33. But see Katznelson and Weir, *Schooling for All.*

34. Wong, "The Politics of Urban Education as a Field of Study."

35. The Institute for Educational Leadership, *School Boards* (Washington, D.C.: Institute for Educational Leadership, November 1986); Jacqueline P. Danzberger, Michael W. Kirst, and Michael D. Usdan, *Governing Public Schools* (Washington, D.C.: Institute for Educational Leadership, 1992); and the Report of the Twentieth Century Fund Task Force on School Governance, *Facing the Challenge* (New York: Twentieth Century Fund Press, 1992).

36. David S. Seeley, *Education through Partnership* (Washington, D.C.: American Enterprise Institute for Public Policy Research, 1985).

37. Joyce L. Epstein, "Parents' Reactions to Teacher Practices of Parent Involvement," *Elementary School Journal* 86 (January 1986): 277–94. And Epstein and Susan L. Dauber,

"School Programs and Teacher Practices of Parent Involvement in Inner-City Elementary and Middle Schools," *Elementary School Journal* 91 (January 1991): 289–305.

38. Bernard Crick, *In Defense of Politics*, 2d ed. (New York: Penguin Books, 1964): 25.

39. Seymour Sarason, *School Change* (New York: Teachers College Press, 1995): 84.

40. For an insightful analysis of the politics of parent engagement, see Shirley, *Community Organizing*. For contrasting city approaches, see Marilyn Gittell, "School Reform in New York and Chicago," *Urban Affairs Quarterly* 30:1 (September 1994): 136–51.

41. Michelle Fine, *Framing Dropouts* (Albany, N.Y.: State University of New York Press, 1991).

42. See, for example, Cibulka and Olson, "Milwaukee Public School System," 73–109.

43. Paul T. Hill, "Urban Education," in *Urban America*, ed. James B. Steinberg, David W. Lyon, and Mary E. Vaiana (Santa Monica, Calif.: Rand, 1992): 138–39.

44. Susan J. Rosenholtz, *Teachers' Workplace* (White Plains, N.Y.: Longman, 1989).

45. John Goodlad, *A Place Called School* (New York: McGraw-Hill, 1983): 354.

46. Gerald Grant, *The World We Created at Hamilton High* (Cambridge, Mass.: Harvard University Press, 1988): 226.

47. Maryland State Department of Education, *The Fact Book* (Baltimore, Md.: Maryland State Department of Education, 1994).

48. Goodlad, *A Place Called School*, 296. See also Allan Odden, "Incentives, School Organization and Teacher Compensation," in *Rewards and Reform*, ed. Susan H. Fuhrman and Jennifer A. O'Day (San Francisco, Calif.: Jossey-Bass, 1996): 226–56.

49. Bryk et al., *Charting Chicago School Reform*, 10.

50. Of special interest are the changes taking place in Chicago and the efforts there to establish greater mayoral control over school administration; see Kenneth K. Wong and others, *Integrated Governance as a Reform Strategy in the Chicago Public Schools* (Chicago: Department of Education and Irving B. Harris Graduate School of Public Policy Studies, University of Chicago Press, January 1997); Michael Kirst and Katrina Bulkley, "'New, Improved' Mayors Take Over City Schools," *Phi Delta Kappan* (March 2000).

51. Susan H. Fuhrman, ed., *Designing Coherent Education Policy* (San Francisco, Calif.: Jossey-Bass, 1993).

52. Quoted in Shirley, *Community Organizing*, 228.

53. Willard Waller, *The Sociology of Teaching* (New York: John Wiley and Sons, 1932). See also Stephen D. Brookfield, *The Skillful Teacher* (San Francisco, Calif.: Jossey-Bass, 1990); and Philip Jackson, *Life in Classrooms* (New York: Teachers College Press, 1990).

54. Charles E. Bidwell, "The School as a Formal Organization," in *The Handbook of Organizations*, ed. James G. March (Skokie, Ill.: Rand McNally, 1965).

55. Richard F. Elmore, Penelope L. Peterson, and Sarah J. McCarthey, *Restructuring the Classroom* (San Francisco, Calif.: Jossey-Bass, 1996).

56. Steve Farkas, Jean Johnson, and Tony Foleno, *A Sense of Calling: Who Teaches and Why* (New York: Public Agenda Foundation, 2000).

57. Betty Malen, Michael J. Murphy, and Ann Weaver Hart, "Restructuring Teacher Compensation Systems," in *Attracting and Compensating America's Teachers*, ed. Kern Alexander and David Monk (Cambridge, Mass.: Ballinger, 1987): 91–141.

58. Milbrey Wallin McLaughlin and David D. Marsh, "Staff Development and School Change," in *Schools as Collaborative Cultures,* ed. Ann Lieberman (New York: Falmer Press, 1990); Goodlad, *A Place Called School.*

59. Malen, Murphy, and Hart, "Restructuring Teacher Compensation Systems."

60. Elmore, Peterson, and McCarthey, *Restructuring the Classroom.* See also Laraine K. Hong, *Surviving School Reform* (New York: Teachers College Press, 1996).

61. Bryk et al., *Charting Chicago School Reform,* 7.

62. Goodlad, *A Place Called School;* Powell, Farrar, and Cohen, *The Shopping Mall High School;* Paul Haubrich, "Student Life in Milwaukee High Schools, 1920–1985," in *Seeds of Crisis;* and Laurence Steinberg, *Beyond the Classroom* (New York: Simon and Schuster, 1996).

63. There is a large literature on this topic. See, for example, R. Patrick Solomon, *Black Resistance in High School* (Albany, N.Y.: State University of New York Press, 1992).

64. Goodlad, *A Place Called School,* 78.

65. Jean Johnson and Steve Farkas with Ali Bers, *Getting By* (New York: Public Agenda, 1997).

66. Quoted in ibid., 13.

67. Mirel, *Rise and Fall;* Rury and Cassell, eds. *Seeds of Crisis,* 17.

68. William J. Wilson, *When Work Disappears* (New York: Alfred A. Knopf, 1996).

69. Some observers go beyond the changing job market and changing demography to talk about broad cultural changes that have also affected student motivation. See Goodlad, *A Place Called School;* Haubrich, "Student Life in Milwaukee High Schools, 1920–1985."

70. Mirel, *Rise and Fall.*

71. Powell, Farrar, and Cohen, *Shopping Mall High School.*

72. Official figures on dropout rates are notoriously unreliable and are measured in various ways. Using high school completion by age nineteen as a measure, the rate is about 50 percent in most large cities. The rate of achieving high school diplomas is higher because of the number of young people who obtain GEDs outside the regular high school process. For a close examination of the dropout problem in one system, see Fine, *Framing Dropouts.*

73. Mary Haywood Metz, "How Social Class Differences Shape Teachers' Work," in *The Contexts of Teaching in Secondary Schools,* ed. Milbrey W. McLaughlin, Joan Talbert, and Nina Bascia (New York: Teachers College Press, 1990).

74. Bryk et al., *Charting Chicago School Reform,* 5.

75. Wilbur Rich, *Black Mayors and School Politics* (New York: Garland, 1996).

76. Jean Anyon, "Race, Social Class, and Educational Reform in an Inner-City School," *Teachers College Record* 97 (fall 1995): 69–94.

77. Hentschke, "Radical Reform Versus Professional Reform."

78. David Cohen, "What Is the System in Systemic Reform?" 9. Note, however, that school officials may be drawn toward special responsiveness to middle-class rather than lower-SES students. The small number of middle-class students represents a potential "exit" threat, hence systems have a strong incentive to be attentive to this less needy group. Without them, the school system will likely look even weaker on various measures of performance, such as high school completion rates and scores on standardized tests.

79. Rich, *Black Mayors and School Politics,* 190.

80. Steinberg, *Beyond the Classroom.*

81. One complicating factor is that the prevailing norms among teachers (often rein-forced in union contracts) and the structure of schooling do little to overcome the isolation of individual teachers—Malen, Murphy, and Hart, "Restructuring Teacher Compensation Systems"; Rosenholtz, *Teachers' Workplace*. Another complication is that those connected to badly performing schools tend to avoid acknowledging the seriousness of the problem. See Anyon, "Race, Social Class, and Educational Reform in an Inner-City School"; Mary Haywood Metz, "Real School," in *Education Politics for the New Century*, ed. Douglas E. Mitchell and M. E. Goertz (Philadelphia: Falmer Press, 1990): 75–91; and Sarason, *School Change*, 111.

82. Bryk et al., *Charting Chicago School Reform*, 4.

83. James P. Comer, *School Power* (New York: Free Press, 1993): viii.

84. Rich, *Black Mayors and School Politics*, 213.

85. Goodlad, *A Place Called School*.

86. See Robert L. Crain, *The Politics of School Desegregation* (Garden City, N.Y.: Anchor Books, 1969).

87. Shirley, *Community Organizing*, 223.

88. Barbara L. Jackson and James G. Cibulka, "Leadership Turnover and Business Mobilization," in *The Politics of Urban Education*, ed. James G. Cibulka, Rodney J. Reed, and Kenneth K. Wong (Washington, D.C.: Falmer Press, 1992); Barbara L. Jackson, *Balancing Act* (Washington, D.C.: Joint Center for Political and Economic Studies, 1995).

89. See, for example, the series on Prince George's County, Maryland, in the *Washington Post*. Even more affluent Montgomery County has compiled less than a sterling record—see Jones and Hill, "Strategy and Tactics in Subsystem Protection."

90. Samuel Casey Carter, *No Excuses: Lessons from 21 High Performing, High-Poverty Schools* (Washington, D.C.: Heritage Foundation, 2000); but see Richard Rothstein, Martin Carnoy, and Luis Benveniste, *Can Public Schools Learn from Private Schools?* (Washington, D.C.: Economic Policy Institute, 1999).

91. Quoted in Rich, *Black Mayors and School Politics*, 209.

92. Jean Anyon, *Ghetto Schooling* (New York: Teachers College Press, 1997): 181; James Comer and others, *Rallying the Whole Village* (New York: Teachers College Press, 1996). Compare with Steve Farkas, *Divided Within, Besieged Without* (a report from the Public Agenda Foundation prepared for the Charles F. Kettering Foundation); and Rich, *Black Mayors and School Politics*, 209–13.

93. Rich, *Black Mayors and School Politics*, 210.

94. See Kathryn M. Doherty, "Changing Urban Education: Defining the Issues," in *Changing Urban Education*, ed. Clarence N. Stone (Lawrence, Kans.: University Press of Kansas, 1998).

95. Frederick M. Wirt, *Power in the City: Decision Making in San Francisco* (Berkeley, Calif.: University of California Press, 1974).

96. Karl E. Weick, "Educational Organizations as Loosely Coupled Systems," *Administrative Science Quarterly* 21 (March 1976): 1–19.

97. See, for example, Stephen J. Caldas and Carl L. Bankston, "Multilevel Examination of Student, School, and District-Level Effects on Academic Achievement," *Journal of Education Research* 93 (November/December 1999): 91–109.

98. Charles E. Lindblom, *The Intelligence of Democracy* (New York: Free Press, 1965); Theodore J. Lowi, *The End of Liberalism*, 2d ed. (New York: Norton, 1979).

99. Peter Bachrah and Morton S. Baratz, "The Two Faces of Power," *American Political Science Review* 56:4 (December 1962): 947–52.

100. Baumgartner and Jones, *Agendas and Instability in American Politics.*

101. On the particular political dynamics surrounding local culture wars, see Elaine B. Sharp, ed., *Culture Wars and Local Politics* (Lawrence, Kans.: University Press of Kansas, 1999). On value conflicts in education, see Robert T. Stout, Marilyn Tallerico, and Kent Scribner, "Values, the 'What' of the Politics of Education," in *The Study of Educational Politics,* ed. Jay D. Scribner and Donald H. Layton (Washington, D.C.: Falmer Press, 1995): 5–20.

102. Metz, "How Social Class Differences Shape Teachers' Work." See also David Tyack and Larry Cuban, *Tinkering toward Utopia: A Century of Public School Reform* (Cambridge, Mass.: Harvard University Press, 1995).

103. Morone, 1998, 275.

104. Marris and Rein, *Dilemmas of Social Reform.*

105. Walsh, *Stories of Renewal;* Bryk et al., *Charting Chicago School Reform.*

106. Tyack and Cuban, *Tinkering toward Utopia,* 3.

107. Bryk et al., *Charting Chicago School Reform,* 10.

108. Ibid.

109. Anyon, *Ghetto Schooling,* 13; see also Halpern, *Rebuilding the Inner City.*

110. Marc K. Landry, "Local Government and Environmental Policy," in *Dilemmas of Scale in American Federal Democracy,* ed. Martha Derthick (Cambridge, UK: Woodrow Wilson Center Press and Cambridge University Press, 1999): 227–60.

111. Metz, "How Social Class Differences Shape Teachers' Work," 40–107; Goodlad, *A Place Called School;* Hentschke, "Radical Reform Versus Professional Reform in American Schools"; Caldas and Bankston, "Multilevel Examination."

CHAPTER 3. THE URBAN CONTEXT: A FIRST LOOK AT THE CASE CITIES

1. The precise figures, for the 1993–1994 school year, were 14,886 districts serving 43,777,237 students. U.S. Department of Education, National Center for Education Statistics. Common Core of Data, "Public Elementary and Secondary Education Agency Universe."

2. Ibid.

3. William Ryan, *Blaming the Victim* (New York: Vintage, 1976).

4. One of the themes of this book is that school politics must be understood in the context of city politics. For that reason, we keep the focus of much of our discussion on cities rather than districts. Some of the data that we present are based on school district boundaries and some are based on cities. Unless otherwise noted, data on population characteristics are based on city boundaries, whereas data on student characteristics, school characteristics, budgets, and policies are based on district boundaries.

5. U.S. Bureau of the Census, *Statistical Abstract of the United States,* 1997, table 237.

6. For example, local contribution to public elementary and secondary education rose 52.9 percent in constant dollars between 1980 and 1994; proportionally local governments accounted for 43.3 percent of expenditures in 1980 versus 45.1 percent in 1994. Ibid.

7. Henig, Hula, Orr, and Pedescleaux, *Color of School Reform.*

8. These issues are explored in greater depth in John Portz, Lana Stein, and Robin R. Jones, *City Schools and City Politics* (Lawrence, Kans.: University Press of Kansas, 1999).

9. Susan Clarke, Rodney Hero, Mara Sidney, Bari Erickson, and Luis Fraga, *The New Educational Populism: The Multi-Ethnic Politics of School Reform* (forthcoming, Duke University Press).

10. St. Louis, for example, although categorized as a "machine-descendant" city based on its 1990 census attributes and its 1993 political configuration, looks similar to the black-led cities in several respects and has drifted closer to them subsequently.

11. This characterization is based on 1990 census data. Since then, population changes have shifted St. Louis into the majority black category.

12. The four cities in which Hispanic incomes are more than marginally greater than those of blacks—Atlanta, Baltimore, Pittsburgh, and St. Louis—are also those in which the number and proportion of Hispanics is quite low (less than 2 percent).

13. Atlanta, Detroit, Houston, Pittsburgh.

14. Albert O. Hirschman writes that "the presence of the exit alternative can . . . tend to *atrophy the development of the art of voice*" [emphasis in the original]. *Exit, Voice and Loyalty* (Cambridge, Mass.: Harvard University Press, 1970): 43. This is especially the case if those who exit tend to be those most sensitive to decline in quality and those most capable of effectively utilizing voice.

15. James S. Coleman et al., *Equality of Educational Opportunity* (Washington, D.C.: U.S. Government Printing Office, 1966); Greg J. Duncan and Jeanne Brooks-Gunn, eds., *Consequences of Growing Up Poor* (New York: Russell Sage, 1997).

16. David Rusk, *Cities without Suburbs,* 2d ed. (Washington, D.C.: Woodrow Wilson Center Press, 1995). The relationship between share of the region's poor and a variable that combines black and Hispanic population is less strong than that with percent black alone ($r = .66$; $p < .03$).

17. D.C. represents the extreme case here; Congress prohibits the district from taxing income earned by suburbanites.

18. Reliable data on school finance are remarkably elusive. Our project collected data directly from local sources as well as national databases such as the *School District Data Book* (produced by the MESA Group under contract to the National Center for Education Statistics) and the annual *Digest of Education Statistics.* As often as not, numbers from these different sources are inconsistent with one another. In this report, we generally rely on the *Digest for Education Statistics* for our expenditure and revenue data, since that provides us with comparable budget categories across places and over time. We use the 1989–1990 figures from the *School District Data Book* in some sections, like this one, where we are interested in drawing comparisons to the suburban districts.

19. This figure is based on the ten cities excluding D.C., where there is no separate state funding.

20. Coleman et al., *Equality of Educational Opportunity;* Eric A. Hanushek, "The Impact of Differential Expenditures on School Performance," *Educational Researcher* 18 (May 1989).

21. Gary Burtless, ed., *Does Money Matter?* (Washington, D.C.: Brookings, 1986); Ronald F. Ferguson and Helen F. Ladd, "How and Why Money Matters: An Analysis of

Alabama Schools," in *Holding Schools Accountable,* ed. Helen F. Ladd (Washington, D.C.: Brookings, 1996): 265–98.

22. Hirschman, *Exit, Voice and Loyalty,* 43.

23. The total loss in persons eighteen and under and total population for each of the cities were Atlanta (37.7%/19.2%), Baltimore (43.9%/21.6%), Detroit (42.5%/38.4%), and D.C. (47.9%/20.6%).

24. This is based on census figures organized by school district. Private school enrollment is proportionally highest in the machine-descendant cities, which have substantial numbers of white, ethnic families with strong attachments to the Catholic church, the dominant provider of private education.

25. Weir, "Central Cities' Loss of Power in State Politics," 23–40.

CHAPTER 4. CIVIC MOBILIZATION IN ELEVEN CITIES

1. Goodlad, *A Place Called School,* 32.

2. Compare with Joel F. Handler, *Down from Democracy* (Princeton, N.J.: Princeton University Press, 1996).

3. Council of Great City Schools, *National Urban Education Goals: 1992–3 Indicators Report* (Washington, D.C.: Council of Great City Schools, 1994).

4. In Pittsburgh the summit meeting was around the school desegregation issue, but its focus was on school improvement.

5. LEARN stands for Los Angeles Educational Alliance for Restructuring Now.

6. Pittsburgh's business-supported Education Fund parallels in some ways the Kansas City Association by working project by project to stimulate reform.

7. Marris and Rein, *Dilemmas of Social Reform,* 160–62.

8. Our thanks to Luis Fraga for stating the issue in this form.

9. The mobilization rankings were developed before the field teams compiled and analyzed the policy data.

10. Emmette Redford, *Democracy and the Administrative State* (New York: Oxford, 1969).

11. See the telling discussion of the limited impact of a key school board member in Diana Tittle, *Welcome to Heights High* (Columbus, Ohio: Ohio State University Press, 1995): 175.

12. The American political tradition reveals some ambivalence about the extent to which schools should be controlled by—or buffered from—political input. Early in the twentieth century, the Progressives' view that education ought to be protected from political meddling was quite influential. One reflection of this is the fact that many school districts have appointed rather than elected boards. Among our eleven cities—as indeed among most large, central-city school districts—elected boards are the norm, as is the expectation that school policies ought to be sensitive to the electorate's values.

13. Crain, *Politics of School Desegregation,* 378.

14. Up to five responses were coded, although most respondents mentioned three or fewer. Because our 300 respondents to this set of questions were not evenly spread over the eleven cities, we present two sets of figures: (a) the proportion of the entire respondent groups mentioning a particular group or actor; (b) the average percentage across the

eleven cities. As can be seen, the differences are minor and affect the rank ordering in two instances toward the lower end of the listing.

15. For example, Coleman et al., *Equality of Educational Opportunity;* J. Epstein, "Parent Involvement: What the Research Says to Administrators," *Education and Urban Society* 19:2 (February 1978): 119–36; S. S. Purkey and M. Smith, "Effective Schools: A Review," *Elementary School Journal* 83 (1983): 427–52.

16. Henig, Hula, Orr, and Pedescleaux, *Color of School Reform.*

17. See ibid. for a more detailed discussion.

18. San Francisco is perhaps a special case in that a progressive countermobilization has largely negated business leadership in the development arena, undoing an earlier pattern of business dominance in development policy.

19. Henig, Hula, Orr, and Pedescleaux make this argument in *Color of School Reform.*

20. Debbi Wilgoren, "School Board Could Shrink: Mayor's Plan to Appoint Members Lacks Council Support," *Washington Post,* January 5, 2000.

21. Barbara L Jackson, "Desegregation: Atlanta Style," *Theory into Practice* 17:1 (1978): 43–53; Joel L. Fleishman, "The Real Against the Ideal—Making the Solution Fit the Problem," in *Roundtable Justice,* ed. Robert B. Goldman (Boulder, Colo.: Westview Press, 1980): 129–80.

22. Stone, "Civic Capacity and Urban School Reform," 267–69.

23. Julie A. White and Gary Wehlage, "Community Collaboration," *Educational Evaluation and Policy Analysis* 17 (spring 1995): 23–38.

24. For a more detailed discussion of Pittsburgh's school politics, see Portz, Stein, and Jones, *City Schools and City Politics.* On Pittsburgh's political evolution more generally, see Barbara Ferman, *Challenging the Growth Machine: Neighborhood Politics in Chicago and Pittsburgh* (Lawrence, Kans.: University Press of Kansas, 1997).

25. Henig, Hula, Orr, and Pedescleaux, *Color of School Reform,* chaps. 2, 5.

26. Kathryn M. Doherty, Cheryl L. Jones, and Clarence N. Stone, "Building Coalitions, Building Communities" (working paper 23 for the National Center for the Revitalization of Central Cities, University of New Orleans, October 1997).

27. The classic statement is found in Thomas R. Dye, *Politics, Economics, and the Public* (Chicago: Rand McNally, 1966).

28. Something that might be expected based on the typically higher rates of political participation and economic clout of urban white households, as well as Albert Hirschman's proposition that a wide-open exit option tends to lead to a degradation of political voice (see Chapter 3).

29. For an extended discussion of the role of race in structuring civic capacity for education reform, see Henig, Hula, Orr, and Pedescleaux, *Color of School Reform.*

30. For an extended discussion of the history and politics of school reform in these cities, see Portz, Stein, and Jones, *City Schools and City Politics.*

31. Note that the dividing line between categories is not always sharp. Baltimore, for example, comes from a machine-politics background, and St. Louis has moved demographically to the black-led cities.

32. For example, Marilyn Gittell, "Education: The Decentralization-Community Control Controversy," in *Race and Politics in New York City,* ed. Jewel Bellush and Stephen M. David (New York: Praeger, 1971): 134–63.

33. Douglas Yates, *The Ungovernable City* (Cambridge, Mass.: MIT Press, 1977). Frederick Wirt similarly characterized school politics as an example of "hyperplura-

lism" in his 1974 study of San Francisco, *Power in the City: Decision Making in San Francisco.*

34. Kenneth K. Wong, "Transforming Urban School Systems" (a report prepared for the cross-Atlantic conference, "A Working Conference on School Reform in Chicago and Birmingham," University of Chicago Gleacher Center, May 11–12, 1998). Note also that Robert Crain's study of school desegregation in the 1960s found that autonomous school boards were less likely to promote peaceful desegregation than those appointed by mayors. Crain explained this pattern by observing that mayors tended to have a broader set of concerns than autonomous school boards did (Crain, *Politics of School Desegregation,* 351).

35. Dorothy Shipps, "The Invisible Hand," *Teachers College Record* 99:1 (1997): 73–116.

36. Baumgartner and Jones, *Agendas and Instability,* chap. 11.

37. Those who oppose aggressive judicial intervention argue that the courts exceed their proper role when they take it upon themselves to set policy and when they move too far from the center of the public's expressed will and values, and they further argue that such efforts usually fail. See, for example, David Armor, *Forced Justice: School Desegregation and the Law* (New York: Oxford University Press, 1995). Those who argue the contrary position hold that the courts sometimes have a legal and moral imperative to intervene, and that when they do so strongly and justly they have proven that they can reshape public attitudes and generate public support for doing the right thing. See, for example, Jennifer Hochschild, *The New American Dilemma: Liberal Democracy and School Desegregation* (New Haven, Conn.: Yale University Press, 1984), and Orfield and Eaton, *Dismantling Desegregation.*

38. Luis Fraga, Bari Erlichson, and Sandy Lee, "Consensus Building and School Reform: The Role of the Courts in San Francisco," in *Changing Urban Education,* ed. Clarence N. Stone (Lawrence, Kans.: University Press of Kansas, 1998): 66–92.

39. See Portz, Stein, and Jones, *City Schools and City Politics.*

40. Clarence N. Stone, *Regime Politics* (Lawrence, Kans.: University Press of Kansas, 1989); Portz, Stein, and Jones, *City Schools and City Politics.*

41. Compare with Peterson, *School Politics, Chicago Style.*

42. Crain, *Politics of School Desegregation,* 210–12.

43. This includes Pittsburgh, Boston, Los Angeles, Baltimore, Houston, and Detroit. There was variation, of course, in the strength and cohesion of these partnerships, but in each case they entailed a formal organizational structure with at least some staff. Fuller discussions of the Pittsburgh and Boston cases can be found in Portz et al., *City Politics and City Schools.* The Baltimore and Detroit experiences are elaborated in Henig, Hula, Orr, and Pedescleaux, Chapter 6, and an even more detailed account of the Baltimore case is available in Marion Orr, *Black Social Capital.* The story of the Greater Houston Coalition for Education Excellence is told in Thomas Longoria Jr., "School Politics in Houston: The Impact of Business Involvement," in *Changing Urban Education,* ed. C. Stone. For Los Angeles see Fernando Guerra and Mara Cohen, "Educational Restructuring in Los Angeles" (December 1994), and David Menefee-Libey, "Building a Political Explanation for School Reform: The Los Angeles Unified School District as a Case Study," presented at the Annual Meeting of the American Educational Research Association, San Francisco, April 19, 1995.

44. Henig et al., *Color of School Reform,* chap. 6. D.C.'s Committee on Public Education tried initially to walk the line between being helpful partner and independent critic,

and quickly tilted more to the latter role. By the end of the 1990s, frustrated with the slow pace of progress, the business organization that initiated COPE allowed it to pass out of existence and in a move of major symbolic import launched, in its place, an organization focused exclusively on supporting charter schools.

45. Portz, Stein, and Jones, *City Politics and City Schools,* provide an excellent comparison of the St. Louis versus Pittsburgh and Boston cases.

46. Ferman, *Challenging the Growth Machine.*

47. Portz, Stein, and Jones, *City Politics and City Schools.*

CHAPTER 5. CONDUCTING POLICY IN AN ILL-STRUCTURED PROBLEM SPACE

1. Baumgartner and Jones, *Agendas and Instability;* Bryan D. Jones, *Reconceiving Decision-Making in Democratic Politics* (Chicago: University of Chicago Press, 1994).

2. The interviews were read by our project staff and coded into categories that allow extended analysis. The project staff employed a coding strategy that ensured highly reliable data. Results reported in this and other chapters are based only on intercoder reliabilities that reached customary social science standards.

3. Herbert Simon, *The Sciences of the Artificial,* 3d ed. (Cambridge, Mass.: MIT Press, 1996): 108.

4. David Rochefort and Roger Cobb, eds., *The Politics of Problem Definition* (Lawrence, Kans.: University Press of Kansas, 1994).

5. Walter R. Rietman, "Heuristic Decision Procedures, Open Constraints, and the Structure of Ill-Defined Problems," in *Human Judgments and Optimality,* ed. Maynard W. Shelly II and Glenn L. Bryan (New York: John Wiley, 1964): 296.

6. Herbert Simon, *Administrative Behavior,* 3d ed. (New York: Free Press, 1976).

7. It is possible that community advocates simply spent more time with our interviewers and thus had the opportunity to elaborate. On the other hand, general influentials named more problems, and elaborations from them did not decline with the third mention (indeed, there is a slight rise).

8. Unfortunately, we did not ask our interviewers to indicate the degree of specificity of responses, but clearly it is likely that the education specialists were more specific here.

9. Simon, *Sciences of the Artificial,* 28–32.

10. Charter schools were a new phenomenon, generally low on the national radar screen, at the time we conducted our interviews.

11. Peterson, *City Limits.*

CHAPTER 6. CIVIC MOBILIZATION AND POLICY EFFORT

1. Janowitz, *On Social Organization and Social Control,* 288–90 [the chapter in this volume on "Models for Urban Education" is based on writings by Janowitz published first in 1969]; see also Hentschke, "Radical Reform Versus Professional Reform in American Schools."

2. Nancy Burns, *The Formation of American Local Governments* (New York: Oxford University Press, 1994).

3. Frederick M. Hess, *Spinning Wheels: The Unpolitics of Urban School Reform* (Washington, D.C.: Brookings, 1999).

4. If a respondent said that the city's performance fell somewhere between two of the choices, our coders subsequently recorded that as a .5 answer (for example, "somewhere between 1 and 2" was coded as 1.5; "somewhere between 2 and 3" was coded as 2.5).

5. Frank M. Howell and Wolfgang Frese, "Size of Place, Residential Preferences and the Life Cycle: How People Come to Like Where They Live," *American Sociological Review* 48 (August 1983): 569–80.

6. Henig, "Civic Capacity and the Problem of Ephemeral Education Reform," presented at the Annual Meeting of the Urban Affairs Association, Portland, Oregon, May 3–6, 1995; Hess, *Spinning Wheels;* Henig et al., *Color of School Reform.*

7. Rich, *Black Mayors and School Politics.*

8. A fuller description of each of the items and its coding is available from the authors.

9. A copy of the instrument is available on request.

10. For the four items scaled 1 to 3, we multiply the scores of "2" and "3" by 1.33.

11. Luis Fraga, Bari Erichson, and Sandy Lee, "Consensus Building and School Reform: The Role of the Courts in San Francisco," in *Changing Urban Education,* ed. Clarence N. Stone (Lawrence, Kans.: University Press of Kansas, 1998): 66–92.

12. John Chubb and Terry Moe, *Politics, Markets, and America's Schools* (Washington, D.C.: Brookings, 1990); Myron Lieberman, *Public Education: An Autopsy* (Cambridge, Mass.: Harvard University Press, 1993).

13. The issue of race and civic capacity receives extended treatment in Henig, Hula, Orr, and Pedescleaux, *Color of School Reform.*

14. An examination of large suburban districts in Maryland did not indicate that Baltimore City was significantly different from its suburban counterparts.

15. Bryk et al., *Charting Chicago School Reform,* 123–24.

16. Associated Black Charities, A Report of a Management Study of the Baltimore City Public Schools (June 26, 1992); MGT of America, A Report on Monitoring and Evaluating Implementation of Management Study Recommendations in Baltimore City Public Schools, submitted to the Maryland State Department of Education (Tallahassee, Fla.: MGT of America, 1995); the McKenzie Group, "An Organizational Review of the St. Louis Schools" (Washington, D.C., September 11, 1995).

17. MGT of America, *Report,* viii–21.

18. For extended discussions of how racial interests and perspective interweave with the patronage function of public school employment see Rich, *Black Mayors and School Politics,* and Henig et al., *Color of School Reform,* chap. 4.

19. William J. Grimshaw, *Union Rule in the Schools* (Lexington, Mass.: Lexington Books, 1979); Paul E. Peterson, *School Politics, Chicago Style* (Chicago: University of Chicago Press, 1976); and Rich, *Black Mayors and School Politics.*

20. Marion Orr, *Dilemmas of Black Social Capital: School Reform in Baltimore, 1986–1998* (Lawrence, Kans.: University Press of Kansas, 1999).

21. Vander Weele, *Reclaiming Our Schools.*

22. Peterson, *School Politics, Chicago Style,* 197–98.

23. Goodlad, *A Place Called School,* 254.

24. Peter Schrag, *Village School Downtown* (Boston: Beacon Press, 1967): 165.

25. Marris and Rein, *Dilemmas of Social Reform.*

26. Comer, *Waiting for a Miracle.*

27. Farkas, *Divided Within, Besieged Without.*

28. Associated Black Charities 1992, iii–42.

29. Goodlad, *A Place Called School,* 259–60.

30. See Theodore Sizer, *Horace's Compromise* (Boston: Houghton-Mifflin, 1985); Elmore, Peterson, and McCarthey, *Restructuring the Classroom.*

CHAPTER 7. IMPLICATIONS AND RECOMMENDATIONS

1. These two needs do not necessarily have to be met with a single theory of nonreform. That is to say, proponents of policy change may have a perspective developed for inside consumption and strategizing that differs from that offered in more public forums.

2. William L. Boyd, "The Public, the Professionals and Educational Policy Making: Who Governs?" *Teachers College Record* 77 (1976): 539–77. For a parallel observation regarding urban redevelopment, see Clarence N. Stone, *Economic Growth and Neighborhood Discontent* (Chapel Hill, N.C.: University of North Carolina Press, 1976).

3. On this general phenomenon, see Mancur Olson, *The Logic of Collective Action* (Cambridge, Mass.: Harvard University Press, 1965, 1971), and James Q. Wilson, *Political Organizations* (New York: Basic Books, 1973). For an application to school politics, see Stone, *Changing Urban Education.*

4. Stanley M. Elam, Lowell C. Rose, and Alec M. Gallup. "The 23rd Annual Gallup/ Phi Delta Kappa Poll of the Public's Attitude toward the Public Schools," *Phi Delta Kappa* (September 1991): 41–56.

5. Farkas, *Educational Reform.*

6. Such as Chubb and Moe, *Politics, Markets, and America's Schools.*

7. Hero, Clarke, and Sidney, "Civic Capacity and Urban Education: Denver."

8. Richard Hula, Richard Jelier, and Mark Schnauer, 1994. "The Politics of School Reform in Detroit," second-year report prepared for the Civic Capacity and Urban Education Project (1994).

9. Lana Stein, "Education Reform and Civic Capacity: St. Louis, Missouri," second-year report prepared for the Civic Capacity and Urban Education Project (1994): 13.

10. John Portz, "Boston: Case Study Report," second-year report prepared for the Civic Capacity and Urban Education Project (1994): 23.

11. D.C. Committee on Public Education, *Our Children, Our Future* (Washington, D.C.: D.C. Committee on Public Education, June 1989).

12. The series, "DC Schools: A System in Crisis," ran daily from February 16 to February 20, 1997.

13. Farkas, *Educational Reform: The Players and the Politics,* 4.

14. Hess, *Spinning Wheels.*

15. Paul T. Hill, Lawrence C. Pierce, and James W. Guthrie, *Reinventing Public Education: How Contracting Can Transform America's Schools* (Chicago: University of Chicago Press, 1997).

16. Paul T. Hill and Mary Beth Celio, *Fixing Urban Schools* (Washington, D.C.: Brookings, 1998).

17. Paul T. Hill, Christine Campbell, and James Harvey, *It Takes a City: Getting Serious about Urban School Reform* (Washington, D.C.: Brookings, 2000): 107.

18. The Annie E. Casey Foundation, *Improving School-Community Connections* (Baltimore, Md., July 1999); Raymond Domanico, Carol Innerst, and Alexander Russo, *Can Philanthropy Fix Our Schools? Appraising Walter Annenberg's $500 Million Gift to Public Education* (Washington, D.C.: Thomas B. Fordham Foundation, April 2000). See also Susan H. Fuhrman, ed., *Designing Coherent Education Policy* (San Francisco: Jossey-Bass, 1993).

19. David Mathews, *Is There a Public for Public Schools?* (Dayton, Ohio: Kettering Foundation Press, 1996): 19.

20. Ibid., 5. An early advocate of a broader approach to school reform is Seymour B. Sarason, *The Culture of the School and the Problem of Change*, 2d ed. (Boston: Allyn and Bacon, 1982). See also various yearbooks of the Politics of Education Association, especially James G. Cibulka, Rodney J. Reed, and Kenneth K. Wong, eds., *The Politics of Urban Education in the United States* (Washington, D.C.: Falmer Press, 1992); and Robert L. Crowson, William L. Boyd, and Hanna Mawhinney, *The Politics of Education and the New Institutionalism* (Washington, D.C.: Falmer Press, 1996).

21. James S. Coleman and Thomas Hoffer, *Public and Private High Schools: The Impact of Communities* (New York: Basic Books, 1987).

22. For example, Anthony S. Bryk, Valerie E. Lee, and Peter B. Holland, *Catholic Schools and the Common Good* (Cambridge, Mass.: Harvard University Press, 1993); Joseph P. Viteritti, *Choosing Equality: School Choice, the Constitution, and Civil Society* (Washington, D.C.: Brookings, 1999); Mark Schneider, Paul Eric Teske, and Melissa Marschall, *Choosing Schools* (Princeton, N.J.: Princeton University Press, 2000).

23. Robert D. Putnam, *Making Democracy Work: Civic Traditions in Modern Italy* (Princeton, N.J.: Princeton University Press, 1993); Robert D. Putnam, *Bowling Alone: The Collapse and Revival of American Community* (New York: Simon and Schuster, 2000).

24. Jean Anyon, *Ghetto Schooling* (New York: Teachers College Press, 1997).

25. Quoted in Walsh, *Eye of the Storm*, 20.

26. Ibid.

27. Otis Johnson quoted in ibid.

28. Orr, *Dilemmas of Black Social Capital*, 143–64.

29. The quoted phrase is from ibid., 146.

30. Henig, Hula, Orr, and Pedescleaux, *Color of School Reform*.

31. Portz, Stein, and Jones, *City Schools and City Politics*, develop this line of argument and provide a rich array of supportive evidence, only some of which we draw on here.

32. Quoted in ibid. 56.

33. Arendt, *Between Past and Future*, 169.

34. See, among others, Albert O. Hirschman, *Shifting Involvements* (Princeton, N.J.: Princeton University Press, 1982); Robert B. Reich, ed., *The Power of Public Ideas* (Cambridge, Mass.: Harvard University Press, 1988); James G. March and Johan P. Olsen, *Rediscovering Institutions* (New York: Free Press, 1989); Charles A. Lindblom, *Inquiry and Change* (New Haven, Conn.: Yale University Press, 1990); and Jane J. Mansbridge, ed., *Beyond Self-Interest* (Chicago: University of Chicago Press, 1990).

35. Ferman, *Challenging the Growth Machine*.

36. Hill, Campbell, and Harvey, *It Takes a City*, 58.

37. Baumgartner and Jones, *Agendas and Instability.*

38. Hill, Campbell, and Harvey, *It Takes a City,* 24.

39. Radio interview on WPFW, May 17, 2000.

40. On Kentucky's pioneering reform legislation, see Stephen K. Clements, "The Changing Face of Common Schooling: The Politics of the 1990 Kentucky Education Reform Act" (Ph.D. diss., Department of Political Science, University of Chicago, 1998). On local reforms across a range of localities, see Annie E. Casey Foundation, "Improving School-Community Connections" (Baltimore, Md.: Annie E. Casey Foundation, 1999); and Hill, Campbell, and Harvey, *It Takes a City.*

41. Goodlad, *A Place Called School;* Susan H. Fuhrman, ed., *Designing Coherent Education Policy* (San Francisco: Jossey-Bass, 1993); Fuhrman and O'Day, eds., *Rewards and Reforms* (San Francisco: Jossey-Bass, 1996); National Research Council, Eric Hanushek, and Dale Jorgenson, eds., *Improving America's Schools* (Washington, D.C.; National Academy Press, 1996).

42. Compare with Hill, Campbell, and Harvey, *It Takes a City.*

43. Perhaps the most eloquent champion of this view is Goodlad, *A Place Called School.* See also the six-city study done by Anthony Bryk, Paul Hill, Dorothy Shipps, Michael Murphy, David Menefee-Libey, and Albert Bennett, summarized in a report by the Annie E. Casey Foundation, *Improving School-Community Connections,* esp. 43.

44. Hill, Campbell, and Harvey, *It Takes a City,* 105.

45. Compare with Hill and Celio, *Fixing Urban Schools.*

46. Donna E. Muncey and Patrick J. McQuillan, *Reform and Resistance in Schools and Classrooms* (New Haven, Conn.: Yale University Press, 1996); Elmore, Peterson, and McCarthey, *Restructuring in the Classroom;* and Tittle, *Welcome to Heights High.*

47. See Kirst and Bulkley, "'New, Improved' Mayors Take Over City Schools," for a broad and sympathetic analysis of this trend.

48. "In 1959 fewer than 25 blacks per 10,000 had white classmates. Not until 1963 did Southern desegregation reach even one percent." Charles S. Bullock III, "Equal Education Opportunity," in *Implementation of Civil Rights Policy,* ed. Charles S. Bullock III and Charles M. Lamb (Monterey, Calif.: Brooks/Cole Publishing, 1984).

49. Colleen O'Dea, "The Price of Parity: Once More into the School Aid Breach," *New Jersey Reporter* 25 (May/June 1996): 7.

50. The high degree of national attention on the Milwaukee experiment has contributed to a situation in which it is difficult to separate the evidence from the ideologically driven controversy in which it is enmeshed. John Witte of the University of Wisconsin issued several yearly reports on a range of outcomes associated with the program. While finding many positive signs—for example, high satisfaction among parents of children using the vouchers—Witte's comparison of choice students to similar children in the Milwaukee Public Schools (MPS) indicated that "test scores did not improve and did not differ from MPS scores, and attrition from the program averaged 30% per year (not including three private schools which went bankrupt in the midst of the school year)." John F. Witte, "Reply to Greene, Peterson and Du," unpublished paper distributed at the annual meeting of the American Political Science Association, August 1996, p. 2. Witte's analysis was challenged by Jay P. Greene, Paul E. Peterson, and Jiangtao Du in "The Effectiveness of School Choice in Milwaukee: A Secondary Analysis of Data from the Program's Evaluation," a paper prepared for presentation at the annual meeting of the American Political Science Association, San Francisco, August 30, 1996. By focusing only

on children who remained in the voucher program for at least three years and comparing them to a small sample of students who applied for the program but were randomly rejected, they found evidence that voucher programs were so successful that "if similar success could be achieved for all minority students nationwide, it could close the gap separating white and minority test scores by somewhere between one-third and one-half" (4). But their analysis also has been challenged (see John F. Witte, *The Market Approach to Education: An Analysis of America's First Voucher Program* [Princeton, N.J.: Princeton University Press, 2000]), and the debate rages on.

51. For some of the context for this pronouncement, see Jeffrey R. Henig, *Rethinking School Choice: Limits of the Market Metaphor* (Princeton, N.J.: Princeton University Press, 1994).

52. "Magnet Schools in Prince George's," *Washington Post,* January 8, 1990.

53. Retha Hill, "In Pr. George's, Business vs. Schools: Superintendent Blamed for Chill in Once Warm Relations," *Washington Post* (January 31, 1994). Orfield and Eaton, *Dismantling Desegregation,* chap. 10.

54. "We can just kiss those programs goodbye," one of the board members who opposed weakening the desegregation regulations concluded. Lisa Frazier, "Pr. George's Schools Vote to End Racial Quotas," *Washington Post* (June 6, 1996).

55. For a general overview see Gerald N. Rosenberg, *The Hollow Hope* (Chicago: University of Chicago Press, 1991).

56. David Kirp, *Just Schools: The Idea of Racial Equality in American Education* (Berkeley, Calif.: University of California Press, 1982): 51.

57. Joseph F. Sullivan, "Improvement Lags After School Takeovers, State Says," *New York Times* (April 25, 1995): B-6. Also, Neil MacFarquhar, "Better Finances, but Not Better Test Scores," *New York Times* (July 9, 1995). Test scores in 1996 apparently did show some improvement, although it is not clear whether those improvements could be attributed to the intervention.

58. Kerry A. White, "N.J. Plans to End Takeover in Jersey City," *Education Week on the Web* (http://www.edweek.org/ew/current/39jersey.h18), June 9, 1999.

59. Maria Newman, "New Jersey Finds No Simple Solutions in Takeover of Schools," *New York Times* (March 21, 1999): 25.

60. Bill Peterson, "Kentucky Public Schools Ruled Unconstitutional," *Washington Post* (June 9, 1989): A-16.

61. Chester E. Finn Jr., *We Must Take Charge: Our Schools and Our Future* (New York: Free Press, 1991): 63.

62. Quoted in Richard F. Elmore, Charles H. Abelmann, and Susan H. Fuhrman, "The New Accountability in State Education Reform: From Process to Performance," in *Holding Schools Accountable,* ed. Helen F. Ladd (Washington, D.C.: Brookings, 1996): 75.

63. For discussions of the rhetoric of crisis in education reform, see Henig, *Rethinking School Choice,* chap. 2; David C. Berliner and Bruce J. Biddle, *The Manufactured Crisis: Myths, Fraud, and the Attack on America's Public Schools* (Reading, Mass.: Addison-Wesley, 1995).

64. Anemona Hartocollis, "Mayor's Remarks on School System Assailed by Crew," *New York Times* (April 27, 1999): A-1.

65. General Electric, *1999 Annual Report,* 2.

Index